Shelley with Benjam

Shelley with Benjamin
A critical mosaic

Mathelinda Nabugodi

⋔UCLPRESS

First published in 2023 by
UCL Press
University College London
Gower Street
London WC1E 6BT

Available to download free: www.uclpress.co.uk

Text © Author, 2023

The author has asserted her rights under the Copyright, Designs and Patents Act 1988 to be identified as the author of this work.

A CIP catalogue record for this book is available from The British Library.

![CC BY-NC logo]

Any third-party material in this book is not covered by the book's Creative Commons licence. Details of the copyright ownership and permitted use of third-party material is given in the image (or extract) credit lines. If you would like to reuse any third-party material not covered by the book's Creative Commons licence, you will need to obtain permission directly from the copyright owner.

This book is published under a Creative Commons Attribution-Non-Commercial 4.0 International licence (CC BY-NC 4.0), https://creativecommons.org/licenses/by-nc/4.0/. This licence allows you to share and adapt the work for non-commercial use providing attribution is made to the author and publisher (but not in any way that suggests that they endorse you or your use of the work) and any changes are indicated. Attribution should include the following information:

Nabugodi, M. 2023. *Shelley with Benjamin*: A *Critical Mosaic*. London: UCL Press. https://doi.org/10.14324/111.9781800083233

Further details about Creative Commons licences are available at http://creativecommons.org/licenses/

ISBN: 978-1-80008-325-7 (Hbk.)
ISBN: 978-1-80008-324-0 (Pbk.)
ISBN: 978-1-80008-323-3 (PDF)
ISBN: 978-1-80008-326-4 (epub)
DOI: https://doi.org/10.14324/111.9781800083233

Бабушке

Contents

List of abbreviations   ix

Preface   xi

Acknowledgements   xxi

Afterlife   1

I: Truth in a name

1   Shells   13

2   Violets   26

3   Footsteps   38

II: Loving knowledge

4   Beauty   53

5   Mosaic   66

6   Love   79

III: Legacies of violence

7   Guilt   97

8   Atonement   116

9   Forgiveness   127

Coda   140

Bibliography   145

Index   150

List of abbreviations

WALTER BENJAMIN

Benjamin is cited in English translation, with reference provided to the original German.

AP	*The Arcades Project*, ed. by Howard Eiland and Kevin McLaughlin (Cambridge, MA: Harvard University Press, 2002)
Briefe	*Briefe*, ed. by Gershom Scholem and Theodor W. Adorno, 2 vols (Frankfurt am Main: Suhrkamp, 1966), cited with volume number 1–2
Correspondence	*The Correspondence of Walter Benjamin: 1910–1940*, ed. by Gershom Scholem and Theodor W. Adorno, trans. by Manfred R. Jacobson and Evelyn M. Jacobson (Chicago, IL: University of Chicago Press, 1994)
EW	*Early Writings: 1910–1917*, trans. by Howard Eiland and others (Cambridge, MA: Harvard University Press, 2011)
GS	*Gesammelte Schriften*, ed. by Rolf Tiedemann and Hermann Schweppenhäuser, 7 vols (Frankfurt am Main: Suhrkamp, 1972–1999), cited with volume number 1–7
Origin	*The Origin of German Tragic Drama*, trans. by John Osborne (London: Verso, 2009)
SW	*Selected Writings*, ed. by Marcus Bullock and Michael W. Jennings, 4 vols (Cambridge, MA: Harvard University Press, 1996–2003), cited with volume number 1–4

PERCY BYSSHE SHELLEY

Shelley's poetry is cited from the Longman edition of *The Poems of Shelley*.

Letters	*The Letters of Percy Bysshe Shelley*, ed. by Frederick L. Jones, 2 vols (Oxford: Clarendon Press, 1964), cited with volume number 1–2
Prose	*Shelley's Prose; or The Trumpet of a Prophecy*, ed. by David Lee Clark (New York, NY: New Amsterdam, 1988)
PS	*The Poems of Shelley*, ed. by Jack Donovan, Cian Duffy, Kelvin Everest, Geoffrey Matthews and Michael Rossington, 4 vols to date (Abingdon: Routledge, 1989–), cited with volume number 1–4
SoL	*Shelley on Love*, ed. by Richard Holmes (London: Anvil Press Poetry, 1980)
SPP	*Shelley's Poetry and Prose*, ed. by Neil Fraistat and Donald H. Reiman, 2nd edn (New York, NY: W. W. Norton and Co., 2002)

Preface

Criticism is a split. Its name is rooted in the Ancient Greek κρῐ́νω – 'to separate, to divide, to split'. The one who criticises divvies up the matter, separates the wheat from the chaff, divides a problem into its constituent elements. In the process, the critic also weeds out personal whims and bugbears from their analysis. When I arrived at university to study English Literature and Philosophy, I did not realise the extent to which the education I was about to receive would separate my intellectual life from my personal development as a young woman of Afro-European heritage. This contrast – between my critical and my private selves – determines the contour of my split.

  A split can also be observed in the two writers who are the subjects of this book: Percy Bysshe Shelley and Walter Benjamin. The first is a British Romantic poet, born in 1792 to a baronetcy, expelled from university 'for contumaciously refusing to answer questions . . . and for also repeatedly declining to disavow a publication titled *The Necessity of Atheism*', yet nonetheless destined to become one of the most canonical poets in the English language.[1] The second is a German Jewish philosopher born exactly a hundred years later, in 1892, into a solidly bourgeois family in Berlin, who was effectively expelled from the academy after his habilitation thesis was deemed incomprehensible. The work was later published as *The Origin of German Tragic Drama* and contributed to making Benjamin one of the most influential critical theorists of the twentieth century. Both were read in their lifetimes but died failures – or they believed. My engagement with their writings opens with a meditation on afterlife that grounds my reading in their own reflections about how literary works live on beyond the author's death.

Shelley with Benjamin: A Critical Mosaic offers a close reading of the two writers, but, equally importantly, it is a critical experiment, an attempt to develop a method for reading out of the materials being read. While posterity has received Shelley as a poet and Benjamin as a theorist, I show how their own works invalidate such distinctions. The term 'mosaic' in the title comes from Benjamin's 'Epistemo-Critical Prologue' to *The Origin of German Tragic Drama*, where he uses it to describe the form of his work, which he conceives as a mosaic of citations. 'Mosaic' is also the name of this book's central chapter, in which I argue that Benjamin's methodological reflections in the 'Prologue' amount to a poetics of philosophical prose of the kind that he is writing. At the same time, the term 'mosaic' cites a passage in Shelley's 'A Defence of Poetry' where he notes the differences between poetical inspiration and critical interpretation, suggesting that criticism is 'to poetry what mosaic is to painting'.[2] My own methodology combines Benjamin's and Shelley's considerations to simultaneously demarcate and suspend the split between poetry and philosophy, creation and contemplation.

In his essay on Johann Wolfgang von Goethe's novel *Elective Affinities*, Benjamin compares the relation between poetry and philosophy to that between two siblings:

> Let us suppose that one makes the acquaintance of a person who is beautiful and attractive but impenetrable, because he carries a secret within him. It would be reprehensible to want to pry. Still, it would surely be permissible to inquire whether he has any siblings and whether their nature could not perhaps explain somewhat the enigmatic character of the stranger. In just this way criticism seeks to discover siblings of the work of art. And all genuine works have their siblings in the realm of philosophy.[3]

The sibling relationship is established by the fact that both works of art and philosophy are oriented towards the unity of beauty and truth. Dissecting this unity is the task that Benjamin sets criticism. His underlying premise, that 'everything beautiful is connected in some way to the true', is inherited from Plato via Goethe and other Romantic poets.[4] 'Beauty is truth, truth beauty, that is all | Ye know on earth, and all ye need to know', as Keats puts it in the closing lines of his 'Ode on a Grecian Urn'.[5] Shelley also shares this view: it is what prompts him to define poetry as 'at once the centre and circumference of knowledge' – its beauty and its truthfulness mutually reinforce one another because poetry 'has a common source with all other forms of order and of beauty according to which the materials of human life are susceptible of being arranged'.[6] I approach Shelley's poetry and Benjamin's philosophical prose as siblings, related in their pursuit of the truth that emerges in writing when it attains the order of the beautiful and the good. Throughout the book, the work of one helps clarify that of the other – so Benjamin's theory of naming, for example, illuminates Shelley's puns on the 'shell' that can be heard in his name, while Shelley's adaptation of Plato's *Symposium* unveils the poetic substratum of Benjamin's reception of the same work.

In the course of the last few decades, Benjamin's reflections on method have influenced not only how critics read his work but also how they carry out their own thinking: concepts such as 'constellation' and 'dialectical image' have become staples in the critical landscape. Part of my aim, however, is to show how comparable concepts are also found in Shelley's poetics; for example, Shelley's claim that all poetical language is 'vitally metaphorical; that is, it marks the before unapprehended relations of things' bears comparison to Benjamin's definition of the dialectical image as 'that wherein what has been comes together in a flash with the now to form a constellation'.[7] In both cases, the impetus is on identifying correspondences between disparate phenomena and making connections that traverse notions of chronological development or linear influence. For this reason, each chapter is anchored in an image or concept that appears in both Shelley's and Benjamin's works, and that therefore acts as the connecting link between them. Although I cite Benjamin in English translation, I am also interested in how key terms in his and Shelley's writings translate into one another. It is well known that Benjamin's thought is tightly bound up with his modes of expression, a feature that renders his work particularly challenging to translate. In addition, he was prone to self-citation, letting words and phrases echo across different texts: such echoes are often lost when these texts are translated by different translators. To recover some of them, I have punctuated my text with Benjamin's German, as well as a few stray words in Greek, Russian and Swedish that have shaped my thinking.

The focus on select images unlocks resonances and affinities across Shelley's and Benjamin's respective oeuvres, allowing me to establish relations between them without appealing to notions of influence, reception or even commensurability between the two. But while concrete images provide the structuring principle, my reading is not only about capturing static relations between things. It also concerns itself with how these relations emerge out of the flux of literary and intellectual history, and thus also about movement in time. Therefore, a sense of tempo is no less important than an eye for imagery. Although Shelley's definition of poetry harks back to the semantic expansiveness of the Ancient Greek ποίησις to encompass all kinds of making, he regards language as the highest form of poetic creation since language is 'a more direct representation of the actions and passions of our internal being, and is susceptible of more various and delicate combinations, than colour [in painting], form [in sculpture] or motion [in dance]'.[8] These 'combinations' involve the relations between the sounds of words and their meaning, and so Shelley argues that poetry in a narrow sense depends on a distinction between 'measured and unmeasured language' (*not* prose and verse).[9] Measure achieves a mimetic correspondence between 'our internal being' and the written work: the rhythms of poetic language imitate the movement of thought. This is why rhythm is as important as imagery: Shelley celebrates poets not only because 'their words unveil the permanent analogy of things by images which participate in the life of truth' but also because 'their periods are harmonious and rhythmical', attuned to the cadences of the human mind.[10]

A comparable interest in rhythm underpins the various terms that Benjamin uses to describe the form of his philosophical prose (including mosaic, picture puzzle, constellation, dialectical image and literary montage). All these terms refer to visual images constructed from divers pieces: Benjamin is primarily concerned with the work of assembling tiny fragments into a bigger picture. He regards each fragment as a fresh start, a new attempt to gain purchase on the problem represented by the text as a whole. 'This continual pausing for breath is the mode most proper to the process of contemplation,' he explains in the 'Epistemo-Critical Prologue'.[11] Like Shelley, Benjamin seeks to secure a mimetic correspondence between the rhythms of writing and of thinking:

> For by pursuing different levels of meaning in its examination of one single object it [the process of contemplation] receives both the incentive to begin again and the justification for its irregular rhythm. Just as mosaics preserve their majesty despite their fragmentation into capricious particles, so philosophical contemplation is not lacking in momentum. Both are made up of the distinct and the disparate.[12]

The various fragmentary forms that Benjamin develops attest to his ongoing search for a composition practice that captures the intermittent rhythm (or momentum) of thought. As in Shelley's poetics, this is a quest for a measured language capable of representing 'the actions and passions of our internal being'. As a result, the concept of 'measure' is a recurrent motif throughout this book, indicating Shelley's and Benjamin's shared interest in verbal rhythmics.

'Sometimes you can see a celestial object better by looking at something else, with it, in the sky,' Anne Carson writes at the outset of her reading of Simonides of Keos with Paul Celan, and the same is true of my constellation of Shelley with Benjamin.[13] The preposition 'with' is important here. Although 'constellation' is a key concept in Benjamin's thought (indeed, so much so that the mere mention of the word evokes his name), this book does not 'apply' Benjamin's theory to a reading of Shelley's poetry. A constellation brings into relation. It connects the disparate and dissimilar. It balances without resolving tensions. But also, as James McFarland has noted, a constellation is a relation not simply between its constituent stars, but also between those stars and the beholder. 'Constellations as such are not "out there" at the edge of the cosmos, they appear to us, from our position, eyes raised, on the surface of the earth.'[14] The visibility of a constellation depends on the when and where of the person viewing it, and therefore also on who that person is – and this is where the critic's own internal 'actions and passions' come into view.

I have been taught to believe that the ideal critic writes a level-headed prose, values arguments over opinions, facts over feelings, and is moved by no passion other than the disinterested pursuit of knowledge. The ideal critic is not hampered by anxiety, racked by menstrual pains or worried about how to pay the rent – such factors might be part of our daily lives, but they do not matter for the life of the mind, which takes place elsewhere: among ideas conveyed in language, words imprinted in black on white, paper or pixels. Intellectually, I was and still am drawn towards Romanticism and its afterlife in twentieth-century literary theory, a movement in many ways preoccupied with questions of subjectivity – but my academic training instructed me to suppress the subjective, to dispel what Shelley called 'the dull vapours of the little world of self' by isolating my critical voice from my lived experience.[15] Yet, as Shelley also knew, self is 'that burr that will stick to one'.[16] Rather than trying to get 'that burr' off me, in this book I make my subjective self visible as part of my critical interpretation.

Notions of 'objectivity', 'discipline' and 'intellectual rigour' give literary criticism a scientific veneer, distinguishing it from dilettantish appreciation, and were therefore important for its establishment in the academy. But they have also served to negate other ways of knowing literary texts, including the forms of knowledge gained from historically situated, embodied experience. 'We are expected to discard, discount, disregard, jettison, abandon, and measure those ways of knowing and to enact epistemic violence that we know to be violence against others and ourselves,' Christina Sharpe writes of Black academics, encouraging us to reject conventional academic protocols of knowledge, to 'become undisciplined' and practise modes of 'knowing otherwise' that exceed the strictures of the White academy.[17] Knowing otherwise is about embracing 'that burr of self' and resisting the separation between academic criticism and the experience of living at the receiving end of gendered racialisation, the split between who we are and how we read.

Embracing one's self in a critical text is an act of resistance. Resistance against the totalitarian universalism of critical objectivity, for one, but also resistance as a generative force in its own right. My understanding of generative resistance draws on Giorgio Agamben's response to the question: 'What is an act of creation?' Agamben begins with the passage from potentiality to actuality in Aristotle: for instance, if I am an architect, I possess the potentiality to build a house and I can actualise this potentiality by building a house. Yet I can also choose not to build a house: alongside the potentiality-to-create is a potentiality-*not*-to-create, which Agamben terms *impotenza* ('impotentiality') or *potenza-di-non* ('potentiality-not-to'). *Impotenza* is present in any act of creation, as a resistance that is integral to that act. 'If creation were only potentiality-to, which cannot but blindly cross into the act, art would lapse into execution, which proceeds with false confidence toward a complete form, since it has repressed the resistance of the potentiality-not-to.'[18] Genuine creation does not overcome its *impotenza*, but transfers it into the created work, where it remains lodged as a disturbance: 'the salvation of imperfection in a perfect form'.[19]

The imperfection that Agamben seeks to salvage can be related to what Sharpe calls 'knowing otherwise' – something in excess of the form given to it, be it the artistic form of the work or the epistemic form of academic disciplines: insofar as criticism is a creative activity, it too must salvage its own imperfections. If the stimulus for a critical interpretation – its potentiality-to – is provided by the literary text, then a certain mode of generative resistance arises from attending to those extra-textual concerns that preclude a disinterested engagement with that text. The critic's recalcitrant self. In 'Truth in a Name', my attempt to salvage the imperfections of my reading appears in the form of marginal annotations. Taking my cue from bell hooks's invitation to occupy the margin as a site of resistance,[20] I place a handful of anecdotes about my name in the margins of my critical argument, which explores the aura of being named in Shelley and Benjamin. These facts from my personal history frame my interpretation even though they obviously are of no relevance for the texts under discussion. Their purpose is to highlight the boundary between the personal and the critical even as they echo some of the central themes in this part of the book: Shelley's and Benjamin's puns on their own names, Benjamin's theory of translation and Shelley's poetics – all of which influence the structure of this book.

The marginal annotations are in excess of my reading of Shelley and Benjamin. In this regard, they can be seen as blemishes or imperfections. Yet, since they reveal the personal motivations that generated my reading, they are also integral to it: the development of my argument cannot be separated from its flaws. In 'Loving Knowledge', I approach the oppositional pull between private self and academic writing from a different angle. Turning to Shelley's and Benjamin's readings of Plato's *Symposium*, I retrace the steps that lead the Platonic philosopher from embodied physicality into intellectual abstraction: a route that takes us beyond bodies, beyond gender, beyond language, beyond even silence towards that point of indifference where only truth remains. For Plato, the true is also the beautiful and the good. This unity of beauty, truth and goodness is a point of convergence in Shelley's definition of a poet and Benjamin's definition of a critic, both of which draw on the *Symposium*'s representation of philosophy as an erotic love of knowledge.

Ultimately, my resistance to academic ideals of literary criticism and desire to pursue modes of knowing otherwise, from the margin, are attempts to reconfigure the relation between fact and fiction, literature and the world – which also encompasses the relation between literary criticism and historical events. It is a question of what kind of extra-textual knowledge is relevant for the interpretation of a particular text. That such knowledge includes facts about the author's biography and historical context seems evident: that it includes comparable information about the critic, less so. I test the boundaries of such relevance in 'Legacies of Violence', which contains a reading of Benjamin's theorisation of tragedy alongside Shelley's tragedy of *The Cenci*, touching on themes such as violence, guilt, justice, capitalism, rights, sacrifice and atonement. This part is punctuated by interlinear interruptions that forcefully insert the transatlantic slave trade and its afterlife between the lines of my interpretation. Like the marginal annotations in the first part, these interruptions exceed my reading of Shelley and Benjamin, neither of whom ever thought about racialised slavery or anti-Black racism at any length. And yet, from my own historical vantage-point, these questions cannot be ignored: they interrupted my reading when the pandemic-struck world erupted into Black Lives Matter protests in the summer of 2020. As academic institutions across the globe issued anti-racist statements that were in equal measure heartfelt and hypocritical, it no longer seemed viable to discuss two canonical European writers without acknowledging the anti-Black violence that saturates European modernity. After all, if any constellation involves the beholder's position, then my constellation of Shelley and Benjamin must be grounded in the historical present in which I read their works.

The interlinear interruptions are in part indebted to M. NourbeSe Philip's *Zong!*, which is one of our time's most haunting confrontations with the legacies of transatlantic slavery. Both *Zong!* and *The Cenci* are based on true historical events. In Philip's poem, it is a court case concerning the slave ship *Zong*, whose captain decided to throw 150 Africans overboard to claim compensation for lost 'cargo'; in Shelley's play, it is an account of Count Francesco Cenci raping his daughter Beatrice, who retaliates by having him assassinated. 'There is no telling this story,' Philip repeatedly insists: words are not able to convey the magnitude of the crime. Yet the story must be told and her poem does the telling, or 'un-telling'.[21] Shelley similarly refers to the incestuous rape as an 'expressionless crime' and his tragedy has to perform an accusation that cannot be spoken. The two works are related because they thematise the failure of language to represent certain forms of violence. While I do not mean to imply that they are commensurable, nor invite facile comparison between an incestuous rape and a massacre at sea, it is the case that both Philip and Shelley took an archival record describing an unspeakable crime and turned it into poetry. This transformation places a demand on their critics – a demand to face the ethical implications of writing and reading poetry about atrocity, to resist the lure of aesthetic redemption.

In *Zong!* this demand is partially encoded in the formatting: the poem has a symphonic structure and its final movement is printed in fading shades of grey – the text appears to sink into the page so as to visually reinforce 'the un-telling of what cannot, yet must, be told'.[22] In the 'Notanda' accompanying the poem, Philip emphasises that she does not wish to misappropriate the suffering of others by speaking for them, but their voices must be rescued from silence. Drawing inspiration from her solution to the problem of giving voice to, without speaking for, victims of historical violence, the interlinear interruptions in the third part of this book are presented in grey. This keeps them distinct from the main text even as it testifies to the near-invisibility of the anti-Black violence on which European culture is built. But while they represent an attempt to bear witness to this history, I do not want to suggest that the interlinear interruptions even come close to adequately acknowledging the horrors of transatlantic slavery. On the contrary, I believe that this is an atrocity whose enormity resists the kind of atonement through literary means that may be associated with the genres of tragedy or elegiac poetry.

Nonetheless, as recent culture wars and the pushback against the Black Lives Matter movement have shown, this is a story that must be told if we wish to understand European history – and this includes literary history. It is still too often the case that, unless a critic is explicitly concerned with enslavement and colonialism, these questions are bypassed in studies of European literature produced in the long centuries when Europeans were enslaving and exploiting peoples across the globe. As Benjamin famously put it: 'There is no document of culture which is not at the same time a document of barbarism.'[23] This insight applies as much to our own critical writing as it does to the works of Benjamin, Shelley or any other writer in the Western tradition. As critics living 'in the wake',[24] it is our responsibility to make this barbarism visible.

Notes

1. Minutes of College Meeting, 25 March 1811, University College, Oxford, UC: GB3/A1/2 fol. 148ʳ; cited in Michael Rossington, 'Shelley's Poetical Essay: About the Text', http://poeticalessay.bodleian.ox.ac.uk/about-the-text/ [accessed 29 June 2022].
2. 'A Defence of Poetry', *SPP*, p. 532.
3. 'Goethe's *Elective Affinities*', *SW1*, p. 333, translation emended; *GS1*, p. 172.
4. 'Goethe's *Elective Affinities*', *SW1*, p. 334; *GS1*, p. 173.
5. John Keats, 'Ode on a Grecian Urn', in *John Keats: The Complete Poems*, ed. by John Barnard, 2nd edn (Harmondsworth, Middlesex: Penguin Books, 1976), ll. 49–50.
6. 'A Defence of Poetry', *SPP*, p. 531, p. 535.
7. 'A Defence of Poetry', *SPP*, p. 512; [N2a,3], *AP*, p. 462; *GS5*, p. 576.
8. 'A Defence of Poetry', *SPP*, p. 513.
9. 'A Defence of Poetry', *SPP*, p. 514.
10. 'A Defence of Poetry', *SPP*, p. 515; for Shelley's take on the 'certain rhythm or order' innate to man, see 'A Defence of Poetry', *SPP*, pp. 511–12.
11. *Origin*, p. 28; *GS1*, p. 208.
12. *Origin*, p. 28; *GS1*, p. 208.
13. Anne Carson, *Economy of the Unlost* (Princeton, NJ: Princeton University Press, 1999), p. viii.
14. James McFarland, 'Sailing by the Stars: Constellations in the Space of Thought', *MLN*, 126 (2011), 471–85 (p. 474).
15. 'A Defence of Poetry', *SPP*, p. 525.
16. *Letters 2*, p. 109.
17. Christina Sharpe, *In the Wake: On Blackness and Being* (Durham, NC: Duke University Press, 2016), pp. 12–13.
18. Giorgio Agamben, 'What Is the Act of Creation?', in *The Fire and the Tale*, trans. by Lorenzo Chiesa (Stanford, CA: Stanford University Press, 2014), pp. 33–56 (p. 42).
19. Agamben, 'What Is the Act of Creation?', p. 42.
20. bell hooks, 'Choosing the Margin as a Space of Radical Openness', *Framework: The Journal of Cinema and Media*, 36 (1989), 15–23 (p. 22).
21. M. NourbeSe Philip, *Zong! As told to the author by Sataey Adamu Boateng* (Middletown, CT: Wesleyan University Press, 2008), p. 189.
22. Philip, *Zong!*, p. 199.
23. 'On the Concept of History', *SW4*, p. 392; *GS1*, p. 696.
24. The formulation cites the title of Sharpe's book, *In the Wake*, and her discussion of existing in the wake of the slave ship hold.

Acknowledgements

This book started life as a doctoral thesis and I will be ever indebted to Tim Beasley-Murray and Paul Hamilton for agreeing to supervise what must initially have seemed a rather nonsensical doctoral project. The former's sceptical gaze arrested countless false starts and the latter's almost mischievously incisive comments encouraged me to explore directions I would never have discovered myself. The thesis was the first to be awarded a PhD in Creative Critical Writing from UCL, and I am very grateful to the programme's convenor, Tim Mathews, for his unwavering enthusiasm and intellectual generosity, and to Stephanie Bird for smoothing my path. Jenny Chamarette, Clare Lees, Florian Mussgnug, Christopher Ohge, Emily Orley, Jane Rendell, Jennifer Richards and John Schad have, in different ways, offered courage and inspiration in pursuing an experimental methodology. Carol Jacobs advised me during an exchange semester at Yale and raised a number of fundamental questions about my citation practice. Anthony Adler, Henry Sussman and Paul North were also generous interlocutors during my time there. A big thank you to Kristen Kreider for telling me to let the light in at a crucial moment, and Peter Zusi for making it clear that there was no way around Benjamin's work on Goethe. Agnes Broome, Liz Harvey, Christiane Luck, Niall Sreenan and Yva Jung shared the various woes and tribulations of doctoral research; these would have been much more difficult to overcome without you.

Michael Rossington has championed my work in more ways than I can name, and I will never forget the moment when we first looked at a Shelley manuscript in the Bodleian Library together. More recently, conversations with Ruth Abbott, Will Bowers, Alexander Freer, John Gardner, Oliver Morgan and Ross Wilson have helped me clarify the stakes of this work. Rebecca Barr and Mary Newbould have radicalised me in the most beautiful ways. Joshua Batts and Stephanie Galasso are the best comrades-in-arms one could wish for. Harriet Truscott is the truest poet I've ever met. I'm grateful to Diarmuid Hester for reminding me to be kind to my past self, and Anahid Nersessian for prompting me to tackle the present. I am also thankful to the two anonymous reviewers for their careful reading of the book, and the hints they gave for how to complete it, as well as the production team at UCL Press who patiently incorporated my requests about formatting and last-minute revisions. But above all I want to thank my mother, for ceaselessly reminding me, *что утро вечера мудренее.*

Afterlife

'I once imagined, that in everything any man ever wrote, spoke, acted, or imagined, is contained, as it were, an allegorical idea of his own future life, as the acorn contains the oak,' Shelley noted in a letter written in May 1820.[1] His own death in a shipwreck two years later has tested the truth of this observation, casting a new light on his various references to drowning: 'if you can't swim | Beware of Providence', Count Maddalo warns Shelley's alter ego Julian in an autobiographical poem based on his conversations with Lord Byron.[2] Mocking an attack on his character published in the *Quarterly*, Shelley jokes:

> It describes the result of my battle with their Omnipotent God; his pulling me under the sea by the hair of my head, like Pharaoh; my calling out like the devil who was *game* to the last; swearing and cursing in all comic and horrid oaths, like a French postilion on Mount Cenis; entreating everybody to drown themselves; pretending not to be drowned myself when I *am* drowned; and, lastly, *being* drowned.[3]

Although the tone here is clearly satirical, in the light of his death it becomes prophetic. 'Shelley's frequent allusions to his being drowned are singular,' Jane, Lady Shelley, solemnly remarked when she published the above comment in her hagiographic *Shelley Memorials* (1859).[4]

Her attempts to clear the poet's name of the radical associations that had made him notorious in his lifetime contributed to making Shelley a poet defined by his death. While most poets are commemorated quill in hand, Shelley is memorialised as a corpse: reposing on a funeral pyre in Louis Édouard Fournier's *The Funeral of Shelley* (1889) or washed up on the shore, strewn with seaweed – either held by his weeping widow, in Henry Weekes's Shelley monument at Christchurch Priory, Dorset (1853–4), or supported by his grieving muse, in Edward Onslow Ford's Shelley memorial at University College, Oxford (1892). 'Surely, no stranger revenge has ever been brought about by the whirligig of time,' *The Times* reported on the unveiling of the latter sculpture: 'The college which expelled Shelley living honours him dead.'[5] Ford's Shelley memorial was originally displayed in a custom-built, darkened chamber to ensure that the viewer was dazzled by the marble body's glistening whiteness: a paragon of the Poet as a dead, white man.

Although these artistic representations of dead Shelley are a peculiarity of his afterlife, they also point to a wider cultural tendency to privilege death as the point around which the meaning of a life crystallises. As Moritz Heinemann has remarked, 'A man who dies at the age of thirty-five ... is at every point in his life a man who dies at the age of thirty-five.' Citing this remark, Benjamin adds:

> Nothing is more dubious than this sentence – but for the sole reason that the tense is wrong. A man – so says the truth that was meant here – who died at thirty-five will appear to *remembrance* at every point in his life as a man who dies at the age of thirty-five.[6]

And to remembrance Benjamin appears as a German Jewish philosopher who took his own life on the Spanish border during an attempt to escape Nazi-occupied France. His failure to cross the border seems all the more fateful since it had just been closed when Benjamin reached it. Hannah Arendt has summed up the tragic coincidence:

> One day earlier Benjamin would have got through without any trouble, one day later the people in Marseilles [whence Benjamin had departed] would have known that for the time being it was impossible to pass through Spain. Only on that particular day was the catastrophe possible.[7]

This account of Benjamin's death first appeared as an article in the *New Yorker* and was later reprinted in 1968 as the introduction to *Illuminations*, the first translation of Benjamin's works into English, which launched his international reception. Benjamin is represented as an otherworldly intellectual out of keeping with his time: according to Arendt, he is supposed to have joked that if he managed to escape to America, 'people would probably find no other use for him than to cart him up and down the country to exhibit him as the "last European"'.[8] In this posthumous context, Benjamin's humorous comment turns into a prophetic premonition: his failure to escape Nazi Europe appears as predestined by his intellectual temperament rather than the tragic accident that it was.

To remembrance, Shelley is the poet who died while composing a poem entitled 'The Triumph of Life'. When his widow, Mary Shelley, published it, she suppressed the final 3.5 lines of the draft, letting it end with a question: '"Then, what is life? I cried."—'[9] The closing dash is an editorial addition: it pierces the fictional framing of the text and gestures towards Shelley's death as if in answer to that final question. 'Shelley's own death, which left the poem "unfinished," has revealed the profound uncertainties in our cultural and critical attitudes toward death and authorship,' Hugh Roberts writes. 'If we read Shelley's life as a narrative totality, the "Triumph" gains special significance as the moment when he looks back on his life and seeks to capture its essence.'[10] Yet the extent to which we can legitimately think of life in terms of narrative totality, that is, read a life as if it were a literary work, is uncertain. The crux is indicated by Paul Hamilton's query regarding the poem's very genre: 'How can we have a "Triumph", in the manner of Petrarch's great series of poems, not of the usual subjects of love, fame or death, but a "Triumph" of life, the very element in which we move and have our being?'[11] Whereas a work of literature has an aesthetic order (even if this order might be deliberately self-contradictory and fragmentary), historical events are governed by contingency and surpass any attempt at aesthetic closure. 'As many commentators have remarked, the attempt to discursively grasp life in this poem is overwhelmed by the unstoppable perpetuation of life itself. There is no ending to speak of here, other than the poem's curtailment in Shelley's death,' Ross Wilson suggests.[12] The shipwreck that took Shelley's life is historically speaking a tragic accident, yet in aesthetic terms it appears as the most satisfactory conclusion imaginable to his final poem. 'The Triumph of Life' ends with life's triumph over Shelley.

This insight prompted Paul de Man to place Shelley's dead body 'in the margins of the last manuscript page', where, he asserts, it 'has become an inseparable part of the poem'.[13] When de Man calls his reading of the poem 'Shelley Disfigured', he refers not only to the disfiguration of the poem's rhetorical figures, but also to Shelley's own disfigured corpse washed up on the Italian shore and embodied in later sculptural representations. This is an instance of a historical accident, in the form of a shipwreck, providing the finishing stroke of a literary work. 'At this point,' writes de Man, meaning the draft's break-off point, 'figuration and cognition are actually interrupted by an event which shapes the text but which is not present in its represented or articulated meaning.'[14] Shelley's death is both inside and outside of his final poem: the accident that interrupted its composition determines the fragmentary form of a work that, apart from its first 48 lines, only exists as a chaotic draft manuscript. It also becomes the framing narrative through which we read the poem. 'The final test of reading, in *The Triumph of Life*, depends on how one reads the textuality of this event, how one disposes of Shelley's body,' de Man concludes.[15] But Shelley's death is just an extreme instance of something that is always the case: literary texts may aim for aesthetic closure but they are products of historical contingency. The test of any critical reading is how it determines the relation between the literary text and its historical contexts – the circumstances in which it was written, transmitted and is now being read. This is why it is not only the poet's body that needs to be disposed of, but also the body of the critic. After all, like Shelley's shipwreck, the critic is not present in the poem's 'represented or articulated meaning', and yet their interpretation contributes to shaping what the text means to its readers.

Poetry originates in the Greek ποιέω ('to make, to create, to produce'). The etymology enables a link between poetic creation and political action – the production of things and events that makes up history. This is why Agamben seamlessly slides from poetics to politics in his discussion of creation. 'I have added the term *politics*', he explains, 'because the attempt to think the *poiesis* – that is, the deeds of man – in a different way cannot but put into question even the way in which we conceive of politics.'[16] But one key difference between the two modes of production – poetic and political – is that each poetic work, unlike each political action, contains the seeds of its own criticism: it is created to be interpreted. Moreover, whereas politics acts in the present, poetry is created to be interpreted in the future. For Shelley, this is what allows poetry to transcend its own historical context: destined to be continually reinterpreted, a poem will remain fresh while factual records fade into irrelevance.

> There is this difference between a story and a poem, that a story is a catalogue of detached facts, which have no other bond of connexion than time, place, circumstance, cause and effect; the

other is the creation of actions according to the unchangeable forms of human nature, as existing in the mind of the creator, which is itself the image of all other minds. The one is partial, and applies only to a definite period of time, and a certain combination of events which can never again recur; the other is universal, and contains within itself the germ of a relation to whatever motives or actions have place in the possible varieties of human nature.[17]

The 'germ of a relation' is one of several organic metaphors that Shelley uses to describe poetry, be it as seed from which all knowledge springs or 'as the first acorn, which contained all oaks potentially',[18] a metaphor that also resonates in his claim, cited at the outset, that a man's writings contain 'an allegorical idea of his own future life, as the acorn contains the oak'.[19]

Benjamin likewise speaks of seeds to capture the distinction between writing that lives on over time, which he here calls story but which closely resembles Shelley's definition of poetry, and writing driven by facts or, in Benjamin's term, information:

> The value of information does not survive the moment in which it was new. It lives only at that moment; it has to surrender to it completely and explain itself to it without losing any time. A story is different. It does not expend itself. It preserves and concentrates its energy and is capable of releasing it even after a long time. . . . It is like those seeds of grain that have lain for centuries in the airtight chambers of the pyramids and have retained their germinative power to this day.[20]

In the present reading, the seeds contained in Shelley's and Benjamin's writings are brought to fruition and intertwined so that their works, effectively, grow together. The procedure is prompted by the peculiar method that Benjamin develops in his doctoral dissertation, *The Concept of Criticism in Early German Romanticism*. Singling out Friedrich Schlegel's theoretical work as representative of Romantic criticism, Benjamin immediately adds that Schlegel's writings will be supplemented by those of his collaborator and friend Novalis.[21] 'The justification for bringing in Novalis' writings along with those of Schlegel is the complete unanimity of both as regards the premises and conclusions of the theory of criticism,' he explains in defence of his method.[22] This is to say that, rather than pursuing the Romantic concept of criticism through a comparative reading of Schlegel and Novalis, he approaches their writings as one oeuvre, alternatingly citing from either author to substantiate his argument. 'The interchangeability of the two figures is now brought to the point where whichever provides the most suitable statement in elaborating the posited common body of thought may be introduced indifferently,' Marcus Bullock writes of Benjamin's procedure: 'They are fused into one.'[23] However questionable from a critical point of view, the method replicates the aesthetic fusion that is central to both Schlegel's and Novalis' conception of *Universalpoesie* ('universal poetry'), in which all artworks are one:

> All the classical poems of the ancients conjoin, inseparably; they form an organic whole, and are, rightly seen, a single poem, the only one in which the art of poetry itself is completely manifest. In a similar way, in perfect poetry all books should be only a single book.[24]

Shelley, with limited knowledge of Schlegel and Novalis, arrived at a similar view of all individual poems as 'episodes' of one 'great poem, which all poets, like the co-operating thoughts of one great mind, have built up since the beginning of the world'.[25] I follow these prompts from Shelley and Benjamin to approach their writings as if they were episodes in one greater work, mining them less for their similarities than for their complementarity: how the work of one can supplement that of the other in thinking through the premises of poetry and criticism.

Shelley's *Adonais* is an elegy for Keats that, because he died just over a year after composing it, appears to remembrance as an elegy for Shelley himself. The elegy charts the relation between a living poet and the universal poem to which he contributes: Keats the biological person may die, but Keats the poet will live on; moreover, the poet will live on in the very realm from which his poetic inspiration sprang:

> Dust to the dust! but the pure spirit shall flow
> Back to the burning fountain whence it came,
> A portion of the Eternal, which must glow
> Through time and change, unquenchably the same[26]

But even as *Adonais* speaks of the 'unquenchably' self-similar eternity of poetry to which the dead poet's spirit returns, the poem acknowledges that poets are in fact forgotten. Alongside allusions to living and dead authors such as Lord Byron, Thomas Moore, Thomas Chatterton, Sir

Philip Sidney and Lucan, Shelley also commemorates 'many more, whose names on Earth are dark, | But whose transmitted effluence cannot die | So long as fire outlives the parent spark'.[27] What matters for literary survival is not the author's name so much as that the seeds contained in their work live on in subsequent writings. 'One might, for example, speak of an unforgettable life or moment even if all men had forgotten it,' Benjamin notes in his essay on translation, where he develops his own take on the relation between biological and literary life.[28]

> The idea of life and afterlife in works of art should be regarded with an entirely unmetaphorical objectivity. . . . The concept of life is given its due only if everything that has a history of its own, and is not merely the setting for history, is credited with life. In the final analysis, the range of life must be determined by history rather than by nature, least of all by such tenuous factors as sensation and soul. The philosopher's task consists in comprehending all of natural life through the more encompassing life of history.[29]

Uwe Steiner terms this Benjamin's 'doctrine of the life and afterlife of works' and argues that it is an implicit refutation of the celebrations of vital power that characterised the *Lebensphilosophie* that was popular at the time. In contrast, Benjamin defines life as a historical process modelled on how texts continue to be read and used by new generations.[30] Where Shelley suggests that poets participate in 'the Eternal' by virtue of their writings, Benjamin relegates even biological life to the realm of textual transmission: life is defined as that which leaves a written record. It follows that we are only alive to the extent that our lives will be legible for posterity: poetic and historical production overlap in a manner captured by the German word *Geschichte*, which means both 'history' and 'story'.

'A text lives only if it lives *on* {*sur-vit*}, and it lives *on* only if it is *at once* translatable *and* untranslatable,' Jacques Derrida writes in his reading of 'The Triumph of Life'.[31] The way in which an original work lives on in a translation, even though every single word might have been changed, serves as a model for how the meaning of a text lives on even if it is completely transformed by future interpretations. But Derrida does not simply use translation as a metaphor for the afterlife of texts in future acts of reading; he quite literally translates the title of Shelley's last poem, 'The Triumph of Life', into 'life's triumph over life' and hence a 'life after life' that he terms 'living-on' to facilitate its literal translation into the French *sur-vivre* and German *über-leben*. The endpoint of this trajectory – *Überleben* – deliberately cites the word in Benjamin's translation essay that is usually rendered into English as 'afterlife'. In thus weaving together Shelley's 'The Triumph of Life' and Benjamin's 'The Task of the Translator', Derrida's essay performs the concept of afterlife (*survivance*) that it theorises, proving that criticism is the medium of a work's afterlife, a mode of 'triumphant translation [that] is neither the life nor the death of the text, only or already its living *on*, its life after life, its life after death'.[32]

If a text lives on by being read in the future, this means that an essential part of its meaning consists in relation to texts which are yet to be written. It is the task of critical interpretation to facilitate the apprehension of new relations between texts, relations, that emerge in the course of time. These new relations may destroy some of the old ones, just as any translation will leave behind aspects of the original work as an untranslated residue. 'The living meaning of his poems might be destroyed,' Luke Donahue notes in a reading of Shelley's 'Ode to the West Wind', 'but this very destruction is precisely what allows them to have a future. Only if they cannot be exhaustively read now, can they be read in the future . . . The death of poetry's full meaning offers it an afterlife.'[33] But focusing exclusively on the destruction of meaning distracts from the extent to which future readings are anticipated by past texts. The relation between my interpretation and the works I interpret is not antagonistic, not one of destruction, but rather one of germination – seeds contained in the work come to fruition in interpretation. Agamben describes such seeds as a work's 'capacity for development', something for the critic to latch on to and work with until reaching 'a point where it is not possible to distinguish between what is ours and what belongs to the author we are reading'.[34] This is the point I am striving for.

Notes

1. Letter to Thomas Love Peacock, 2 May 1820, in *Letters 2*, p. 192.
2. 'Julian and Maddalo', ll. 117–18.
3. Letter to Charles Ollier, 15 October 1819, in *Letters 2*, p. 128.
4. *Shelley Memorials: From Authentic Sources* (Boston, MA: Ticknor and Fields, 1859), p. 134. Jane, Lady Shelley, was the poet's daughter-in-law and his fiercest champion in the Victorian era.
5. Cited by David J. Getsy, in *Body Doubles: Sculpture in Britain, 1877–1905* (New Haven, CT: Yale University Press, 2004), p. 129. As Getsy points out, the installation was a success for Jane, Lady Shelley, yet '[b]eyond the suspect politics Lady Shelley hoped to sanitize, and despite his popular appeal, Shelley's reputation as a poet was far from secure' (p. 129), and the mere fact

of a Shelley memorial (conceived and paid for by Lady Shelley) should not be taken as proof of Shelley's complete rehabilitation at his alma mater.
6 'The Storyteller', *SW3*, p. 156; *GS2*, p. 456.
7 Hannah Arendt, 'Introduction: Walter Benjamin: 1892–1940', in *Illuminations*, ed. by Hannah Arendt, trans. by Harry Zohn (London: Jonathan Cape, 1970 [1968]), pp. 1–51 (p. 18).
8 Arendt, 'Introduction', pp. 17–18.
9 'The Triumph of Life', in *The Posthumous Poems of Percy Bysshe Shelley*, ed. by Mary Shelley (London: Hunt, 1824), pp. 71–95 (p. 95).
10 Hugh Roberts, *Shelley and the Chaos of History: A New Politics of Poetry* (University Park, PA: Pennsylvania State University Press, 1997), p. 198; relevant section reprinted in *SPP*, pp. 760–8 (pp. 760–1).
11 Paul Hamilton, 'Poetics', in *The Oxford Handbook of Percy Bysshe Shelley*, ed. by Michael O'Neill and Anthony Howe (Oxford: Oxford University Press, 2012), pp. 177–92 (p. 181).
12 Ross Wilson, *Shelley and the Apprehension of Life* (Cambridge: Cambridge University Press, 2013), p. 167.
13 Paul de Man, 'Shelley Disfigured', in *The Rhetoric of Romanticism* (New York, NY: Columbia University Press, 1984), pp. 93–123 (p. 120).
14 de Man, 'Shelley Disfigured', p. 120.
15 de Man, 'Shelley Disfigured', p. 121.
16 Agamben, 'What Is the Act of Creation?', pp. 50–1.
17 'A Defence of Poetry', *SPP*, p. 515.
18 *SPP*, p. 528; cp. p. 522; p. 531.
19 *Letters 2*, p. 192.
20 'The Storyteller', *SW3*, p. 148; *GS2*, pp. 445–6.
21 *The Concept of Criticism in Early German Romanticism*, *SW1*, p. 118; *GS1*, p. 14. At the time when Benjamin was doing his research, parts of Schlegel's corpus that have since been recovered were still lost, which may have been a reason for Benjamin to turn to Novalis' writings in order to substantiate his argument. Winifred Menninghaus has traced the limitations of Benjamin's corpus of Schlegel's and Novalis' works as he was preparing his dissertation and the extent to which he extrapolates from his materials in 'Walter Benjamin's Exposition of the Romantic Theory of Reflection', in *Walter Benjamin and Romanticism*, ed. by Andrew Benjamin and Beatrice Hanssen (London: Continuum, 2002), pp. 19–50.
22 *The Concept of Criticism in Early German Romanticism*, *SW1*, p. 119; *GS1*, p. 15.
23 Marcus Bullock, *Romanticism and Marxism: The Philosophical Development of Literary Theory and Literary History in Walter Benjamin and Friedrich Schlegel* (New York, NY: Peter Lang, 1987), p. 83.
24 Cited in *SW1*, p. 167; *GS1*, p. 90.
25 *SPP*, p. 522. Shelley had, however, read August Wilhelm Schlegel's *Lectures on Dramatic Art and Literature* in John Black's translation, so it is possible that he was influenced by F. Schlegel's ideas via A. W. Schlegel's *Lectures*, which he read in 1818.
26 *Adonais*, ll. 338–41.
27 *Adonais*, l. 264, l. 268, l. 399, l. 401, l. 404, ll. 406–8.
28 'The Task of the Translator', *SW1*, p. 254; *GS4*, p. 10.
29 'The Task of the Translator', *SW1*, p. 255; *GS4*, p. 11.
30 Uwe Steiner, 'Exemplarische Kritik: Anmerkungen zu Benjamins Kritik der *Wahlverwandtschaften*', in *Benjamins Wahlverwandschaften: zur Kritik einer Programmatischen Interpretation*, ed. by Helmut Hühn, Jan Urblich and Uwe Steiner (Berlin: Suhrkamp, 2015), pp. 37–67 (p. 60).
31 Jacques Derrida, 'Living On: Border Lines', in *Deconstruction and Criticism*, ed. by Harold Bloom and others, trans. by James Hulbert (London: Routledge & Kegan Paul, 1979), pp. 75–176 (p. 102).
32 Derrida, 'Living On', pp. 102–3. In 'Des Tours de Babel', Derrida follows Benjamin in making literary survival into the model for his conception of (biological) life, noting that 'it is rather starting from the notion of a language and its "sur-vival" in translation that we could have access to the notion of what life . . . mean[s]. This reversal is operated expressly by Benjamin.' 'Des Tours de Babel', in *Difference in Translation*, ed. and trans. by Joseph F. Graham (Ithaca, NY: Cornell University Press, 1985), pp. 165–207 (p. 178); further references in text. Towards the end of the footnote that spans the length of 'Living On: Border Lines', Derrida acknowledges that the essay draws on a seminar he gave in Paris on Benjamin's 'The Task of the Translator'

and confesses that his initial title for his reading of Shelley was 'Living On – In Translation' or even simply 'Translations' (pp. 166–8).
33 Luke Donahue, 'Romantic Survival and Shelley's "Ode to the West Wind"', *European Romantic Review*, 25.2 (2014), pp. 219–42 (p. 220).
34 Agamben, 'What Is the Act of Creation?', p. 34.

I
Truth in a Name

1
Shells

The Homeric *Hymn to Hermes* relates how the trickster god Hermes killed a tortoise, fashioned a lyre out of its shell and, as he began to sing to its tune, invented the lyric art. The Greek word χέλυς 'denotes both the tortoise and the lyre made from its shell'[1] – the lyre names lyric poetry, whereas the shell becomes an allegorical emblem for the art and its practitioners. In the Romantic period, this iconography was sufficiently well established for William Wordsworth to use a shell to symbolise poetry in the visionary dream of *The Prelude*'s 'Book V: Books'. But 'shell' is also a word that fortuitously resonates in Shelley's proper name. That he was aware of the sound of the shell in 'Shelley' is evidenced by some of his nicknames, such as the Nautilus and the Conchoid, and this awareness also enters his translation of the Homeric *Hymn to Hermes*, which Shelley renders as 'Hymn to Mercury'.

'A useful godsend are you to me now,' are the trickster god's first words to the tortoise in Shelley's translation,[2] and the Homeric shell is clearly a useful godsend for Shelley as well: as Gary Farnell has argued, the pun on χέλυς/Shelley enables the poet to claim the allegorical account of the origins of lyric poetry 'as emblem of his own general project . . . he makes it look as if it is indeed Homer who is putting the shell in Shelley'.[3] For Farnell, this is an example of what Geoffrey Hartman has termed the 'Romance of Being Named'. Searching for a linguistic equivalent to Lacan's mirror phase, in which a child 'sees itself for the first time as a coordinated being and, triumphantly, jubilantly, assumes that image', Hartman wonders whether it is 'possible to discern a specular word, logos phase, or imago of the proper name in the development of the individual'.[4] In literary writing, such a 'specular name or identity phrase' would function like a playful signature disseminated throughout the author's work: it 'is reaffirmed *in time* by a textual mimicry, joyful, parodistic, or derisory ... The repetition of the specular name gives rise to texts that seem to be anagrammatic or to conceal an unknown-unknowable key, a "pure" signifier.'[5]

A survey of Shelley's shell imagery suggests that his shells do indeed function as specular names: take, for instance, the shell that appears at the climax of his lyrical drama *Prometheus Unbound*. As he is released, Prometheus instructs The Spirit of the Hour to 'Go, borne over the cities of mankind' and 'breathe into the many-folded shell, | Loosening its mighty music'.[6] The music so loosened from the many-folded shell is the herald of a liberated future, representing Shelley's hopes for his poetry to become the catalyst of a cultural and imaginative revolution. Peter Butter's suggestion that the shell 'contained the prophecy of Prometheus' victory' identifies its importance, but is too narrow: the shell does not contain a specific prophecy but stands for the power of poetry as a whole to drive intellectual as well as political emancipation – for Shelley poets are, after all, 'the unacknowledged legislators of the World'.[7] Earl Wasserman is closer to the mark when he reads the shell 'as an analogue of the other caves of potentiality' found in Shelley's poetry, turning it into an emblem for ποίησις.[8] Equally importantly, G. Wilson Knight emphasises its sheer beauty, 'how with its mystic sea-music, itself ocean-born, it blends the aerial and the solid, time and space, its patterns perhaps suggesting a rainbow light, its curve the geometric harmony'.[9] This sampling of interpretations shows how this particular shell is allegorically overdetermined: it can be read variously as apocalyptic prophecy and the blast that heralds it, both metonym and metaphor for poetry (music of the shell), or symbol of political and epistemological potentiality. However, it is not only the object's intrinsic allegorical potential that determines Shelley's choice of specifically a shell to announce the post-apocalyptic restitution of the lyrical drama's final act, but also the echo that it carries of his own proper name: Shelley himself is the agent whose song will liberate the future.

Hartman's discussion of the 'Romance of Being Named' is based on a reading of Benjamin's short auto-mythographical sketch 'Agesilaus Santander'. 'When I was born,' the text opens, 'it occurred to my parents that I might perhaps become a writer. If that happened, it would be a good idea if people did not immediately notice I was a Jew. This is why they gave me two names in addition to my first name.'[10] This text is dated 12 August 1933, a time when the Nazi seizure of power had forced Benjamin into exile. From that time onwards, he was frequently forced to use German-sounding pseudonyms to publish his work, but he never used the two middle names – Benedix (the name of his paternal grandfather) and Schönflies (his mother's maiden name) – that he alludes to in this short text. Speaking of himself in the third person, Benjamin admits that rather than 'making the two prophylactic names public with his works, he kept them to himself [*schloß er sie in sich ein*; lit. "locked them into himself"]'.[11] But although he did not publish under these two names, they do enter his writings in more oblique ways, as in this passage from his essay on Goethe's *Elective Affinities*, where Benjamin introduces the name 'Schönflies' through a citation from Julius Walter's *Geschichte der Ästhetik im Altertum* (*History of Aesthetics in Antiquity*):

When I was born (in Belarus, then the Soviet Union), my mother did not want to give me a patronymic name, as is the custom among speakers of Russian. So, for instance, in the name of Russia's greatest poet, Alexander Sergeyevich Pushkin, the name in the middle is a patronymic indicating that his father's name was Sergey.

How I came by my patronymic is a family anecdote. Scene: my mother at the social services, registering my birth to make a Soviet citizen of me. Social worker: 'Given name?' 'Mathelinda.' 'Patronymic?' 'None.' 'What do you mean, "none"? Doesn't she have a father?' 'No, but…' 'She doesn't have a father, you just got her out of thin air.' 'Well, of course she has one, but he's not…' 'What's his name?' 'Apollo.' 'Then Apollovna it is.'

Later my family moved to Sweden, where my patronymic became a middle name. But it troubled me. Whether it was the knowledge that it had been coined by an anonymous social worker or embarrassment about it marking me out as part Russian, in my teens I had it officially changed to Apolona. My intention was to remove some of the patronymic's embarrassing foreignness, yet I clearly did not have the guts to just get rid of it, as my mother did with hers. Instead, I keep it to myself, as Benjamin kept his Schönflies.

> In the element from which the goddess [Aphrodite] arose, beauty appears truly to be at home. She is praised at the flowing rivers and fountains; one of the Oceanides is named *Schönfließ* [Beautiful Flow]; among the Nereids the beautiful form of Galatea stands out; and numerous beautiful-heeled daughters arise from the gods of the sea. The mobile element, as it first of all washes round the foot of the walker, moistens the feet of the goddesses, dispensing beauty; and silver-footed Thetis always remains the model for the poetic imagination of the Greeks when they depict this part of the body in their creations.[12]

Benjamin ostensibly cites Walter's observation on the classical association between beauty and water to further his interpretation of Ottilie, the heroine of Goethe's novel – except that, as Jochen Hörisch has noted, the citation has little relevance to the context in which it appears. The purported similarity between Ottilie and the Oceanides, Nereids and

SHELLS

other Greek beauties is a 'beautifully violent interpretation – if it succeeds, it is for the sake of one thing, for the sake of his name'.[13] Benjamin's citation of Walter is chosen less for its bearing on Goethe's novel than for the homophony between the Oceanide name that translates into German as *Schönfließ* and the maiden name of Benjamin's mother, Schönflies, that became one of his own secret names.

Benjamin must also have taken pleasure in citing an author whose surname was identical with his own given name. Noting its etymological connection to the German word for violence, *Gewalt*, Derrida suggests that the name 'Walter' resonates in Benjamin's 'Critique of Violence', written in the same period as 'Goethe's *Elective Affinities*'. The essay's closing sentence, which much like Shelley's Promethean shell-song announces the arrival of a new moral order, places this order under the sign of violence. 'Divine violence [*Gewalt*], which is the sign and seal but never the means of sacred dispatch, may be named "sovereign" violence [*mag die waltende heißen*].'[14] Highlighting the sonic relations between the name 'Walter', the noun *Gewalt* and the adjective *waltende*, the word that names violence, Derrida reads this sentence 'like the discreet seal and the first name of its signature',[15] that is, the sign and seal of divine violence but also of Benjamin's own name discreetly inserted at the climax of his text:

> Chance of language and of the proper name, chance [*aléa*] at the juncture of the most common and the most singular, law [*loi*] of the unique fate, this 'play' between *Walten* and *Walter*, this very game, here, between this particular Walter and what he says of *Walten*, one must [*il faut*] know that it cannot provide any knowledge, any demonstration or any certainty. . . . But, touching on the absolute secret, this 'play' is in no way ludic and gratuitous. For we also know that Benjamin was very interested, notably in his 'Goethe's Elective Affinities,' in the contingent [*aléatoire*] and significant coincidences of which proper names are properly the site.[16]

Walter's *waltende* is akin to Shelley's shells: in addition to their referential meaning, these words function as specular names and convey a private joke between the author and his text. Nor does it matter whether Benjamin or Shelley intended for their readers to be able to identify the veiled self-reference. What matters, rather, is that they introduce an additional stratum of signification where meaning is playful and elusive. As Hartman concludes: 'What emerges with startling clarity' in this transitory illumination is 'the *aura* of being named or imaged'.[17]

The aura of being named suffuses Shelley's transformation of the Homeric *Hymn to Hermes* into his own 'Hymn to Mercury', an allegory depicting the birth of lyric poetry out of his own proper name. 'Sing, Muse,' Shelley's translation of the hymn opens in a conventional enough manner, yet the invocation is belied by one of the hymn's central scenes in which Apollo, dazzled by Mercury's song, demands: 'What Muse, what skill, what unimagined use, | What exercise of subtlest art has given | Thy songs such power?'[18] Apollo's question is the more remarkable coming from the god of lyric poetry. 'And I, who speak this praise, am that Apollo | Whom the Olympian muses ever follow,' he goes on.[19] In this line Shelley departs from the original, which can be more accurately rendered as 'For I too am a follower of the Olympian Muses'.[20] Shelley's alteration, which turns Apollo from a follower to the leader of the Muses, is not accidental: he drafted a note explaining that 'The literal is – who ever follow or minister to, the Olympian Muses – but without regard to them the relation expressed by οπηδως [adj. = following, accompanying] may be considered as a convertible term.'[21]

Even if we accept Shelley's argument that the term is convertible, it is telling that he decides to convert it: where the Greek has Apollo acknowledge both himself and Mercury as followers of the Muses, Shelley's conversion places Mercury's song in opposition to Apollo and his accompanying Muses. Since Apollo has just asserted that 'such a strain of wondrous, strange, untired | And soul-awakening music sweet and strong | Yet did I never hear except from thee', this alteration implies that the Muses in Apollo's wake have never inspired such song as emanates from Mercury's lyre.[22] Jennifer Fraser has pointed out that 'although he is the God of Poetry, when Apollo hears Hermes's lyre, he hears poetic song for the first time'.[23] It is a peculiar displacement whereby Apollo cannot fulfil his divine function as god of lyric poetry until he receives the lyre from his trickster brother. Shelley's translation targets this displacement by emphasising moments when Apollo is bewildered by Mercury's invention, as in the following passage in which Apollo has discovered that Mercury has stolen and sacrificed his oxen and now wants to take vengeance on his younger brother, who, in his turn, is trying to figure out a means of escape:

> Sudden he [Mercury] changed his plan, and with strange skill
>   Subdued the strong Latonian [Apollo] by the might
> Of winning music, to his mightier will;
>   His left hand held the lyre, and in his right
> The plectrum struck the chords – unconquerable
>   Up from beneath his hand in circling flight
> The gathering music rose[24]

Playing on his shell-lyre, Mercury demonstrates that his will is mightier than Apollo's wrath. Apollo, duly subdued, nonetheless misunderstands the nature of Mercury's 'winning music'. The very question he poses to Mercury, 'Whether the glorious power you now show forth | Was folded up within you at your birth, | Or whether mortal taught or God inspired | The power of unpremeditated song[?]',[25] is based on a mistaken assumption about the source of Mercury's power. Mercury answers Apollo's question by handing him the instrument:

> The lyre – be mine the glory giving it –
>   Strike the sweet chords, and sing aloud, and wake
> The joyous pleasure out of many a fit
>   Of trancèd sound – and with fleet fingers make
> Thy liquid-voicèd comrade talk with thee,–
> It can talk measured music eloquently.[26]

Rather than being inborn, 'mortal taught or God inspired', Mercury's song lies entranced within the instrument and is awoken by playing it: it is the shell-lyre itself that 'talk[s] measured music eloquently'. Therefore, playing on the lyre is not about exercising mastery over a tool, but more like participating in a conversation. 'I | Present thee with this music-flowing shell, | Knowing thou canst interrogate it well,' Mercury adds to complete his gift, which will thenceforth be known as the Apollonian lyre and an emblem of lyric poetry.[27]

The idea that lyric power is a quality inherent in the shell-lyre, rather than the person playing it, is anticipated in a slight adjustment that Shelley makes to the opening description of the tortoise whose shell furnishes the material for the first lyre. Mercury encounters the tortoise as he leaves the cavern of his nativity:

> Out of the lofty cavern wandering
>   He found a tortoise, and cried out – 'a treasure!'
> (For Mercury first made the tortoise sing)
>   The beast before the portal at his leisure
> The flowery herbage was depasturing,
>   Moving his feet in a deliberate measure
> Over the turf.[28]

Mercury may be the first to make the tortoise sing, but the basic elements of this song are already present in the 'deliberate measure' with which the tortoise treads the ground – a measure still reverberating in the 'measure | Of the sweet lyre' that so impresses Apollo.[29] Claudine Kahan notes that 'the tortoise which merely "waddles along" in the original poem, moves "his feet in deliberate measure" [sic] in his translation . . . and this precision, however slight, prepares the ground for the later description of the lyre'.[30] Kahan supports her argument by comparing H. G. Evelyn-White's and Shelley's translations of Mercury's address to Apollo as he hands him the lyre: καλὰ καὶ εὖ κατὰ κόσμον ἐπιστάμενος ἀγορεύειν – 'you are skilled in good well-ordered utterance,' says Evelyn-White's Hermes to Apollo; 'It can talk measured music eloquently,' says Shelley's Mercury.[31] Shelley's editors confirm the deviation: 'S. mistranslates the original . . . "skilled at uttering beautifully and in good order," which applies to Apollo, not the lyre.'[32] However, this change is not a mistranslation but a purposeful alteration of the original: the 'measured music' of the shell-lyre is an echo of the 'deliberate measure' of the tortoise's tread while still alive. 'Where the Greek text makes the mastery of social and orderly speech an attribute of Apollo,' Kahan notes, 'Shelley makes it a predicate of the lyre.'[33] The small changes that he introduces into his translation amount to a claim for the primacy of Shelley's art over even the god of lyric poetry: the lyric measure that dazzles Apollo is an intrinsic property of Shelley's namesake shell.

The translation contains another remarkable departure from the original that Kahan only notes in passing. '*Agoreuein*,' she writes, 'which Shelley translates as "measured music," and rendered as "good, well-ordered utterance" by H. G. Evelyn-White, indeed refers to public speech.'[34] Shelley purposefully transforms a beautifully ordered rhetorical performance fit for a public assembly into 'measured music' emanating from the shell-lyre; that is, he turns public rhetoric into poetry, because in Shelley's poetics it is precisely measure that distinguishes poetic language: 'It is necessary', he writes in the 'Defence', 'to determine the distinction between measured and unmeasured language; for the popular division into prose and verse is inadmissible in accurate philosophy.'[35] Jessica Quillin suggests that, since Shelley turns measure into the primary

The name Mathelinda is an imperial hangover: it was the English name of my Ugandan grandmother. It often causes consternation, sliding into sonically similar names: Mathilda, Melinda, Maddalena, Metheld and so on.

Given the historical background, I am particularly impatient with British people who struggle to pronounce my name, asking me for short forms like Mattie or Lindy. Or asking me what it means, because 'African names have such beautiful meanings'. My default answer is that *linda* means 'pretty' or 'beautiful' in Spanish and that, coupled with *Mathe-*, it celebrates the beauty of mathematics.

Like literature, maths deals with figures; like poetry, it is a science of numbers, of measuring thoughts rather than things. These associations contributed to making measure one of the central concepts of this book.

feature of poetic language, 'music becomes the sole identifying characteristic of a poet'.[36] His translation of ἐπιστάμενος ἀγορεύειν as 'measured music' supports Quillin's point, though it must be remembered that measure is not about musicality for its own sake; rather, Shelley values it because it enables the poet to recapture the 'certain rhythm or order' that is innate to man 'and from which the hearer and the spectator receive an intenser and purer pleasure than from any other'.[37] This is why 'measured' and 'well-ordered' are convertible equivalents when it comes to translating ἀγορεύειν.

When Shelley turns the waddle of the Homeric tortoise into measured music, he specifies that the tortoise is '[m]oving his *feet* in a deliberate measure';[38] a foot being the basic prosodic unit by which poetry is measured. This invites us to interpret the hymn's repeated descriptions of moving feet as figures for its own measure. When Mercury steals Apollo's oxen, for example, 'being ever mindful of his craft | Backward and forward drove he them astray | So that the tracks which seemed before, were aft'.[39] In addition, he disguises his own footsteps: 'for each foot he wrought a kind of raft | Of tamarisk, and tamarisk-like sprigs | And bound them in a lump with withy twigs'.[40] Mercury's ploy is meant to confound Apollo and it works a charm. 'What wonder do mine eyes behold!', Apollo exclaims when he discovers the tracks:

> 'Here are the footsteps of the hornèd herd
>   Turned back towards their field of asphodel –
> But these! – are not the tracks of beast or bird,
>   Grey wolf or bear or lion of the dell
> Or manèd Centaur – sand was never stirred
>   By man or woman thus! – Inexplicable!
> Who with unwearied feet could e'er impress
> The sand with such enormous vestiges?[41]

When Apollo later reports the theft to their father, Zeus, he yet again emphasises his inability to comprehend the marks of Mercury's passage:

> *His* steps were most incomprehensible –
>   I know not how I can describe in words
> Those tracks – he could have gone along the sands
> Neither upon his feet nor on his hands –[42]

Since feet are a pun on metric feet, and treading is a synecdoche for poetry's musical measure, Apollo's consternation when faced with the traces of Mercury's 'unwearied feet' is analogous to his stunned reaction to the 'measure | of the sweet lyre'.[43]

Apollo's bedazzlement is further developed by Shelley's use of light imagery, which anticipates the imagery he will use to describe poetry in 'A Defence of Poetry', written in the year following the translation of the Homeric *Hymn*. Thus, when Apollo comes looking for the culprit who stole his cows, we learn that Mercury wraps himself up in his 'swaddling-clothes . . . As among fire-brands lies a burning spark | Covered, beneath the ashes cold and dark'.[44] The simile 'as a burning spark' is repurposed in Shelley's description of Dante's poetry: 'His very words are instinct with spirit; each is as a spark, a burning atom of inextinguishable thought; and many yet lie covered in the ashes of their birth'.[45] This self-citation is a two-way movement. If translating the *Hymn to Hermes* helped Shelley discover imagery that he would later employ in formulating his poetics, it is also the case that his poetics determined his translation choices, as in his introduction of 'deliberate measure' to describe the tortoise's tread. Another example of this practice is found in his choice of 'Clothe in the light of his loud melodies' to render ἐγέραιρεν ἀοιδῇ.[46] Tom Phillips notes that this translation is 'transparently recognizable as a product of his own imagistic repertoire' that has no counterpart in the Greek – but it is precisely by translating something that is not immediately apparent in the original that Shelley transforms our understanding of the *Hymn*.

> Employing a metaphorical register alien to the Greek, Shelley encourages readers to find in his translation the discovery of an 'unapprehended relation', as his line projects or discovers behind ἐγέραιρεν ἀοιδῇ a moment in which a mode of intelligibility opens up that neither Apollo nor (more importantly) the poet responsible for the *Hymn to Hermes* can adequately capture. On this account, Shelley's retrojections are not only a virtuosic parading of his own poetic identity and concerns, but a means of writing moral and imaginative possibilities back into the imaginative domain of which the original text is a 'trace'[47]

The 'retrojections' through which Shelley reshapes the original to make it reflect his own poetic concerns indicate how the *Hymn* lives on within his translation: he does not simply recreate the Greek original in his own English, he transforms it in a way that generates new opportunities for meaning within the ancient text. Shelley's 'Hymn to Mercury' retrospectively endows the Homeric *Hymn to Hermes* with new significance and, in so doing, corroborates its status as the classical account of the birth of lyric poetry. It is a gift, mirroring how Apollo, belatedly, became the god of this art by receiving the shell-lyre from Hermes.

In the early 1930s, as it was becoming increasingly clear that he would never be able to return to the city of his birth, Benjamin began work on *Berlin Childhood around 1900*, a series of autobiographical thought-images that recover lost times and places from his personal history. He intended to head the sequence with a section called 'Die Mummerehlen', which contains a portrait of himself as a child: 'like a mollusk in its shell, I had my abode in the nineteenth century, which now lies hollow before me like an empty shell. I hold it to my ear.'[48] The sounds unloosened from Benjamin's shell need to be heard in his original German:

> Was höre ich? Ich höre nicht den Lärm von Feldgeschützen oder von Offenbachscher Ballmusik, auch nicht das Heulen der Fabriksirenen oder das Geschrei, das mittags durch die Börsensäle gellt, nicht einmal Pferdetrappeln auf dem Pflaster oder die Marschmusik der Wachtparade. Nein, was ich höre, ist das kurze Rasseln des Anthrazits, der aus dem Blechbehälter in einen Eisenofen niederfällt, es ist der dumpfe *Knall*, mit dem die Flamme des Gasstrumpfs sich entzündet, und das *Klirren* der *Lampenglocke* auf dem Messingreifen, wenn auf der Straße ein Gefährt vorbeikommt. Noch andere Geräusche, wie das Scheppern des *Schlüsselkorbs*, die beiden *Klingeln* an der Vorder- und der Hintertreppe; endlich ist auch ein *kleiner* Kindervers dabei. »Ich will dir was erzählen von der Mummerehlen.«[49]

What do I hear? Not the noise of field artillery or of dance music à la Offenbach, or the howling of factory sirens, or the cries that resound through the Stock Exchange at midday – not even the stamping of horses on the cobblestones, or march music announcing the changing of the guard. No, what I hear is the brief clatter of the anthracite as it falls from a coal scuttle into a cast-iron stove, the dull pop [*Knall*] of the flame as it ignites in the gas mantle, and the clinking [*Klirren*] of the lamp shade [*Lampenglocke*] on its brass ring when a vehicle passes by on the street. And other sounds as well, like the jingling of the basket of keys [*Schlüsselkorbs*], or the ringing [*Klingeln*] of the two bells at the front and back steps. And, finally, there is a little [*kleiner*] nursery rhyme. 'Listen to my tale of the mummerehlen.'[50]

The consonantal reverberations in this passage recreate what Werner Hamacher has termed the 'tonal world' of Benjamin's childhood – a world Peter Fenves brings out in his translation of Hamacher's essay: 'the *c*lap and *c*latter of the *l*amp *c*lock, in the tassle of the *l*ock cord, in the *kl*ing and the *cl*ipped children's verse and finally in the *sl*ack and *fl*aking of the small glass sphere: *Kn*all, *Kl*irren, Lampeng*l*ocke, Schlüsse*l*korb, *Kl*inge*l*n, *kl*einen, *L*ockeren, *Fl*ockigen, *kl*einen *Gl*askuge*l*n'.[51] Robert Ryder has further added to this list of sonic correspondences:

> the 'z' of *kurz* and the 'ra-' of *Rasseln* are echoed in the German pronunciation for the word, *Anthrazits*. . . . the syllables that reverberate between 'der d**umpf**e Kn**all**' and 'die **Fl**amme des Gas**str**umpfs' . . . the phrase 'd**as Kl**irren der **L**ampeng**l**ocke' . . . the alliteration of 'das **Schepp**ern des **Sch**lüsse**l**korbs' . . . the last two syllables of the words, 'er-*zählen*' and 'Mummer-*ehlen*.'[52]

This dense patterning of sound indicates that 'Die Mummerehlen' is an example of measured language, even if it is not cast in verse. While Benjamin's text is littered with objects from the nineteenth century, the actual act of reminiscence is not carried out among these things. Rather, it is the writerly act of awakening long-lost echoes in words that captures the process of remembering. The passage's lyricism confirms that the shell that child Benjamin holds to his ear is an emblem of lyric poetry, a kind of poetry that, for the adult Benjamin, is being torn apart by the ruptures of modernity. In fashioning this self-portrait with a shell, Benjamin is not merely listening for echoes from the past (in the way that, proverbially, a shell allows one to hear the echoes of the sea), he is also hearkening after a certain lyric sensibility that risks slipping out of his grasp together with the Berlin of his childhood.

Notes

1 *Homeric Hymns, Homeric Apocrypha, Lives of Homer*, ed. and trans. by Martin L. West (Cambridge, MA: Harvard University Press, 2003), n. 24, p. 115.
2 'Hymn to Mercury', l. 33.
3 Gary Farnell, 'Rereading Shelley', *ELH*, 60 (1993), 625–50 (p. 637). While it was not uncommon to use Latin names in translations from the Greek, Farnell suggests that 'it is surely not insignificant that "Mercury" was . . . one of the poet's many nicknames' (p. 634). He notes a comment by Shelley's friend Leigh Hunt: 'I used to tell him [Shelley] that he had come from the planet Mercury'. *The Autobiography of Leigh Hunt*, ed. by J. E. Morpurgo (London: Cresset Press, 1949), p. 331.
4 Geoffrey Hartman, *Saving the Text: Literature/Derrida/Philosophy* (Baltimore, MD: Johns Hopkins University Press, 1981), p. 100–1.

5   Hartman, *Saving the Text*, p. 102.
6   *Prometheus Unbound*, III.iii.76, III.iii.80–1.
7   Peter Butter, *Shelley's Idols of the Cave* (Edinburgh: Edinburgh University Press, 1954), p. 198; 'A Defence of Poetry', *SPP*, p. 535.
8   Earl J. Wasserman, *Shelley: A Critical Reading* (Baltimore, MD: Johns Hopkins University Press, 1971), p. 348.
9   G. Wilson Knight, *The Starlit Dome: Studies in the Poetry of Vision* (London: Methuen and Co., 1968), pp. 212–13.
10 'Agesilaus Santander', *SW2*, p. 714; *GS6*, p. 520.
11 'Agesilaus Santander', *SW2*, p. 712; *GS6*, p. 520.
12 Cited in *SW1*, p. 342; *GS1*, p. 183.
13 'Eine Deutung von schöner Gewaltsamkeit – erfolgt sie doch um eines, um seines Namen willen.' Jochen Hörisch, 'Der Satanische Engel und das Glück – Die Namen Walter Benjamins', *Spuren – Zeitschrift für Kunst und Gesellschaft* (1986), 38–42 (p. 41), my translation. Thomas Schestag has also discussed this citation from Walter: 'In dem Zitat Walters aber zitiert Benjamin, und ruft – lautlos – das Wort *beim Namen*, den Mädchennamen der Mutter Walter Benjamins, Pauline *Schoenflies*. Und mehr als das. Denn *Schoenflies* ist, neben *Bendix*, dem Vornamen des väterlichen Großvaters, einer der beiden Vornamen, die Walter Benjamin trug, und genauer, »in sich ein[...]schloß«.' Thomas Schestag, 'Lampen', in *Übersetzen: Walter Benjamin*, ed. by Christiaan L. Hart Nibbrig (Frankfurt am Main: Suhrkamp, 2001), pp. 38–79 (p. 75). ('In the citation from Walter, Benjamin cites, and calls – soundlessly – the word *by its name*, the maiden name of Walter Benjamin's mother, Pauline *Schoenflies*. And more than that. Because *Schoenflies* is, beside *Bendix*, the name of his paternal grandfather, one of the two given names that Walter Benjamin carried, and, to be more precise, "locked into himself".' My translation.) While I agree with the range of personal allusions that Schestag evokes, I am surprised by his suggestion that Benjamin calls his hidden name 'soundlessly' (*lautlos*): after all, it is all about the sound of *Schönfließ* and *Schönflies*.
14 'Critique of Violence', *SW1*, p. 252, translation emended; *GS2*, p. 203.
15 Jacques Derrida, 'Force of Law', in *Acts of Religion*, ed. by Gil Anidjar, trans. by Mary Quaintance (London: Routledge, 2002), pp. 230–98 (p. 264).
16 Derrida, 'Force of Law', n. 47, pp. 292–3.
17 Hartman, *Saving the Text*, p. 113.
18 'Hymn to Mercury', ll. 597–9.
19 'Hymn to Mercury', ll. 603–4.
20 *PS3*, p. 536, n. to ll. 603–4.
21 Cited in *PS3*, p. 536, n. to ll. 603–4. Material in square brackets is part of the original.
22 'Hymn to Mercury', ll. 593–5.
23 Jennifer Fraser, 'Intertextual Turnarounds: Joyce's Use of the Homeric "Hymn to Hermes"', *James Joyce Quarterly*, 36 (1999), 541–57 (pp. 551–2).
24 'Hymn to Mercury', ll. 557–63.
25 'Hymn to Mercury', ll. 587–90.
26 'Hymn to Mercury', ll. 639–44.
27 'Hymn to Mercury', ll. 658–60.
28 'Hymn to Mercury', ll. 25–31.
29 'Hymn to Mercury', ll. 568–9.
30 Claudine T. Kahan, 'Shelley's "Hymn to Mercury": Poetic Praxis and the Creation of Value', *Studies in Romanticism*, 31 (1992), 147–69 (p. 154).
31 *Hymn to Hermes*, trans. Evelyn-White, l. 479; 'Hymn to Mercury', trans. Shelley, l. 644.
32 *PS3*, n. to l. 644.
33 Kahan, 'Shelley's "Hymn to Mercury"', p. 150.
34 Kahan, 'Shelley's "Hymn to Mercury"', p. 150.
35 'A Defence of Poetry', *SPP*, p. 514.
36 Jessica K. Quillin, *Shelley and the Musico-Poetics of Romanticism* (Farnham, Surrey: Ashgate Publishing, 2012), p. 40.
37 'A Defence of Poetry', *SPP*, p. 512.
38 'Hymn to Mercury', l. 30; emphasis added.
39 'Hymn to Mercury', ll. 96–8.
40 'Hymn to Mercury', ll. 100–2.
41 'Hymn to Mercury', ll. 285–93.

42 'Hymn to Mercury', ll. 453–60.
43 'Hymn to Mercury', ll. 568–9.
44 'Hymn to Mercury', ll. 307–9.
45 'A Defence of Poetry', *SPP*, p. 528.
46 'Hymn to Mercury', l. 576; *Hymn to Hermes*, l. 429. West translates these words as 'he honoured in his song', in *Homeric Hymns*, p. 147.
47 Tom Phillips, 'Unapprehended Relations', *Classical Receptions Journal*, 12.1 (2020), 109–27 (pp. 118–19).
48 'The Mummerehlen', *SW3*, p. 392, translation emended; *GS4*, p. 261.
49 'The Mummerehlen', *GS4*, p. 262; my emphasis.
50 'The Mummerehlen', *SW3*, p. 392.
51 Werner Hamacher, 'The Word *Wolke* – If It Is One', trans. by Peter Fenves, in *Benjamin's Ground: New Readings of Walter Benjamin,* ed. by Rainer Nägele (Detroit, MI: Wayne State University Press, 1986), pp. 147–75 (p. 164).
52 Robert G. Ryder, 'Walter Benjamin's Shell-Shock', *New Review of Film and Television Studies*, 5 (2007), 135–55 (p. 149).

2
Violets

It is somewhat ironic that Shelley's allegory of the birth of lyric poetry takes place in translation – an art of which he himself said that 'it were as wise to cast a violet into a crucible that you might discover the formal principle of its colour and odour, as seek to transfuse from one language into another the creations of a poet'.[1] For Shelley, translating poetry is only worthwhile when the act of translation simultaneously becomes one of poetic creation. 'At times, indeed, Shelley's translations are quite obviously variations on a theme. Whether deliberately or not, Shelley uses the framework of the original as a trellis round which to wrap some of his own images and ideas,' Timothy Webb has noted.[2] Such a practice, demonstrated in the creative licence of his translation of the 'Hymn to Mercury', runs against the grain of Benjamin's view of translation, which he defines as an art form distinct from poetic creation: 'Just as translation is a form of its own, so, too, may the task of the translator be regarded as distinct and clearly differentiated from the task of the poet.'[3] In seeking to separate these two tasks, Benjamin's 'The Task of the Translator' is effectively a poetics of translation, an attempt to determine its artistic form. 'The text is a poetics, a theory of poetic language, so why does Benjamin not go to the poets?' de Man asks in his lecture on the essay, offering the

> This chapter is about violet, the flower, yet I also want you to hear the word 'violet', the colour close to purple. This is a colour associated with St Lydia, or Lydia of Thyatira, sainted for being the first European converted to Christianity. Before finding God, she was a seller of purple.

following answer: 'One of the reasons why he takes the translator rather than the poet is that the translator, per definition, fails. The translator can never do what the original text did.'[4] He reads the translator's *Aufgabe* ('task') in terms of *aufgeben* ('to give up'), thereby reiterating common critical prejudices about the inferiority of translation, and how it fails to live up to the original. However, Benjamin explicitly rejects the notion that the translation should do whatever the original did in a new language; instead, translation 'ultimately serves the purpose of expressing the innermost relationships of languages to one another'.[5] Understanding these relationships between languages entails retracing Benjamin's theory of language, which received an early canonical formulation in the 1916 essay 'On Language as Such and on the Language of Man'.

One of the central aims of Benjamin's essay 'On Language' is to refute what he terms 'the bourgeois view of language', by which he means the hypothesis 'that the word has an accidental relation to its object, that it is a sign for things (or knowledge [*Erkenntnis*] of them) agreed by some convention. Language never gives *mere* signs.'[6] The notion that the word is an arbitrary sign, and that the relation between signifier and signified, the sound of a word and its meaning, is purely conventional, is a key concept of Ferdinand de Saussure's *Course in General Linguistics*, which appeared in print in 1916, the same year in which Benjamin composed his essay 'On Language'. Saussurean ideas about the arbitrariness of the linguistic sign underpin most twentieth-century theories of language, which is why Benjamin's attempt to prove that words are *not* arbitrary signs – and even more so his reliance on biblical exegesis in doing so – is at odds with many of our critical habits. For the purposes of my reading, I consider Benjamin's account of the origins of language as an allegory that does not require literal faith in the passages from Genesis that he draws on any more than tracing the birth of lyric poetry in the Homeric *Hymn to Hermes* requires us to believe in the Ancient Greek pantheon. Benjamin says as much himself:

> If in what follows the nature of language is considered on the basis of the first chapter of Genesis, the object is neither biblical interpretation nor subjection of the Bible to objective consideration as revealed truth, but the discovery of what emerges of itself from the biblical text with regard to the nature of language.[7]

Benjamin begins at the very beginning, with what he terms 'the threefold rhythm of the creation of nature': 'Let there be – He made (created) – He named.'[8] The divine λόγος ('word') both creates and names the world. For

Benjamin, one passes into the other: God creates the world by naming it. Furthermore, Benjamin links the divine λόγος to knowledge, *Erkenntnis*. This noun and its cognates appear frequently in his work, but it is difficult to find an English equivalent that captures its range – meanings include 'knowledge', 'cognition', 'recognition', 'realisation', 'discovery' and 'perception'. In addition to the theological associations that Benjamin directly evokes here – the biblical Tree of Knowledge, for instance, is called *der Baum der Erkenntnis* in German – the term also recalls Immanuel Kant's transcendental philosophy, where *Erkenntniskritik* is the branch that determines the nature and limits of human knowledge (in this context, *Erkenntniskritik* can be translated as 'epistemology'). The term returns in Benjamin's 'Erkenntniskritische Vorrede' to *The Origin of German Tragic Drama*, which John Osborne translates as 'Epistemo-Critical Prologue', and again in Benjamin's late work, where the 'dialectical image' flashes up in the *Jetzt der Erkennbarkeit* ('now of recognizability').[9]

In 'On Language', Benjamin identifies the creative power of the divine λόγος with naming and knowing. 'God's word is cognizant [*erkennend*] because it is name. . . . The absolute relation of name to knowledge [*Erkenntnis*] exists only in God; only there is name, because it is inwardly identical with the creative word, the pure medium of knowledge [*Erkenntnis*].'[10] The primary import of the biblical passage, then, is to establish the unity of λόγος, name and knowledge. This unity leads Benjamin to a very specific view of nature according to which each thing contains within itself the knowledge of the name with which it was made. 'For God created things; the creative word in them is the seed of the cognizing name [*Keim des erkennenden Namens*].'[11] Things are, however, mute. The task of human language – represented by Adam's naming of the animals – is to translate their names into sound. 'Naming, knowledge [*Erkenntnis*] and translation are here synonymous terms,' Irving Wohlfarth explains. 'The Adamic language knows [*erkennt*] nature, because it is the translation of nature.'[12] As a translator, Adam is not a name-giver; rather, his act of naming germinates the seed of the *erkennender Name* implanted in each thing at its creation. 'This means that God made things knowable in their names,' Benjamin explains. 'Man, however, names them according to knowledge [*maßen der Erkenntnis*].'[13] The word 'according' here translates *maßen*, a verb formed from the noun *Maß* ('measure'). Adamic naming proceeds in the measure of knowledge, transforming the seeds of divine λόγος embedded in mute nature into the sounds of human language.

Benjamin furthermore adds that Adam's 'translation of the mute into the sonic' is 'the translation of an imperfect language into a more perfect [*vollkommenere*, lit. 'more complete'] one'.[14] With the same belated logic whereby Hermes' gift of the lyre completes Apollo's divine vocation as the god of lyric poetry, Adam's voicing of creative Names in human sounds completes the divine fiat of linguistic creation. This is why sound is so important to Benjamin's theory of language:

> The incomparable feature of human language is that its magical community with things is immaterial and purely mental, and the symbol of this is sound. The Bible expresses this symbolic fact when it says that God breathes his breath [*Odem*] into man: this is at once life and mind and language.[15]

The word *Odem* that Benjamin uses is the common German equivalent of the Hebrew *ruach*, a theologically overdetermined term. As M. H. Abrams has noted in a discussion of Romantic poetics, the Latin *spiritus* as well as *anima*, 'the Greek *pneuma*, the Hebrew *ruach*, the Sanskrit *atman*, as well as the equivalent words in many other languages, some of them totally unrelated' all signify 'wind' and 'breath' and 'soul' and all are intimately related to notions of an invisible life-force that sets inert matter into motion.[16] In stating that sound – which he also defines as 'the pure formal principle of language'[17] – symbolises the divine breath (*Odem* or *ruach*) with which God breathes life into man, Benjamin effectively offers a novel interpretation of Genesis 1:2–3: 'The earth was without form, and void; and darkness was on the face of the deep. And the Spirit [*ruach*] of God was hovering over the face of the waters. Then God said, "Let there be light"; and there was light.' The divine *ruach* that moved upon the waters *before* He created light is 'the pure formal principle of language', which is to say the measurability of sound that is the precondition for that first articulation, 'Let there be light,' which, in its turn, created light, knowledge and the world that followed.

Adam voices the names of things *maßen der Erkenntnis*, in the measure of knowledge, which guarantees the non-arbitrary relation between the sound of a word and the divine λόγος with which it was made: in the original human language, sound perfectly corresponds to sense – or, to use another distinction that Benjamin introduces in his translation essay, what is meant, *das Gemeinte*, aligns with the manner of meaning, *Art des Meinens*.[18] The sole exception – the one kind of word that is not translated from the language of God – is the proper name, which we choose for ourselves: 'Of all beings, man is the only one who names his own kind, as he is the only one whom God did not name.'[19] Since neither sound nor proper names are derived from God's word, the sound of one's own name is the measure of a uniquely human linguistic creativity.

These considerations form the backdrop of Benjamin's play with the echo of 'Walter' in *Gewalt* or *waltende*, or the homophony between *Schönflies* and *Schönfließ*. It also means that proper names were not affected by the Fall in the same way that the rest of language was. For Benjamin, the Fall of Man coincides with a Fall of Language, in which the perfect equivalence between divine λόγος and human sound was shattered: 'the Fall marks the birth of the *human word*, in which name no longer lives intact and which has stepped out of name-language'.[20] If the prelapsarian name-language was invented to voice the *erkennender Name* embedded in things and was, as such, an end in itself, fallen language has a new function: communication. The imperative to communicate represents a separation from the *erkennender Name*. This rift is inscribed within the very word for communication, *Mitteilung*. As noun, *Teil* means 'part' or 'segment', while the verb *teilen* means 'to divide' or 'to split'. Adding the preposition *mit-* ('with') and suffix *-ung* (used to form nouns from verbs), *Mitteilung* could be literally rendered as 'with-dividing'. Sonically, it also evokes the word *Mittel* ('means') – the opposite of an end in itself. 'In stepping outside the purer language of name, man makes language a means [of communication]', Benjamin writes, 'and therefore also, in one part at any rate, a *mere* sign; and this later results in the plurality of languages.'[21] That is, the multiplicity of human languages arises when the correspondence between sound and sense, what is meant and the manner of meaning, that characterised Adamic language falls into disarray.

> When I was christened, the priest said that 'Mathelinda' would not do, they would have to choose a name from the Saints' Calendar – and so I became a Lydia, chosen for its resemblance to Linda, which is what my family called me. I have never used this name, nor am I religious, but growing up I took some pleasure in having a secret name 'in front of God', as it were. When researching this chapter, I decided to look up St Lydia and discovered that she was known as 'The Woman of Purple', which seemed to give some supernatural sanction both for my predilection for this colour and the reading I was engaged in.

Even though it is broken and disordered, each vernacular language is nonetheless a fractured remnant of the Adamic language. It follows that the translator's materials are broken shards, which Benjamin illustrates with another biblical image, that of a broken vessel:

> Fragments of a vessel that are to be glued together must match one another in the smallest details, although they need not be like one another. In the same way a translation, instead of imitating the sense of the original, must lovingly and in detail incorporate the original's

way of meaning, thus making both the original and the translation recognizable [*erkennbar*] as fragments [*Bruchstück*] of a greater language, just as fragments [*Bruchstück*] are part of a vessel.[22]

Carol Jacobs's reading of this simile shows that in 'the joining together of translation and original, language remains a *Bruchstück*'.[23] That is, for Benjamin, translation does not mend or restore the language that was fractured in the Fall. Rather, it allows different manners of meaning to supplement one another, much as pieces in a puzzle or mosaic supplement one another in creating a single image: 'the great motif' of translation, he writes, is 'an integration of many tongues into one true language . . . in which . . . the languages themselves, supplemented and reconciled in their manner of meaning, become as one'.[24] To illustrate how such supplementation works in practice, Benjamin chooses the example of 'bread' in German and French: the two words *pain* and *Brot* 'signify the very same thing' but they signify it differently – there is no sonic resemblance between them, for instance. 'Even though the manner of meaning in these two words is in such conflict, it supplements itself [*ergänzt sie sich*] in each of the two languages from which the words are derived; to be more specific, the manner of meaning in them supplements itself [*ergänzt sich*] in its relation to what is meant.'[25] *Pain* and *Brot*, no less than the English word *bread*, supplement one another in denoting 'bread', whose meaning is, however, not exhausted by these three words for it.

By marking the divergent ways in which languages mean, translation records the changes that they have undergone since their Fall from their shared origin in the Adamic language of names. The task of the translator is, however, not to reconstitute this original language, but to assemble target and source language in such a way that the two are *ergänzt und versöhnt* (supplemented and reconciled) but not *erlöst* (redeemed); that is, the Word (λόγος) is not made whole. Not restitution, but supplementation, in all its forms, reverberates throughout Benjamin's discussion of the pure language that emerges in translation: as verb *sich ergänzen* (appears thrice), as noun *Ergänzung* (appears twice), as adjectival coupling *ergänzt/unergänzt*.[26]

> For in the individual, unsupplemented [*unergänzten*] languages, what is meant is never found in relative independence, as in individual words or sentences; rather, it is in a constant state of flux – until it is able to emerge as the pure language from the harmony of all the various ways of meaning.[27]

The task of the translator, therefore, consists in creating a contrapuntal interplay in which the different manners of meaning in the two (or more) languages concerned are harmonised. Picking up on Benjamin's reference to the Pythagorean concept of *musica universalis* ('the music of the spheres'), Wohlfarth describes the language of Benjaminian translation as an embodiment of the 'pre-established harmony of all language spheres'.[28] Drawing on the same celestial imagery, Rainer Nägele speaks of it as a 'complementary language-harmony' that is 'not phenomenally perceptible' because it exists on a syntactical rather than a sonic level.[29] In other words, this is a kind of harmony that cannot be heard in the measure of a line, but only perceived in the constellation of multiple languages.

If the multiplicity of languages is the central stimulus of translation, it is also one for poetry. 'Languages imperfect insofar as they are many; the absolute one is lacking,' Stéphane Mallarmé writes in a passage of 'Crisis of Verse' that Benjamin cites in 'The Task of the Translator'.[30] Without an absolute language, words cannot mean absolutely. Which is to say that the Fall of Language brought about not only a multiplicity of languages but also a multiplicity of meanings in a single word, and since words do not mean singly, they appear to mean arbitrarily – for how else could a single word mean several things? 'Only, be aware,' Mallarmé continues, 'that *verse would not exist*' had it not been for such variability of meaning: 'it, philosophically, makes up for language's deficiencies, as a superior supplement'.[31] In other words, it is only because language is inherently fractured and inadequate that we need verse. 'What a strange mystery: and, from no lesser intentions [than supplementing language's deficiency], metrics appeared, during incubatory times.'[32]

Mallarmé's line of reasoning reverses the idea that language originates in poetry, which has been around at least since Giambattista Vico's *New Science* (1730). Instead he argues that metrics – or, in Shelley's phrasing, measure – arose to compensate for the discrepancies between the sensuous feel of words and their meaning, those moments when 'discourse fails to express objects by touches corresponding to them in shading or bearing', as he puts it in the paragraph that Benjamin cites.[33] As an example of such expressive failure, Mallarmé offers the 'perversity' of the contradiction between the 'dark' sound of *jour* ('day') and the 'light' sound of *nuit* ('night'). The contradiction demonstrates a disalignment of what Benjamin, in the paragraph following the Mallarmé citation, calls the '*Gefühlston*'[34] ('tone of feeling') with which the meant (*das Gemeinte*) binds itself to the manner of meaning (*Art des Meinens*) in a particular word. In poetically measured language, by contrast, sound and sense supplement one another to create lines whose sonic shading corresponds to the tone of feeling that the poet wishes to express. In this way, a measured arrangement of words can transmit *Gefühlstöne* not found in the individual words.

Such supplementation is necessarily distorted in translation, which will never be able to reproduce a poem's particular combination of sound and sense in another language. This is exactly what prompts Shelley to assert its vanity. 'Sounds as well as thoughts have relations,' he writes, 'both between each other and towards that which they represent'[35] – these relations of sounds towards that which they represent are equivalent to what Mallarmé describes as the sonic 'touches' that may or may not correspond to a word's meaning. For Shelley,

> a perception of those relations [of sounds] has always been found connected with a perception of the order of the relations of thought. Hence the language of poets has ever affected a certain uniform and harmonious recurrence of sound, without which it were not poetry, and which is scarcely less indispensable to the communication of its influence, than the words themselves, without reference to that peculiar order. Hence the vanity of translation; it were as wise to cast a violet into a crucible that you might discover the formal principle of its colour and odour, as seek to transfuse from one language into another the creations of a poet. The plant must spring again from its seed or it will bear no flower – and this is the burthen of the curse of Babel.[36]

Shelley's response to this curse is to assert that the translator must create a new poem in their own language. Benjamin, who separates the tasks of poet and translator, excludes musical measure from the purview of translation. For him, music is the 'last remaining universal language since the tower of Babel',[37] and the musically measured language of lyric poetry demarcates the outer boundary of translation. 'The limit: music needs no translation. Lyric poetry: closest to music – and posing the greatest difficulties for translation.'[38] He therefore advises the translator to focus on syntax rather than sound, creating literal translations that court their own incomprehensibility by recreating how the foreign language means syntactically rather than sonically.

Mallarmé promotes a kind of literary montage technique that will become Benjamin's model when he develops his own poetics of translation. A book of verse, Mallarmé writes, must be composed in such a way that 'any cry possesses an echo – motifs of the same type balance each other, stabilizing each other at a distance . . . an arrangement of fragments, adding up to a total rhythm, which would be the poem stilled, in the blanks'.[39] If the poet has to balance fragments of sound within a language so as to bring the poem to a standstill, Benjamin makes it the translator's task to arrange fragments across languages. The emphasis is not on how words sound, but their manner of meaning – how they convey sense: in the ideal translation, sense itself will be stilled in the blanks.

Friedrich Hölderlin's translations from the Ancient Greek offer an example of sense at a standstill. Benjamin considers them to be 'prototypes of their form': 'In them the harmony of the languages is so profound that sense is touched by language only the way an Aeolian lyre is touched by the wind.'[40] Rendering the Greek word by word, and sometimes even syllable by syllable, into his own German, Friedrich Hölderlin lets the two languages supplement one another to such an extent that meaning is lost between them. 'For this very reason,' Benjamin concludes, 'Hölderlin's translations in particular are subject to the enormous danger inherent in all translations: the gates of a language thus expanded and modified may slam shut and enclose the translator in silence.'[41] While his contemporaries regarded the translations as tokens of impending madness, for Benjamin they are 'stilled, in the blanks' between the two languages. Hölderlin himself offers an alternative take on rhythmic standstill in a note to his translation of Sophocles' *Oedipus*, which Benjamin cited on repeated occasions: 'For the tragic transport is actually empty, and the least restrained. – Thereby, in the rhythmic sequence of representations wherein the transport presents itself, there becomes necessary what in poetic meter [*Sylbenmasse*; lit. 'syllabic measure'] is called caesura, the pure word, the counter-rhythmic rupture[.]'[42] In terms of translation, the caesura, 'pure word' or 'counter-rhythmic rupture' is a limit case where one language rips through another, suspending its sense-making transport.

Despite Benjamin's insistence on the difference between poetry and translation, Hölderlin's translation practice and Mallarmé's poetics combine to inform the composition principle of his own *Berlin Childhood around 1900*. I have already discussed some of the sound–sense relations in 'Die Mummerehlen'. Hamacher has captured further examples of sounds that reverberate throughout Benjamin's autobiographical text, such as the echoing of 'Walter, violation and *Gewalt*, theft, *viol* and *vol*': these sounds perform a 'complex play of translations between and within the French and German languages' (as well as their English translations).[43] In an expansion of Mallarmé's ideas about sonic supplementation within a language and in imitation of the cross-linguistic supplementarity that characterises Hölderlin's translations, the French and German languages are made to supplement one another in setting the tone of Benjamin's writing. Moreover, all the *v*-sounding words that Hamacher singles out are visually tied to the appearance of the colour violet in different passages of the *Berlin Childhood*. The colour thus becomes the *Gefühlston* that shades the whole text.

My own example of sonic supplementation between languages: in Russian, the standard short form for 'Lydia' is 'Lida'. In Swedish, the word *lida* is a verb meaning 'to suffer'. Of course, it worried me that my secret name was the name of suffering. A false note.

Sound is a signifying property of language that is interrelated with its sense-making elements; in other words, sound–thought relations are supplementary. This is the enabling condition of poetic language, which hinges on a fluid and ever-shifting alignment of sound and sense: it is because

Another false note rang out in a common playground taunt. 'Lida' also happens to be the name of a city in western Belarus where trainers were made. У кого кроссовки "Лида", тот похож на инвалида. 'Whoever wears trainers from Lida, looks like an invalid.' The rhyme, in its childish cruelty, would ineluctably connect my secret name to disability.

the sound of the word *rose* is not fully a flower that it can also name a woman, a colour or the sun's appearance on the eastern horizon yesterday. This circumstance saves us from 'the terror in which everything said is one with meaning and everything meant is one with its effects', as Hamacher says of a 'universal language' in a slightly different context.[44] In this sense, the Fall of Language, which releases meaning from the God-ordained Name, gives us the double gift of poetry and translation – two arts that, in their distinct ways, live on by manipulating the supplementary relations between sound and sense. Casting a violet in a crucible will not help you discover the 'formal principle of its colour and odour', as Shelley says, but setting it in a series of sonic transitions and translations – say from *violet* to *violence* to *violins*, or gliding from the English *violet* to the colour *purple*, to the Russian *сиреневый* ('purple') named after the flower *сирень* ('lilac'), which back in English sounds like *sirens*, which in its turn leads to the *silence* into which the Benjaminian translator, ultimately, is shut – helps us perceive (*erkennen*) the uniquely linguistic phenomenon that Mallarmé celebrates: 'I say: A flower! And, out of the oblivion where my voice casts every contour, insofar as it is something other than the known bloom, there arises, musically, the very idea in its mellowness; in other words, what is absent from every bouquet.'[45] The flower that is absent from every bouquet is present only in the sounds of the word *flower*, and only to the extent that this word does not overlap with 'the known bloom' – its *erkennender Name* in the creative language of God. Whereas Adam's task was to voice the known name in human sounds, the task of the poet working in a postlapsarian language concerns 'something other than the known bloom'.

Notes

1. 'A Defence of Poetry', *SPP*, p. 514.
2. Timothy Webb, *The Violet in the Crucible: Shelley and Translation* (Oxford: Clarendon Press, 1976), p. 99.
3. 'The Task of the Translator', *SW1*, p. 258; *GS4*, p. 16.
4. Paul de Man, '"Conclusions" on Walter Benjamin's "The Task of the Translator": Messenger Lecture, Cornell University, March 4, 1983', *Yale French Studies*, 97 (2000), 10–35 (pp. 19–20).
5. 'The Task of the Translator', *SW1*, p. 255; translation emended; *GS4*, p. 12.
6. 'On Language as Such and on the Language of Man', *SW1*, p. 69; *GS2*, p. 150.
7. 'On Language as Such and on the Language of Man', *SW1*, p. 67; *GS2*, p. 147.
8. 'On Language as Such and on the Language of Man', *SW1*, p. 68; *GS2*, p. 148.
9. *Origin*, p. 27; *SW1*, p. 207; [N9,7], *AP*, p. 473; *GS5*, pp. 591–2.
10. 'On Language as Such and on the Language of Man', *SW1*, p. 68; *GS2*, p. 148.
11. 'On Language as Such and on the Language of Man', *SW1*, p. 70, translation emended; *GS2*, p. 151.
12. 'Benennung, Erkenntnis und Übersetzung sind hier synonyme Termini. Die adamitische Sprache erkennt die Natur, weil sie deren Übersetzung ist.' Irving Wohlfarth, 'Das Medium der Übersetzung', in *Übersetzen: Walter Benjamin*, ed. by Christiaan L. Hart Nibbrig (Frankfurt am Main: Suhrkamp, 2001), pp. 80–130 (p. 95), my translation.
13. 'On Language as Such and on the Language of Man', *SW1*, p. 68; *GS2*, p. 148.
14. 'On Language as Such and on the Language of Man', *SW1*, p. 70; *GS2*, p. 151.
15. 'On Language as Such and on the Language of Man', *SW1*, p. 67; *GS2*, p. 147.
16. M. H. Abrams, 'The Correspondent Breeze: A Romantic Metaphor', in *English Romantic Poets: Modern Essays in Criticism*, 2nd edn (Oxford: Oxford University Press, 1975), pp. 37–54 (p. 44).
17. 'On Language as Such and on the Language of Man', *SW1*, p. 67; *GS2*, p. 147.
18. 'The Task of the Translator', *SW1*, p. 257; *GS4*, p. 14.
19. 'On Language as Such and on the Language of Man', *SW1*, p. 69; *GS2*, p. 149.
20. 'On Language as Such and on the Language of Man', *SW1*, p. 71; *GS2*, p. 153.
21. 'On Language as Such and on the Language of Man', *SW1*, p. 71; *GS2*, p. 153.
22. 'The Task of the Translator', *SW1*, p. 260; *GS4*, p. 18.
23. Carol Jacobs, 'The Monstrosity of Translation', *MLN*, 90 (1975), 755–66 (p. 762).
24. 'The Task of the Translator', *SW1*, p. 259, translation emended; *GS4*, p. 16.
25. 'The Task of the Translator', *SW1*, p. 257, translation emended; *GS4*, p. 14.
26. See *GS4*, pp. 14–18.
27. 'The Task of the Translator', *SW1*, p. 257; *GS4*, p. 14.
28. 'prästabilierte Harmonie aller Sprachsphären unter einander', Wohlfarth, 'Das Medium der Übersetzung', p. 95, my translation.
29. '... Ideal der komplementären Sprachharmonie ... Eben diese Harmonie ist phänomenal nicht faßbar', Rainer Nägele, 'Echolalie', in *Übersetzen: Walter Benjamin*, ed. by Christiaan L. Hart Nibbrig (Frankfurt am Main: Suhrkamp, 2001), pp. 17–37 (p. 23, n. 11). ('... ideal of complementary language-harmony ... Precisely this harmony is not phenomenally perceptible', my translation.)
30. Stéphane Mallarmé, 'Crisis of Verse', in *Divagations*, trans. by Barbara Johnson (Cambridge, MA: Harvard University Press, 2007), pp. 201–11 (p. 205); cited in 'The Task of the Translator', *SW1*, p. 259; *GS4*, p. 17.
31. Mallarmé, 'Crisis of Verse', pp. 205–6.
32. Mallarmé, 'Crisis of Verse', p. 206.
33. Mallarmé, 'Crisis of Verse', p. 206.
34. In 'Echolalie', Nägele offers a different poetic source for Benjamin's *Gefühlston* in Hölderlin's 'Poetik der Töne und des Tonwechsels' (p. 25; 'poetics of tones and tonal shifts', my translation). The German *Ton*, like the English *tone*, has two meanings that can be said to supplement each other in this discussion: 'shade' (as in colour) and 'note' (as in music).
35. 'A Defence of Poetry', *SPP*, p. 514.
36. 'A Defence of Poetry', *SPP*, p. 514.
37. *Origin*, p. 214; *GS1*, p. 388.
38. 'Translation – For and Against', *SW3*, p. 250; *GS6*, p. 159.
39. Mallarmé, 'Crisis of Verse', pp. 208–9.

40 'The Task of the Translator', *SW1*, p. 262; *GS4*, p. 21.
41 'The Task of the Translator', *SW1*, p. 262; *GS4*, p. 21.
42 Friedrich Hölderlin, 'Annotations to Oedipus'; cited in 'Goethe's *Elective Affinities*', *SW1*, pp. 340–1; *GS1*, p. 181.
43 Hamacher, 'The Word *Wolke*', p. 151.
44 Werner Hamacher, '"Lectio": de Man's Imperative', in *Premises: Essays on Philosophy and Literature from Kant to Celan*, trans. by Peter Fenves (Cambridge, MA: Harvard University Press, 1996), pp. 181–221 (p. 216).
45 Mallarmé, 'Crisis of Verse', p. 210.

3
Footsteps

The Oceanide *Schönfließ*, whose name Benjamin calls in the citation from Walter, symbolises the ancient association between beauty and water. Aphrodite is born out of sea foam and is often represented floating ashore in a shell. 'In the element from which the goddess arose, beauty appears truly to be at home,' Walter writes, and as his argument unfolds, it becomes clear that the relation between water and beauty is mediated through feet, pacing the shore where water meets land:

> She [Aphrodite] is praised at the flowing rivers and fountains; one of the Oceanides is named *Schönfließ* [Beautiful Flow]; among the Nereids the beautiful form of Galatea stands out; and numerous beautiful-heeled [*schönfüßige*; lit. 'with beautiful feet'] daughters arise from the gods of the sea. The mobile element, as it first of all washes round the foot of the walker, moistens the feet of the goddesses, dispensing beauty; and silver-footed [*silberfüßige*] Thetis always remains the model for the poetic imagination of the Greeks when they depict this part of the body in their creations.[1]

This emphasis on footsteps on the shoreline – the foot being the basic unit of poetic metre, so called after the practice of stamping out a poem's rhythm – invites us to read the flows of ocean, rivers and fountains as metaphors for the flow of sound in musically measured language. Shelley may well have had this classic iconography in mind when composing one of the key scenes of 'The Triumph of Life', a vision in which Rousseau encounters a 'shape all light'. The scene is another allegory on the birth of poetic language. Like the opening of the 'Hymn to Mercury', it is set in a cavern at dawn:

'And as I looked the bright omnipresence
   Of morning through the orient cavern flowed,
And the sun's image radiantly intense

 'Burned on the waters of the well that glowed
Like gold, and threaded all the forest maze
   With winding paths of emerald fire – there stood

'Amid the sun, as he amid the blaze
   Of his own glory, on the vibrating
Floor of the fountain, paved with flashing rays,

   'A shape all light[']'[2]

The floor of the fountain is a surface paved with flashing rays, in the midst of which the shape all light appears in likeness to the sun's appearance amid the blaze of his own glory. It is an image of light contoured against light. But since the flashing rays in whose midst the shape appears are themselves reflections of the sun's blaze, the simile lacks a term of comparison: the shape all light stands amid the sun's reflected blaze *like* the sun stands amid his own blaze. Light is like light. Any distinction between these layers of light is only made possible by the reflection on the 'vibrating | Floor of the fountain' that splits reflected from unreflected rays and thereby gives a minimal differentiation of light against light that may be termed a 'shape'. But, as de Man notes in 'Shelley Disfigured', neither light nor water has shape on its own: 'Water, which has no shape of itself, is moulded into shape by its contact with the earth . . . it generates the very possibility of structure, pattern, form or shape by way of the disappearance of shape into shapelessness,' and similarly, 'light, the necessary condition for shape, is itself, like water, without shape'.[3] In making the reflection of light in water into the central image of this vision, Shelley gives us precious little to visualise – in de Man's words, the shape all light is 'referentially meaningless'.[4] Only when she begins to move down the river does the narrative offer some reprieve from the blazing light:

               – the fierce splendour
   Fell from her as she moved under the mass

'Of the deep cavern, and with palms so tender
   Their tread broke not the mirror of its billow,
Glided along the river . . .

          so this shape might seem

> 'Partly to tread the waves with feet which kissed
> The dancing foam, partly to glide along
> The airs that roughened the moist amethyst, . . .

And her feet, ever to the ceaseless song

> 'Of leaves and winds and waves and birds and bees
> And falling drops moved in a measure new . . .[5]

The shape's descent coincides with the fall of 'the fierce splendour' (a term consistently associated with light in this poem[6]). As the 'referentially meaningless' shape treads down the river, her feet perform a transition from blinding light to ceaseless song. 'The birth of form as the interference of light and water', de Man observes, 'passes through the mediation of sound.'[7] The form being born here is the musical form given to a poem by the measure of its feet. The pun recalls Shelley's translation of the Homeric hymn, where 'foot' was likewise used to denote at once a metric unit and a body part. Here, the shape all light's gliding tread represents a shift from the visual to the audible and sets up a supplementary relation between the poem's sound and its shapeless imagery – the metric regularity is the most concrete feature in a scene where the imagery consists of light on light.

But if the appearance of the shape's feet comes with a sense of material relief in an otherwise shapeless scene, the materiality in question is that of the sonic features of the poem's language: the shapeless imagery is held in shape by the poem's strict *terza rima*. In other words, the movement of the shape all light's feet over water is a self-reflective representation of the formal principle that holds together the poem's disparate and ever-mutable content. The image combines different senses of the word 'foot' with the sounds articulated in Shelley's use of metric feet, in accordance with his definition of poetic language as marking 'before unapprehended relations of things' – in this case, relations between the various meanings and the metric weight of the word 'foot'. It furthermore suggests that the shape can be understood as 'referentially meaningless' in an additional sense: it is not a figure for any semantic content expressible in language, but for the sonic means through which language is expressed, what Benjamin termed 'the pure formal principle of language – namely, sound'.[8] That language sounds is a precondition of linguistic articulation, and therefore also signification, but sound does not in itself signify any definite conceptual meaning. As a metaphor for metric measure, the shape is a figure for how poetic language works. This also means that, as the shape moves over water, the scene anticipates

Benjamin's take on Genesis 1:2–3 according to which 'the Spirit [*ruach*] of God hovering over the face of the waters' is 'the pure formal principle of language', that is, the measurability of sound that prefigures the first divine articulation: 'Let there be light'.

In a reflection on Keats's *Endymion*, Shahidha Bari observes that the 'metrically measured movement of verse effects imaginative transportation; poetic form enables a recalcitrant, wayward straying from the straight and narrow'.[9] This seems to suggest that, whereas prose strides ahead, purposeful and single-minded in delivering its meaning, poetry twists and turns to capture rhymes and musical effects: wayward, fickle. Of course, nothing could be further from the truth: the stricter the measure, the straighter and narrower the poet's path. This is because measure, in forcing the poet to consider how words sound in addition to what they mean, strictly delimits the range of available word choices. Metre is a forcefield in which tensions between sound and signification play out. In 'The Triumph of Life', these tensions can be sensed in the dancing feet of the shape all light, which spark the process of disfiguration that gives de Man's essay its name. Initially, the shape glides down 'with palms so tender | Their tread broke not the mirror of its billow'; however, by 'the end of the section, we have moved from "thread" to "tread" to "trample," in a movement of increased violence':[10]

> 'As one enamoured is upborne in dream
>   O'er lily-paven lakes mid silver mist
> To music [   ], so this shape might seem
>
>   'Partly to tread the waves with feet which kissed
> The dancing foam, partly to glide along
>   The airs that roughened the moist amethyst, . . .
>
>   'And still her feet, no less than the sweet tune
> To which they moved, seemed as they moved, to blot
>   The thoughts of him who gazed on them; and soon
>
> 'All that was seemed as if it had been not,
>   As if the gazer's mind was strewn beneath
> Her feet like embers, and she, thought by thought
>
>   'Trampled its fires into the dust of death,
> As Day upon the threshold of the east
>   Treads out the lamps of night[11]

Here, too, the figuration of light against light challenges the bounds of imaginative vision as the rising sun treads out the stars – light is extinguished by more light. But, more crucially for de Man's reading, the feet that just stood for the poem's measured language are now trampling the embers of Rousseau's mind. Accordingly, de Man interprets measure as menace:

> [S]ince measure is any principle of linguistic organization, not only as rhyme and meter but as any syntactical or grammatical scansion, one can read 'feet' not just as the poetic meter that is so conspicuously evident in the *terza rima* of the poem, but as any principle of signification. Yet it is precisely these 'feet' which extinguish and bury the poetic and philosophical light.[12]

Having identified the shape as a self-reflective figure for the poem's metric measure, de Man now turns it into a figure for its own disfiguration, one that represents the craft of metric composition as a perpetual destruction of sense by measure.

This move places de Man's interpretation in direct conflict with Shelley's poetics, which is based on the premise that sounds and thoughts are interrelated.[13] As Ross Woodman puts it, '"a certain uniform and harmonious recurrence of sound" . . . governs, for Shelley, poetic thought. Without it, thought would be dead. For de Man, on the other hand, recurrence of sound induces oblivion.'[14] However, it is not recurrence as such that forms the main point of difference (in a different context, Shelley similarly describes our mental faculties as being 'blunted by reiteration'[15]), but the fact of sonic modulation or measure. Tellingly, 'Shelley Disfigured' makes no mention of Shelley's own distinction between measured and unmeasured language; instead, de Man situates disfiguration as a result of 'the bifurcation between the semantic and the non-signifying, material properties of language', placing sound among the non-signifying properties:

> The latent polarity implied in all classical theories of the sign allows for the relative independence of the signifier and for its free play in relation to its signifying function. If, for instance, compelling rhyme schemes such as 'billow,' 'willow,' 'pillow,' or transformations such as 'thread' to 'tread' or 'seed' to 'deed' occur at crucial moments in the text, then the question arises whether these particularly meaningful movements or events are not being generated by random and superficial properties of the signifier rather than by the

constraints of meaning. The obliteration of thought by 'measure' would then have to be interpreted as the loss of semantic depth and its replacement by what Mallarmé calls 'le hasard infini des conjonctions' (*Igitur*).[16]

In this regard, de Man agrees with most twentieth-century language theory in seeing the connection between sound and sense as arbitrary – precisely what Benjamin dismissed as 'the bourgeois view of language'. This view of language is also at odds with Shelley's poetics, which courts the relations between sound and thought. From de Man's perspective, endowing the sonic correspondence between the sound of Shelley's name and one of the possible English translations of the Greek word χέλυς with significance is nonsensical: despite the ease with which metonymic correspondences between shell, poetry and poet come into play in his treatment of the Homeric hymn, Shelley's name has only a coincidental, sonic similarity to the signifier, 'shell', that in its turn has an arbitrary relation to the shell it signifies – proven by the fact that a different context may render the Greek χέλυς as 'lyre' in English. Yet, as Shelley's translation of the Homeric *Hymn to Hermes* also demonstrates, poetic creation is in large part about attending to such aleatory coincidences. Sound is not arbitrarily linked to sense – on the contrary, it is this linkage that makes poetry possible.

> Much as the coincidental associations that I have with my own name have enabled me to recognise (*erkennen*) the aura of being named in Shelley and Benjamin.

Jürgen Blasius translates 'Shelley Disfigured' as *Shelleys Entstellung*,[17] thereby naming de Man's reading of Shelley with a word, *Entstellung*, that is central in the theory of language that Benjamin developed in the early 1930s, not least in 'Die Mummerehlen':

> There is an old nursery rhyme that tells of Muhme Rehlen. Because the word *Muhme* meant nothing to me, this creature became for me a spirit: the mummerehlen. The misunderstanding disarranged [*verstellte*] the world for me. But in a good way: it lit up the paths to the world's interior. The cue could come from anywhere. Thus, on one occasion, chance willed that *Kupferstichen* [copperplate engravings] were discussed in my presence. The next day, I stuck my head out from under a chair; this was a *Kopf-verstich* [a head-stickout]. If, in this way, I distorted [*entstellte*] both myself and the word, I did only what I had to do to gain a foothold in life. Early on,

I learned to disguise myself [*mich zu mummen*] in words [*Worte*], which really were clouds [*Wolken*].[18]

The homophony between the nursery rhyme character *Muhme Rehlen* ('Aunt Rehlen') and the imagined name *Mummerehlen*, or that between the real word *Kupferstich* ('copperplate engraving') and the imagined word *Kopf-verstich* ('head-stickout'), enables the child Benjamin to disguise (*mummen*) and disfigure (*entstellen*) himself in words, which are really clouds. That is, the cloudiness arises precisely from the sonic supplementarity between real and imaginary, a slippage also at work in the similarity between the German words *Worte* and *Wolke*, 'words' and 'clouds' – for in what other sense can we imagine words to be like clouds?

In 'The Word *Wolke* – If It Is One', Hamacher addresses this question through a transposition of what he elsewhere calls 'de Man's most radical text': 'Shelley Disfigured'.[19] For de Man, the 'shape all light' that appears in Shelley's 'The Triumph of Life' represents the 'repetitive erasures by which language performs the erasure of its own positions', a process that he terms 'disfiguration'.[20] Throughout his reading of Benjamin, Hamacher refers to the word *Wolke* as a 'figure of defiguration' and links it to erasure:

> For in the *Worte*, 'word,' due to its likeness to *Wolke*, 'cloud,' language *stands on the threshold of forgetting* everything that may be meant in it. *Cloud – but not this single word, for it is disfigured*; not the thing, which is never one and never assumes a lasting form; not the vague representation or idea, for what is an idea, if it is vague? – 'cloud' is, in a certain sense, the forgetting of ascertained meaning, of linguistic convention and everything that can enter into its space.[21]

This means that, at this juncture in their afterlives, Benjamin's *Wolke* is an equivalent to Shelley's 'shape all light'. In the course of his reading, Hamacher uses a critical procedure that resembles Shelley's tripartite use of the word 'feet': Shelley literally describes the 'feet' of the 'shape all light', but these feet also figuratively represent the poem's own poetic measure, even as they are themselves metric feet within its *terza rima* structure. Hamacher literally talks about the clouds in Benjamin's *Berlin Childhood*, but these clouds are figures for Benjamin's poetically measured prose even as they themselves evoke the morphology of clouds that are nothing but 'the various appearances of water suspended in the Atmosphere', in the definition of Luke Howard, whose *On the Modifications of Clouds* (1803) introduced the modern system of classifying clouds and sparked a craze in cloud-gazing.[22] In this manner, Hamacher demonstrates that the word *Wolke* is not one: it is not one word (but several); it is not even a word (but a 'figure of defiguration') – a state of not-being-one that is functionally equivalent to the shapeless shaping of the shape all light.

'The most continuous and gradual event in nature, the subtle gradations of the dawn, is collapsed into the brusque swiftness of a single moment,' de Man writes about the opening of 'The Triumph of Life' in which 'the Sun sprang forth | Rejoicing in his splendour'.[23] Shelley's splendid Sun is, for de Man, an allegory for language, which springs forth 'of its own unrelated power'.[24] The analogy is carried over into the poem's later figurations of light: de Man reads the shape all light as a figure for the very medium – language – in which she is figured. Building on this reading, Hamacher argues that 'the first meaning we connect with the arbitrary acts of an absolutely positing language is the constitution of meaningful language itself'.[25] However, insofar as the constitution of language is itself a meaningful linguistic act, it presupposes a pre-existing language in which it is uttered. Without a constituted language, the positing cannot make sense. Without a positing, language cannot be constituted. This is one reason why de Man calls 'the positional power of language' an '*imposition*'; it turns 'a positional act', like the Sun springing forth, 'which relates to nothing that comes before or after', into 'the narrative sequence of an allegory'– in this case, the allegory of the birth of language that he reads into Shelley's poem.[26]

Although de Man claims to take the word '*imposition*' from 'the vocabulary of the poem',[27] his italics are masking what is in fact an inaccurate citation:

And in succession due, did Continent,

   Isle, Ocean, and all things that in them wear
The form and character of mortal mould
   Rise as the Sun their father rose, to bear

Their portion of the toil which he of old
   Took as his own and then imposed on them[28]

The scene narrates precisely the kind of gradual succession that de Man claims is absent from the poem's opening. Yet if we accept that the Sun's springing forth stands for the positing power of language, what is being imposed on 'all things that in them wear | The form and character of mortal mould' is the toil of producing meaning. In other words: the task of interpretation. Embracing this implication, Hamacher translates de Man's imposition into an imperative – the 'imperative of language, of reading, [that] considered as an act directed toward the future, contains the promise of a future language'.[29] This imperative is the foundation of literary criticism, which is born with the promise that there *is* significance in literary works, that this significance *will* develop in the course of their afterlives, and that literary criticism – itself part of a work's afterlife – will realise its significance through interpretation.

The crux: the foundational promise that a literary work from the past contains a meaning that will be unfolded in its future (that is, in the present of our reading) is itself posited, or indeed imposed, by the very act of reading that then proceeds to expose this promised meaning – much as de Man's disfiguration of the language of 'The Triumph of Life' rests on his having imposed an equivalence between the poem's figurations of light and the positing power of language. But one could just as easily – and as validly – impose another interpretation onto Shelley's light imagery. Such interpretative fluctuations undermine what Hamacher defines as the imperative of reading: 'The imperative commands, before all "real" language, that there ought to be (one) language – (one) meaning, (one) interpretation.'[30] If there were one such meaning, then critical interpretation would be a straightforward process of deciphering that one meaning; however, this 'ought' will not be fulfilled – no language, no meaning, no interpretation is ever one.

In this regard, the impositions of literary criticism both participate in and suspend the aporia of all absolute positing: interpretation imposes the meanings that it uncovers, but it also sets off a process of disfiguration that de-posits the posited. 'Die Sprache verspricht (sich)', as de Man puts it in a wordplay that Hamacher cites: language promises (*die Sprache verspricht*) and exposes itself (*verspricht sich*) – and this is true of criticism as well, which will never definitively deliver the meaning it promises. Hamacher coins the word 'afformative' to describe this 'condition of formation *and* as de-formation, as a pure positing *and* as a deposing, ex-position'.[31] The afformative force is that power of language which, in one stroke, imposes and suspends meaning: figure and its simultaneous disfiguration. This is the process that Hamacher, in another act of imposition, reads into Benjamin's clouds. They are not 'to be taken here as metaphors at all, for they do not mean something else that could be said more appropriately, and they are not sensuous images of a noumenal content: rather, they mean that they do not mean, and indeed do mean this "not"'.[32]

The 'shape all light' appears as the radiant heat of the sun is burning on the waters of a well – a phenomenon that would produce a mist, in other words a terrestrial modification of cloud, that is illuminated by the same sun whose warmth generates it. The 'shape all light', then, is a form of cloud, which may well be the most minimal kind of visual shaping imaginable. 'Clouds are the realm of the visible invisible,' as Mary Jacobus observes in a study that draws connections between the materiality of clouds and lyric poetry; 'their representation involves the double relation of the work of perception and the work of art, along with our complex, subjective, yet always predetermined relation to both.'[33] Although a cloud is a heavy material thing (considering the sheer weight of water), its contours are ever-shifting, flowing out into the ether, demanding an imaginative intervention to fix it in the mind's eye. The same is true of the 'shape all light', except that she is not made of water but of metric measure, only gaining material shape with the appearance of her treading feet, metonymic of the poem's own *terza rima* that is made to contain the otherwise shapeless imagery.

In her cloudiness, the shape is related to other clouds in Shelley's work, for instance the 'clouds of glimmering dew' that illustrate the nature of words in the 'Ode to Liberty':

> O, that the words which make the thoughts obscure
>   From which they spring, as clouds of glimmering dew
>   From a white lake blot heaven's blue portraiture,
>   Were stripped of their thin masks and various hue
> And frowns and smiles and splendours not their own,
>   Till in the nakedness of false and true
>   They stand before their Lord, each to receive its due.[34]

The relation between individual words and thought is here parallel to the relation between the individual human and the divine 'power unknown'. The 'Lord' of l. 240 is not God, but Imagination, which, according to Shelley, is the source of language but also related to the unknown power that animates all of life. But the passage overall suggests that words are to be taken to task by the power which created them. The comparison of 'words' to 'clouds of glimmering dew' emphasises their ephemeral and shapeshifting nature: words are veiled in 'thin masks and various hue | And frowns and smiles and splendours not their own' that obscure the meaning they would communicate, 'the nakedness of false and true'. So the splendours of language 'blot' its sense like clouds 'blot' the skies (a surprisingly strong word for something which is thin and of various hue).

Yet even as the 'Ode to Liberty' expresses a desire to strip language of its cloudiness by reducing words to the bare simplicity of 'false and true', its complex lyric structure undercuts its abnegation of linguistic splendour. It is not so much a manifesto for unequivocal language, as a play with the glimmering nature of its own words.

This play is taken further in the ode's companion piece 'The Cloud' (both were published in the 1820 *Prometheus Unbound* volume). This poem consists of six stanzas, where 'each stanza portrays an individual state of a cloud according to the best meteorology of Shelley's day', which is to say Howard's *On the Modifications of Clouds*.[35] Since the poem's various stanzas in fact depict distinct meteorological phenomena, Shelley's cloud is not one but rather a series of clouds appearing under differing atmospheric conditions; only the definite article of the title, 'The Cloud', unites these different modifications of cloud into one coherent figure that, in the fourth stanza, also becomes a figure for poetic language:

> That orbèd maiden with white fire laden
>   Whom mortals call the moon,
> Glides glimmering o'er my fleecelike floor,
>   By the midnight breezes strewn;
> And wherever the beat of her unseen feet,
>   Which only angels hear,
> May have broken the woof of my tent's thin roof,
>   The stars peep behind her, and peer[36]

Since the Moon is laden with 'white fire', her passage over the cloud is – like that of the 'shape all light' – a movement of light over water suspended mid-air. Furthermore, as in the 'Hymn to Mercury' and 'The Triumph of Life', the word 'feet' can here be read as a self-reflective pun on the poem's own metric measure. The unseen – because heard – feet of the moon tread over the cloud with a 'beat' so delicately light that it is described as 'gliding', a word that Shelley will use again when describing the shape all light's movement.[37] Lucy Neely McLane's analysis of 'The Cloud' in terms of its 'sound values' beautifully captures the phonetic texture of this glimmering woof: 'For her [the moon's] sake the fire of *i*'s is distilled with the dew of *l*'s and *m*'s, the pearl-roundness of *o*'s is confined by the etherealizing force of *b*'s and *r*'s, the invisible spirit of motion is caught in a net of *e*'s tied with monosyllables and rimmed by *l*'s.'[38] McLane's focus on assonance and consonance points towards the similarity between the 'sound values' of 'The Cloud' and the 'tonal world' of Benjamin's childhood – their measure is woven out of the texture of the words themselves, interlaced to form a glimmering 'woof' of language.

But just as the shape all light tramples the beholder's mind into the dust of death, so the Moon's gliding feet tear a rent in the cloud's woof. On the one hand, as the glimmering woof on which the beat of metric feet is imprinted, the cloud represents the language of poetry; but, on the other hand, it is also the metric feet that destroy it. 'Woof' is a word that Shelley often uses to describe poetry; for instance, in 'The Witch of Atlas' where the witch is 'broidering the pictured poesy | Of some high tale upon her growing woof'.[39] Sometimes, this woof becomes a 'figured curtain' that poetry 'spreads' over reality; at other times, it is a 'dark veil' that poetry withdraws 'from before the scene of things'.[40] Which is to say that just as often as Shelley likens poetry to the woven texture of a woof, figured curtain or glimmering veil, he insists that poetry unveils that which obscures our perception: 'Poetry lifts the veil from the hidden beauty of the world' or 'it strips the veil of familiarity from the world' and 'purges from our inward sight the film of familiarity which obscures from us the wonder of our being'.[41]

In 'The Cloud', these two aspects of poetry – veiling and unveiling – are figured in the flow of the moon's metric feet over the cloud's surface, water suspended in the atmosphere. To borrow a phrase from J. Hillis Miller, this is 'the moment in a work of literature when its own medium is put in question':[42] poetry's measured footsteps tearing the veil that poetry weaves. However, the rent opens onto a view of the skies denied in the 'Ode to Liberty'. The fourth stanza concludes:

> When I widen the rent in my wind-built tent,
>   Till the calm rivers, lakes, and seas,
> Like strips of the sky fallen through me on high,
>   Are each paved with the moon and these.[43]

The rent in the cloud's surface, which has been broken open by the moon's poetic feet, allows the skies to be mirrored in the 'calm rivers, lakes, and seas'. If the cloud – a glimmering woof – is the medium of poetry, then it is also the work of poetry that tears it apart so that the true light of the stars (so many distant suns) can be mirrored in the earth's flowing waters.

Notes

1 Julius Walter, *Geschichte der Ästhetik im Altertum* (History of Aesthetics in Antiquity); cited in 'Goethe's *Elective Affinities*', SW1, p. 342; GS1, p. 183.
2 'The Triumph of Life', ll. 343–52.
3 de Man, 'Shelley Disfigured', p. 107, p. 109.
4 de Man, 'Shelley Disfigured', p. 109.
5 'The Triumph of Life', ll. 359–77.

6   See 'The Triumph of Life', l. 3, l. 87, l. 359, l. 413, l. 444.
7   de Man, 'Shelley Disfigured', p. 107.
8   'On Language as Such and on the Language of Man', *SW1*, p. 67; *GS2*, p. 147.
9   Shahidha K. Bari, *Keats and Philosophy: The Life of Sensations* (New York, NY: Routledge, 2012), p. 92.
10 'The Triumph of Life', ll. 361–2; de Man, 'Shelley Disfigured', p. 111.
11 'The Triumph of Life', ll. 367–90.
12 de Man, 'Shelley Disfigured', p. 113.
13 'A Defence of Poetry', *SPP*, p. 514.
14 Ross Woodman, 'Figuring Disfiguration: Reading Shelley after de Man', *Studies in Romanticism*, 40 (2001), 253–88 (p. 259, n. 7).
15 'On Life', *SPP*, p. 508.
16 de Man, 'Shelley Disfigured', p. 114.
17 Paul de Man, 'Shelleys Entstellung', in *Die Ideologie des Ästhetischen*, ed. by Christoph Menke, trans. by Jürgen Blasius (Frankfurt am Main: Suhrkamp, 1993), pp. 147–82.
18 'The Mummerehlen', *SW3*, p. 390; *GS4*, pp. 260–1; my emphasis.
19 Hamacher, '"Lectio"', p. 213. Hamacher does not relate de Man's and Benjamin's works nor does he explicitly discuss the thematic affinities between his own essays on Benjamin and on de Man, but these can be perceived in the conceptual overlay of both pieces. 'The Word *Wolke* – If It Is One' is first published in *Studies in Twentieth Century Literature*, 11.1 (1986) and reprinted in *Benjamin's Ground: New Readings of Walter Benjamin*, ed. by Rainer Nägele (Detroit, MI: Wayne State University Press, 1986), pp. 147–75. According to a footnote at the close of '"Lectio"', the essay was written in April 1985 (n. 21, p. 221), that is, little more than a year before the appearance of 'The Word *Wolke*', which places their dates of composition in close proximity to one another. '"Lectio"' first appears in *Reading de Man Reading*, ed. by Lindsay Waters and Wlad Godzich (Minneapolis, MN: University of Minnesota Press, 1989). A revised version is published in *Entferntes Verstehen: Studien zu Philosophie und Literatur von Kant bis Celan* (Frankfurt am Main: Suhrkamp, 1998), pp. 151–94; and translated into English in *Premises: Essays on Philosophy and Literature from Kant to Celan*, trans. by Peter Fenves (Cambridge, MA: Harvard University Press, 1996), pp. 181–221. In German, Hamacher uses the three words '*Defiguration*', '*Disfiguration*' and '*Entstellung*', which Peter Fenves's translation renders with the English 'defiguration' (translating *Defiguration*, p. 195; p. 196; p. 197), 'disfiguration' (translating *Disfiguration*, p. 192) and 'distortion' (translating *Entstellung*, p. 210).
20 de Man, 'Shelley Disfigured', p. 119.
21 Hamacher, 'The Word *Wolke*', p. 147; emphasis added.
22 Luke Howard, *On the Modifications of Clouds* (London: J. Taylor, 1803 [repr. 1969]), p. 3.
23 de Man, 'Shelley Disfigured', p. 117; 'The Triumph of Life', ll. 2–3.
24 de Man, 'Shelley Disfigured', p. 116.
25 Hamacher, '"Lectio"', p. 213.
26 de Man, 'Shelley Disfigured', p. 116, p. 117.
27 de Man, 'Shelley Disfigured', p. 117.
28 'The Triumph of Life', ll. 15–20.
29 Hamacher, '"Lectio"', p. 217.
30 Hamacher, '"Lectio"', p. 214.
31 Hamacher, '"Lectio"', p. 218, n. 18.
32 Hamacher, 'The Word *Wolke*', p. 163.
33 Mary Jacobus, *Romantic Things: A Tree, A Rock, A Cloud* (Chicago, IL: University of Chicago Press, 2012), p. 34.
34 'Ode to Liberty', ll. 234–40.
35 Donald H. Reiman, *Percy Bysshe Shelley: Updated Edition* (Boston, MA: Twayne Publishers, 1990), p. 96.
36 'The Cloud', ll. 45–52.
37 'The Triumph of Life', l. 363, l. 371.
38 Lucy Neely McLane, 'Sound Values in "The Cloud"', *The English Journal*, 22 (1933), 412–14 (p. 413).
39 'The Witch of Atlas', ll. 252–3.
40 'A Defence of Poetry', *SPP*, p. 533.
41 'A Defence of Poetry', *SPP*, p. 517, p. 533.
42 J. Hillis Miller, 'The Critic as Host', in *Deconstruction and Criticism*, ed. by Harold Bloom and others (London: Routledge & Kegan Paul, 1979), pp. 217–53 (p. 250).
43 'The Cloud', ll. 55–8.

II
Loving Knowledge

4
Beauty

'Lift not the painted veil which those who live | Call Life', opens a sonnet that Shelley wrote in the same month as he completed a translation of Plato's *Symposium*.[1] The poem suggests that what the living call life is not true life but a mere projection screen devoid of substance: 'unreal shapes be pictured there, | And it but mimic all we would believe | With colours idly spread'.[2] The phrase 'unreal shapes' is cited from the *Symposium* translation, a passage at the climax of Socrates' discourse on love where he describes the Idea of Beauty as being 'simple, pure, uncontaminated with the intermixture of human flesh and colours, and all other idle and unreal shapes attendant on mortality'.[3] On one side of the painted veil: real life, manifested in the serene, self-sustaining grandeur of the Platonic εἴδωλον, 'Ideas' or 'Forms'. On the other side: the mutable mess of humanity.

For Shelley's generation, the image of the veil directly evoked the philosophy of Plato. 'Could there be anything more Platonic than the sonnet of 1818, beginning "Lift not the painted veil which those who live call life,"' David Newsome wonders.[4] His summary of the Romantic reception of Plato will serve as my entry point into a discussion of Shelley's and Benjamin's respective engagements with the *Symposium*. As Newsome puts it:

> These Forms were the original ideas of all created things – divine and immutable within the eternal order, but finite and changing

within the temporal, visible world. The actual world may be ugly, confused, nonsensical – a pointer to the degree to which finite minds can forget or depart from the divine original; so that as time passes, they believe that the formless mockery of their own invention is in fact reality, when it is only a shadow or reflection of the perfection which once had been and actually (within the eternal order) still is. If knowledge of reality were purely an empirical process, the real world of Forms could never be apprehended by man. Here Platonists tended to elaborate upon their master, in the elevation of the role of intuition to penetrate the veil which separated the finite from the infinite, phenomena from *noumena*. They might call the process different names – intuition, 'the mind's eye', vision or imagination – but they were all confident that once the veil was pierced, confusion would become order, ugliness would become beauty, the indefinite would acquire measure and the many would be seen as one.[5]

On this reading, the veil demarcates the separation between phenomena and noumena, order and chaos. Newsome inscribes this split on a temporal axis that can also be read in theological terms: the world falls away from and forgets its original divine order, much as, for Benjamin, the divine λόγος is shattered and language fallen into a confusion of the tongues, or 'chatter'.[6] Piercing the veil would amount to recovering the Adamic language of Names. Benjamin, however, is not pursuing linguistic redemption as much as ways of working with the shards of language at hand. If divine λόγος and profane chatter are two linguistic extremes, he is interested in the area between: the veil rather than what is behind it In 'The Cloud', Shelley represents the cloud as a veil being rent by the metric feet of poetry – but the veil itself is also woven by the measure of poetry. Like Benjamin, he is less interested in what lies beyond the veil than in making its presence visible.

Newsome's suggestion that the Platonic 'Forms were the original ideas of all created things' furthermore hints at the proximity between the Platonic εἴδωλον and Benjamin's conception of the divine λόγος at the core of creation.[7] In 'philosophical contemplation', Benjamin notes, 'the Idea [εἴδωλον] is released from reality's innermost interior as a Word [λόγος]. Reclaiming its name-giving rights. Ultimately, however, this is not the attitude of Plato, but the attitude of Adam, the father of the human race and the father of philosophy.'[8] The statement is taken from the 'Epistemo-Critical [*Erkenntniskritische*] Prologue' to *The Origin of German Tragic Drama*, whose opening sections contain a careful recapitulation of the *Symposium*, and it indicates the extent to which Benjamin's reading of Plato is filtered through the theory of language that he had developed in his essays 'On Language as Such and on the Language of Man' and 'The Task of the Translator'. In Benjamin's thought, the divine λόγος guarantees the truth of language; after his reading of Plato, λόγος approximates εἴδωλον and, more importantly, Beauty enters the picture. For Benjamin, the *Symposium*'s primary significance is that it 'develops truth – the realm of Ideas – as the essential content of Beauty. It declares that truth is beautiful.'[9] Or conversely, that the beautiful is true.

Benjamin therefore argues that an 'understanding of the Platonic view of the relationship of truth and beauty is not just a primary aim in every investigation into the philosophy of art, but it is indispensable to the definition of truth itself'.[10] Not surprisingly, his definition of truth will be intimately tied up with language – and the word *Erkenntnis*- in the title of the 'Prologue' echoes the *erkennender Name* with which God created all things according to the language philosophy he had advanced in his earlier work. Benjamin links the divine language of Names to Platonic Ideas by means of a citation from Hermann Güntert: 'Plato's Ideas are fundamentally . . . nothing other than deified [*vergöttlichte*] Words.'[11] Güntert argues that Plato could only have invented his doctrine of Ideas because he was monolingual, which led him to confuse arbitrary words with immutable concepts. Be that as it may, for the Ancient Greeks only one language mattered: their word for foreign modes of speaking, βαρβᾰρισμός – the root of 'barbarian' and 'barbarism' – is an onomatopoeia that reflects what they perceived as the disordered babbling of all languages but their own. Benjamin draws on Güntert's suggestion to represent the philosopher as a latter-day Adam who knows words by their proper Name. 'Philosophy is meant to name the idea, as Adam named nature,'[12] he wrote in a letter to Florens Christian Rang in which he outlined some preliminary considerations for the 'Epistemo-Critical Prologue'. And since, in naming the idea, philosophy is speaking truth, and truth is beautiful, philosophy can be defined as the art of naming beauty in words.

The Platonic linkage of truth and beauty is also key to Shelley's reading of the *Symposium*. It allows him to conclude that poets, in shaping their language into beautiful forms, have a more immediate relationship to truth than other writers. 'Plato was essentially a poet,' he asserts in the 'Defence'; 'the truth and splendour of his imagery and the melody of his language is the most intense that it is possible to conceive.'[13] Plato is not called a poet simply because he presents true imagery in intensely melodic language; rather, his ideas are the *more* true precisely *because* they are melodically expressed. Poetic metre is now the guarantor of truth. In other words, Plato writes in a beautifully measured language (recalling Shelley's key distinction between measured and unmeasured language) and it is the beautiful measure of his language that testifies to the truth of his words. This indicates the formal essence of Beauty: it inheres not in the propositional content of words or statements, but in the measure that turns confusion into order, chatter into poetry.

There is an apparent analogy between the 'unreal shapes' pictured on Shelley's painted veil and the unreal shadows projected onto the wall in Plato's famous allegory of the cave. This analogy is, however, negated in the sonnet's next turn: what lies beyond the veil is not the sunlit realm of true Ideas that the Platonic philosopher encounters on stepping out of the cave, but 'Fear | And Hope, twin Destinies; who ever weave | Their shadows, o'er the chasm, sightless and drear'.[14] Far from obscuring the truth, the painted veil shields us from the sightless chasm behind it. If we read the veil as an allegory of poetry, poetry emerges as a protective layer between us and a true sense of life: there is a blessing in not knowing life 'in the nakedness of false and true' 'The mist of familiarity obscures from us the wonder of our being,' Shelley states in the essay 'On Life', written a year after the sonnet. 'Life, the great miracle, we admire not, because it is so miraculous. It is well that we are thus shielded by the familiarity of what is at once so certain and so unfathomable from an astonishment which would otherwise absorb and overawe' our faculties.[15] Philosophy, however, can serve to disperse this mist. Shelley continues:

> The most refined abstractions of logic conduct to a view of life which, though startling to the apprehension, is in fact that which the habitual sense of its repeated combinations has extinguished in us. It strips, as it were, the painted curtain from this scene of things. I confess that I am one of those who am unable to refuse my assent to the conclusions of those philosophers, who assert that nothing exists but as it is perceived.[16]

The metaphorical landscape has already shifted: the painted veil (the protective shield of poetry) is transformed into a painted curtain (familiarity and habituation) that obscures life from us. But this kind of shiftiness is precisely the purpose of poetic language; as Shelley writes in the 'Defence', such language 'is vitally metaphorical; that is, it marks the before unapprehended relations of things'.[17] What matters is not which particular metaphor we choose to represent life, but how our perception of life is conditioned by the various metaphors we use to describe it. Each new metaphor revives our apprehension of life. The value of poetic language is that it 'perpetuates' our 'apprehension' of such relations, '*until the words which represent [these relations], become through time signs for portions or classes of thoughts, instead of integral thoughts; and then if no new poets should arise to create afresh the associations which have been thus disorganized, language will be dead to all the nobler purposes of human intercourse*'.[18]

Without appealing to a theological framework, as Benjamin does, Shelley fundamentally agrees with Benjamin's view of language as being in a state of freefall, continually falling away from its creative origin. But whereas Benjamin makes it the task of the translator to reassemble the fragments of fallen language, Shelley tasks poets with continually reviving language by coining new metaphors. In so doing, the language of poets neither veils nor unveils a truth, but rather represents the ever-shifting relations between things. The truth is not hidden, but consists in these relations, always in motion, dancing. Any given metaphor is like a freeze-frame that captures a particular movement in this dance. The problem arises when we become habituated to it, so that we see only the fixed image and not the dance which it partakes in. This is how the process of habituation blunts our perception of life and the world. And since 'nothing exists but as it is perceived', renewing our perception amounts to creating a new world, for us. In calling our attention to how we perceive life, poetry and philosophy heighten our awareness of the discrepancy between how things are and how they appear, and this, in turn, makes visible the separation between a *perception* of something and the *thing perceived*. This separation is captured in the image of the veil that interferes between the two and, in so doing, alerts us to the mediating nature of all perception, which both reveals and re-veils reality. Jennifer Wallace highlights the political stakes of this process (and what she says of Shelley and Plato is also true of Benjamin): 'Both saw political change occuring [*sic*] as a result of a change of perception. As a result, Shelley's claims about the importance of the poet resonate with the claims of Plato about the philosopher.'[19] To this we may add the claims that Benjamin makes for the critic. All three are engaged in unsettling what we think we know.

Shelley's sonnet and the essay 'On Life' can be read as ripostes to Plato's expulsion of the poets from his ideal state in *The Republic*. There Plato argues that poetry deals with nothing but copies of copies: an artistic representation of a veil is a copy of a phenomenal veil that is itself but an imperfect copy of the noumenal Idea of a veil. The main issue is not the second-hand status, but the deceptive potential: mimetic artworks conjure a semblance of reality, invite us to confuse an imitation with the real thing. German Romantic poets and theorists faced this challenge head on, arguing that art may copy reality, but that it simultaneously represents itself as copy. As Timothy Stoll puts it, 'a distinctive feature of artistic illusions is that they are precisely not intended to deceive'.[20] In *On the Aesthetic Education of Man*, Friedrich Schiller asserts that aesthetic semblance (*Schein*) is at once '*honest* (expressly renounces all claims to reality)' and '*autonomous* (dispenses with all support from reality)'.[21] This split between art and the real refutes those who, following Plato, claim that aesthetic semblance is deceptive, that the lifelike nature of mimetic artworks is a false truth. For the artist is not a forger trying to pass off a counterfeit copy of the really real; 'we are rarely, if ever, *deceived* into thinking that works of art are the thing they depict', as Stoll puts it.[22] Nor do we react to an artistic representation in the way we react to a real thing or event: dead bodies might pile up on the stage but no one calls the police.

For Schiller, *Schein* ('semblance') names the quality in an artistic work that alerts us to its status as a work of art and 'which we love just because it is semblance, and not because we take it to be something better'.[23] Put differently, *Schein* is the degree of separation between the mimetic work of art and the reality that it imitates. This separation persists even when the artwork is torn from that reality, as is the case with Marcel Duchamp's 'readymades', for instance, which are sculptural artworks constructed from found objects, many of which were industrially and anonymously produced. Duchamp's note on the minimal difference between near-identical objects – such as that between one of his own readymade artworks and its quotidian doubles – can also help illustrate the modality of *Schein*: '2 forms stamped from the same mould differ from each other by an infra-thin [*inframince*] value of separation.'[24] The pleasure we take in art derives from our awareness of this separation. Regardless of how infinitesimal it might be, it guarantees the non-deceptive essence of art: even when it perfectly coincides with reality, art remains split off from the real. Hence its formal nature: *Schein* is not about the representational content of a work of art – in Plato's terms, it is not about the phenomenal table copied in a picture of a table – but rather it is about the slight adjustment that a real-life table undergoes as it is made into art, which results in an infra-thin separation between any mass-produced table from IKEA and a readymade IKEA table in the style of Duchamp. The distinction is particularly crucial for poetry because, like a readymade, it exists in a medium – language – that is mass-produced and ubiquitous in everyday life. Poetic semblance manifests itself as the infra-thin separation between the language of poetry and commonplace chatter. What separates the two is, of course, measure, to which we can add that measure is a manifestation of *Schein*, an infra-thin separation, the difference that matters.

Schiller's *On the Aesthetic Education of Man*, much like Shelley's 'Defence of Poetry', makes art indispensable for a moral social order. Aesthetics segues into ethics. The same can be said of Plato's *Symposium*. Setting the dialogue within Plato's wider philosophical project, Frisbee Sheffield suggests that it is oriented towards attaining εὐδαιμονία ('the good life').[25] Philosophy, literally the love of wisdom (φιλοσοφία), leads to the good life, which can also be defined as the beautiful life: the life that all men (ought to) desire. 'Wisdom is one of the most beautiful of all things,' the prophetess Diotima explains to Socrates, who in turn recounts her words to his auditors at the *Symposium*. 'Love [Ἔρως] is that which thirsts for the beautiful, so that Love is of necessity a philosopher.'[26] One of the most striking aspects of the *Symposium* is that it represents the philosophical love of wisdom as being identical in kind to the erotic desire one might feel for a beautiful person. This is fundamentally an aesthetic desire, mediated through the eyes. 'And ἔρως (love) is so called because it flows in (ἐσρεῖ) from without,' Socrates states in *Cratylus*, 'and this flowing is not inherent in him who has it, but is introduced through the eyes; for this reason it was in ancient times called ἔσρος [influx], from ἐσρεῖν [flowing in].'[27] First we see, then we lust for what we've seen, and eventually we come to know.

This passage from sensuous beauty to moral truth also informs Benjamin's thought when he addresses 'the old question ... whether beauty is semblance' as part of his engagement with Goethe's *Elective Affinities*:[28]

> Beautiful life, the essentially beautiful, and semblance-like [*scheinhaft*] beauty – these three are identical. In this sense, the Platonic theory of the beautiful is connected with the still older problem of semblance, since, according to the *Symposium*, it first of all addresses physically living beauty.[29]

Physically living beauty is on the life-side of the infra-thin separation between life and art. The *Symposium*, above all the prophetess Diotima's discourse repeated by Socrates, demonstrates how to move to the other side of this split: from a love of sensuous bodily beauty to a love of beautiful order (including in works of art as well as in social institutions) and, finally, towards the good life, devoted to contemplating the Idea of Beauty itself. '"Such a life, as this, my dear Socrates," exclaimed the strange prophetess,' in Shelley's translation, '"spent in the contemplation of the beautiful, is the life for men to live; which if you chance ever to experience, you will esteem far beyond gold and rich garments, and even those lovely persons whom you and many others now gaze on with astonishment[."]'[30]

The route to Ideal Beauty is fuelled by desire (ἔρως). As Sheffield explains, 'Socrates is locating sexual desire within a larger context which explains what this desire is a desire *for*. Sexual *erōs*, apparently, is just one manifestation of a definitive longing for happiness.'[31] The would-be philosopher can achieve the progress from lust to εὐδαιμονία by following the 'correct system of Love' laid out by Diotima, 'proceeding as on steps from the love of one form [σώματα; lit. 'body'] to that of two, and from that of two, to that of all forms which are beautiful; and from beautiful forms to beautiful habits and institutions, and from institutions to beautiful doctrines', until eventually the philosopher will 'arrive at that which is nothing else than the doctrine of supreme beauty in itself, in the knowledge and contemplation of which at length they repose'.[32] There is therefore a continuity between real bodies, man-made artefacts and institutions, and Beauty itself.

The Platonic philosopher's smooth ascent from real bodies to ideal Beauty is at odds with Benjamin's theological intuitions, which lead him to separate divine from artistic creation: whereas God creates *Geschöpfe*, the artist creates *Gebilde*. The aesthetic category of Beauty does not apply to divine creation and therefore not to the living body, 'for everything living (the higher the quality of its life, the more this is so) is lifted up beyond the domain of the essentially beautiful'.[33] This is the domain of art. Furthermore: 'Everything essentially beautiful' – which is to say, all man-made art – 'is always and in its essence bound up, though in infinitely different degrees, with semblance [*Schein*].'[34] *Schein* is that which separates divine from human creation, but it is also that which brings the two into relation: we praise artworks and consider them beautiful when they appear to have a life of their own – living images over dead metaphors. So Benjamin argues that 'there dwells in all beauty of art that semblance – that is to say, that verging and bordering on life – without which beauty is not possible'.[35] *Schein* is his name for the infra-thin separation between the most perfectly life-like work of art and the most artistically shaped living body.

Beauty is essentially impossible without semblance, but semblance does not in itself circumscribe the essence of beauty. Benjamin argues that this essence is to be found in a dynamic balancing act between *Schein* and something else, 'what in the work of art in contrast to the semblance may be characterized as the expressionless [*das Ausdruckslose*]'.[36] Semblance and expressionless stand in a contrapuntal relation that Benjamin illustrates with the image of a veil: 'semblance belongs to the essentially beautiful as the veil', he writes, but the essence of Beauty encompasses both veil and what is veiled in it – the expressionless that 'neither appears in art nor can be unambiguously named' in any other way than as that which semblance veils.[37] It is a 'chasm, sightless and drear' to use the phrasing of Shelley's sonnet.[38] The veil's Platonic associations might invite us to read both Shelley's and Benjamin's veils as representations of phenomenal appearances veiling noumenal contents (the Idea of Beauty, or Love, or Truth), but, given that in both cases the veil is slung over something 'sightless' and 'expressionless', such a reading would annihilate the realm of Platonic Ideas, replacing it with a void.

Benjamin outright dismisses the notion that 'the truth of the beautiful can be unveiled' as 'philosophical barbarism',[39] and, like Shelley, directs attention to veiling as ontological process:

> Beauty is not a semblance [*Schein*], not a veil [*Hülle*] covering something else. It is itself not appearance [*Erscheinung*] but purely essence – one which, of course, remains essentially identical to itself only when veiled [*unter der Verhüllung*]. Therefore, even if everywhere else semblance is deception, the beautiful semblance is the veil [*Hülle*] thrown over that which is necessarily most veiled [*notwendig Verhülltesten*]. For the beautiful is neither the veil [*Hülle*] nor the veiled object [*verhüllte Gegenstand*] but rather the object in its veil [*Hülle*]. Unveiled, however, it would prove to be infinitely inconspicuous [*unendlich unscheinbar*].[40]

If semblance is a veil (*Hülle*), then what is 'necessarily most veiled' (*notwendig Verhülltesten*) is the expressionless, which, in the moment of unveiling – in coming to expression – turns into something else, becomes *unendlich unscheinbar*: at once infinitely inconspicuous and infinitely devoid of semblance (*Schein*). In life, semblance might function like a 'painted curtain' that obscures our perception, but, in a work of art, the same semblance candidly points to the truth of art: it is not life. The figures it presents are veils inhabited by no bodies, empty shells. Which is to say that it is the nature of aesthetic deception to highlight its own deceptiveness, and thereby represent the truth about its own deception. And this is where ethics and aesthetics meet also in Benjamin's discussion:

> The expressionless is the critical violence [*kritische Gewalt*] which, while unable to separate semblance from essence in art, prevents them from mingling. It possesses this violence as a moral dictum. In the expressionless, the sublime violence of the true appears as that which determines the language of the real world according to the laws of the moral world.[41]

Benjamin's moral world is not identical with the Platonic realm of Ideas, yet both are governed by a higher truth. If an artwork can aspire to capture such truth, this would not appear in its propositional contents (especially not if these are understood as phenomenal copies of noumenal Ideas) but as a self-reflective awareness of its own falsity, the shattering of its own illusions.

But is Benjamin really talking about a veil? Although this is the English equivalent favoured by most of Benjamin's translators, his own word is *Hülle*, whose range of meaning includes 'shell', as in husk, casing, sheath, cover: any protective structure that snugly fits the object it encases. Of course, the word also carries an echo of Shelley's name. 'For the beautiful is neither the shell [*Hülle*] nor the shelled object [*verhüllte Gegenstand*], but rather the object in its shell [*Hülle*].'

The truth of poetry cannot be *enthüllt* ('unshelled' or 'unveiled'), and so Shelley's sonnet ends on a cautionary note:

> I knew one who had lifted it [the painted veil] – he sought,
> For his lost heart was tender, things to love,
> But found them not, alas! nor was there aught
> The world contains, the which he could approve.
> Through the unheeding many he did move,

> A splendour among shadows, a bright blot
> Upon this gloomy scene, a Spirit that strove
> For truth, and like the Preacher found it not.[42]

The unnamed person sought for love and truth, yet what he found beneath the veil was so infinitely inconspicuous (*unendlich unscheinbar*) that it does not even warrant a description: we are only told that he 'found . . . not'. This is not to be confused with finding nothing at all: a 'not' can also be a something – albeit a something that cannot be expressed in any other way than with a *not*. To recall Hamacher's reading of the *Berlin Childhood*, where he argued that the word *Wolke* and other similarly polyvalent words structuring Benjamin's memoir are not 'to be taken here as metaphors at all, for they do not mean something else that could be said more appropriately, and they are not sensuous images of a noumenal content: rather, they mean that they do not mean, and indeed do mean this "not"'.[43]

We have already encountered this 'not' in the shape of Shelley's clouds, which are veils imprinted with, and torn by, the metric measure of poetry. The process is repeated in the sonnet. If we regard the painted veil as *Schein* and the 'not' found beneath it as *das Ausdruckslose*, Shelley's sonnet becomes legible as a parable on the *Idee der Untenthüllbarkeit* that Benjamin's discussion of beauty builds up towards: 'Thus, in the face of everything beautiful, the idea of unveiling [*Idee der Enthüllung*] becomes that of the impossibility of unveiling [*Unenthüllbarkeit*].'[44] Stanley Corngold's rendition of *Unenthüllbarkeit* as 'impossibility of unveiling' is a bit of compromise: the German word carries two negative prefixes, *un-* and *ent-*, and would be more accurately, if awkwardly, rendered as 'un-unveilability'. 'It is the idea of art criticism,' Benjamin goes on. 'The task of art criticism is not to lift the veil but rather, through the most precise knowledge of it as a veil, to raise itself for the first time to the true view of the beautiful.'[45]

Truth is beautiful, but the essence of beauty is the *Idee der Unenthüllbarkeit*. This suggests that truth is also essentially *unenthüllbar*; it is essentially veiled. For this reason, truth is incompatible with any inquisitive intention, the spirit of curiosity that would strip off every veil: 'This, indeed, is just what is said by the story of the veiled image of Saïs,' Benjamin writes, 'the unveiling of which was fatal for whomsoever thought thereby to learn the truth. It is not some enigmatic cruelty in the state of affairs that brings this about, but the very nature of truth, in the face of which even the purest fire of the spirit of inquiry is quenched.'[46] This is what happened to the person in Shelley's sonnet, who only found a 'not'. Just as the veiled object transforms into something *unendlich unscheinbar*, so truth evaporates when unveiled. 'Veil after veil may be undrawn,' as Shelley has it in the 'Defence', 'and the inmost naked beauty of the meaning never exposed.'[47] This is why criticism should not seek to expose the truth contained in a literary work. It can only help us perceive the various ways in which this truth cannot be unveiled.

Notes

1. 'Sonnet: "Lift not the painted veil"', ll. 1–2. For date of composition, see *PS2*, p. 413.
2. 'Sonnet: "Lift not the painted veil"', ll. 2–4.
3. 'The Symposium, or The Banquet, translated from Plato', in *SoL*, pp. 115–72 (p. 159).
4. David Newsome, *Two Classes of Men: Platonism and English Romantic Thought* (London: John Murray, 1974), p. 21.
5. Newsome, *Two Classes of Men*, p. 5.
6. Peter Fenves, *'Chatter': Language and History in Kierkegaard* (Stanford, CA: Stanford University Press, 1993).
7. Newsome, *Two Classes of Men*, p. 5.
8. *Origin*, p. 37, translation emended; *GS1*, p. 217.
9. *GS1*, p. 210, my translation.
10. *Origin*, p. 30; *GS1*, p. 210.
11. Hermann Güntert, *Von der Sprache der Götter und Geister* (Halle (Saale): Verlag von Max Niemeyer, 1921), p. 49; cited in *GS1*, p. 216; my translation.
12. To Florens Christian Rang, 9 December 1923, *Correspondence*, p. 224; *Briefe 1*, p. 233.
13. 'A Defence of Poetry', *SPP*, p. 515.
14. 'Sonnet: "Lift not the painted veil"', ll. 4–6.
15. 'On Life', *SPP*, p. 505.
16. 'On Life', *SPP*, p. 506.
17. 'A Defence of Poetry', *SPP*, p. 512.
18. 'A Defence of Poetry', *SPP*, p. 512; emphasis added.
19. Jennifer Wallace, 'Shelley, Plato and the Political Imagination', in *Plato and the English Imagination*, ed. by Sarah Hutton and Anna Baldwin (Cambridge: Cambridge University Press, 1994), pp. 229–41 (p. 236).
20. Timothy Stoll, 'Nietzsche and Schiller on Aesthetic Semblance', *The Monist*, 102 (2019), 331–8 (p. 333).
21. Friedrich Schiller, *On the Aesthetic Education of Man in a Series of Letters*, ed. and trans. by Elizabeth M. Wilkinson and L. A. Willoughby (Oxford: Clarendon Press, 1967), p. 197.
22. Stoll, 'Nietzsche and Schiller', p. 334.
23. Schiller, *On the Aesthetic Education*, p. 193.
24. Marcel Duchamp, 'Inframince', in *Duchamp du signe*, ed. by Michel Sanouillet and Paul Matisse (Paris: Flammarion, 2008), p. 290, n. 35rv; cited in Johanna Malt, 'The Space-Time of the Surrealist Object', in *Thinking Through Relation: Encounters in Creative Critical Writing*, ed. by Florian Mussgnug, Mathelinda Nabugodi and Thea Petrou (Oxford: Peter Lang, 2021), pp. 85–96 (p. 92).
25. Frisbee C. C. Sheffield, *Plato's Symposium: The Ethics of Desire* (Oxford: Oxford University Press, 2009).
26. 'The Symposium', *SoL*, pp. 150–1.
27. Plato, *Cratylus*, in *Plato in Twelve Volumes*, trans. by Harold N. Fowler, 12 vols (Cambridge, MA: Harvard University Press, 1921), xii, 420a-b. Accessed via http://www.perseus.tufts.edu/ [accessed 1 June 2022]. E. Douka Kabitoglou makes this link in *Plato and the English Romantics* (London: Routledge, 1990), p. 100.
28. 'Goethe's *Elective Affinities*', *SW1*, p. 350; *GS1*, p. 193.
29. 'Goethe's *Elective Affinities*', *SW1*, p. 350; *GS1*, p. 194.
30. 'The Symposium', *SoL*, p. 159.
31. Sheffield, *Plato's Symposium*, p. 78.

32 'The Symposium', *SoL*, pp. 158–9.
33 'Goethe's *Elective Affinities*', *SW1*, p. 350; *GS1*, p. 194.
34 'Goethe's *Elective Affinities*', *SW1*, p. 350; *GS1*, p. 194.
35 'Goethe's *Elective Affinities*', *SW1*, p. 350; *GS1*, p. 194.
36 'Goethe's *Elective Affinities*', *SW1*, p. 350; *GS1*, p. 194.
37 'Goethe's *Elective Affinities*', *SW1*, p. 350; *GS1*, p. 194.
38 'Sonnet: "Lift not the painted veil"', l. 6.
39 'Goethe's *Elective Affinities*', *SW1*, p. 351; *GS1*, p. 195.
40 'Goethe's *Elective Affinities*', *SW1*, p. 351; *GS1*, p. 195.
41 'Goethe's *Elective Affinities*', *SW1*, p. 340; *GS1*, p. 181.
42 'Sonnet: "Lift not the painted veil"', ll. 7–14.
43 Hamacher, 'The Word *Wolke*', p. 163.
44 'Goethe's *Elective Affinities*', *SW1*, p. 351; *GS1*, p. 195.
45 'Goethe's *Elective Affinities*', *SW1*, p. 351; *GS1*, p. 195. The idea of *Unenthüllbarkeit* takes its place alongside other Benjaminian coinages that end with the suffix *-barkeit*, or '-ability', such as criticizability (*Kritizierbarkeit*), translatability (*Übersetzbarkeit*), citability (*Zitierbarkeit*) and recognizability (*Erkennbarkeit*). As Samuel Weber has shown, the potentialities inherent in the suffix are an important aspect of Benjamin's critical method. Samuel Weber, *Benjamin's -abilities* (Cambridge, MA: Harvard University Press, 2010).
46 *Origin*, p. 36, translation emended; *GS1*, p. 216.
47 'A Defence of Poetry', *SPP*, p. 528.

5
Mosaic

'Truth is discovered in the essence of language,' Benjamin writes towards the end of his essay on Goethe's *Elective Affinities*, and in the 'Epistemo-Critical Prologue' he picks up that thread again, orienting his work towards 'that area of truth towards which language is directed'.[1] The Platonic doctrine of Ideas helps Benjamin determine the manner of writing that is best capable of representing that region. 'If philosophy is to remain true to the law of its own form, as the representation of truth and not as a guide to the acquisition of knowledge, then the exercise of this form – rather than its anticipation in the system – must be accorded due importance.'[2] The move recalls 'The Task of the Translator', where Benjamin defined translation as a form of its own. If that essay set out the translator's task, then the 'Prologue' explicates the task of the philosophical critic.[3] Moreover, in emphasising questions of form over system-building, Benjamin reinforces the literary aspect of philosophical writing: it must be exercised as an artistic practice in its own right. In other words, the 'Prologue' is a poetics: at once theoretical exposition and practical manual on writing philosophical prose – or, more specifically, a treatise, which is Benjamin's term for the form of *The Origin of German Tragic Drama*. In a letter to Gershom Scholem, Benjamin described the book as being composed with 'the craziest mosaic technique one can imagine'.[4] More explicitly, it is a mosaic of citations. Whereas systematic thought relies on mathematical proofs, in 'the canonic form of the treatise the only element of an intention . . . is the authoritative citation'.[5] Such citations are the pieces out of which Benjamin constructed his text: 'what I have written consists, as it were, almost entirely of citations,' he confides to Scholem – a statement that is not strictly speaking true as there is quite a lot of Benjamin's own writing to join the citations together.[6]

As a poetics, the 'Prologue' has further affinities with the poetics of translation presented in 'The Task of the Translator'. 'Translation thus ultimately serves the purpose of expressing the innermost relationship of languages to one another,' he wrote in that essay.[7] In an analogous manner, the philosophical treatise serves the purpose of expressing the innermost relationship between language and truth. 'It cannot possibly reveal or establish this hidden relationship itself; but it can represent it by realising it in embryonic [*keimhaft*: lit. 'seed-like'] or intensive form.'[8] Benjamin views all languages as shattered fragments of the divine language of Names: translation represents the relationship between languages by assembling these fragments into a harmoniously balanced whole. The treatise is likewise an assemblage of fragments – Benjamin describes its separate sections as *Denkbruchstücke* ('thought-fragments'), recalling his description of words as *Bruchstücke* of prelapsarian language. It is this fragmentary form that allows the treatise to establish a relationship to truth: the treatise mimetically re-enacts the process of thought through which we approach truth:

> Tirelessly the process of thinking makes new beginnings, returning in a roundabout way to its original object. This continual pausing for breath is the mode most proper to the process of contemplation. For by pursuing different levels of meaning [*Sinnstufen*] in its examination of one single object it receives both the incentive to begin again and the justification for its intermittent rhythm.[9]

Pausing. Starting again. What is at stake in this 'intermittent rhythm' is the measure of thought. This is not captured in the prosodic structure of a sentence, but in the conceptual arrangement of prose paragraphs, each paragraph a fragment carefully taking its place in a greater whole, this whole being nothing less than truth itself.

Benjamin's approximation between divine λόγος and Platonic εἴδωλον, moreover, introduces a visual aspect: whereas the λόγος is heard, the εἴδωλον is seen. And so Benjamin's image for the form of a philosophical treatise is appropriately pictorial: it is like a mosaic. 'Just as mosaics preserve their majesty despite their fragmentation into capricious particles, so philosophical contemplation is not lacking in momentum. Both are made up of the distinct and the disparate.'[10] The mosaic is recognisably a variant on the image of the broken vessel that Benjamin used in his essay on translation, where he argued that a translation must make 'both the original and the translation recognizable [*erkennbar*] as fragments [*Bruchstück*] of a greater language, just as fragments [*Bruchstück*] are part of a vessel'.[11] The same holds true for the mosaic (and, by implication, the treatise). The small pieces of glass, stone or ceramic that make up a mosaic are not like to one another, yet by being perfectly matched and assembled, they serve to depict one image.

Ultimately, then, the 'Prologue' is a lesson in how to represent the process of thought that leads to truth in language. Each little *Denkbruchstück* represents a conceptual step (*Sinnstufe*, lit. 'step of meaning') on the ladder of interpretation: 'I have never been able do research and think in any sense other than, if you will, a theological one, namely, in accordance with the Talmudic teaching about the forty-nine levels of meaning [*Sinnstufen*] in every passage of Tora,' Benjamin wrote in a letter outlining his research method.[12] Yet, despite these theological overtones, the philosophical mosaic is also conspicuously like to Mallarmé's definition of books of verse in which 'motifs of the same type balance each other, stabilizing each other at a distance ... an arrangement of fragments, adding up to a total rhythm, which would be the poem stilled, in the blanks'.[13] The treatise is a kind of complex philosophical poem. Of course, divining multiple levels of meaning in a single word, phrase or passage is also characteristic of literary criticism and is, for Shelley at least, one of the features that distinguishes criticism from poetic composition. Making reference to 'the fifty-six various readings of the first line of the Orlando Furioso', Shelley does not deny the presence of multiple layers of meaning in a poetic line, but argues that this is not compatible with a poet's creative process, which captures the whole before developing the parts.[14]

> For Milton conceived the Paradise Lost as a whole before he executed it in portions. We have his own authority also for the Muse having 'dictated' to him the 'unpremeditated song,' and let this be an answer to those who would alledge the fifty-six various readings of the first line of the Orlando Furioso. Compositions so produced are to poetry what mosaic is to painting.[15]

Today Shelley's intention may be more forcefully captured in a contrast between mosaic and photography: the true genius conceives his unpremeditated work in a flash, as a snapshot of the whole, while the inferior poet (or critic) scrambles together fragments of meaning into an image that displays its laborious composition. While painting and photography conjure a semblance of the real to the extent that they can, at a quick glance, be mistaken for reality, the mosaic always retains a trace of its own constructedness: we see the smaller pieces it is made of.

Shelley's rejection of the mosaic composition principle follows on from one of his most famous statements, that 'the mind in creation is as a fading coal which some invisible influence, like an inconstant wind, awakens to transitory brightness . . . like the colour of a flower which fades and changes as it is developed, and the conscious portions of our nature are unprophetic either of its approach or its departure.'[16] Such statements have earned Shelley the reputation of being, in Carl Grabo's phrase, 'a kind of inspired idiot, producing beautiful poetry without clearly knowing what he was about',[17] yet we can also read his depiction of the 'mind in creation' as performative: not describing how he actually writes, but representing poetic practice in accordance with Romantic ideals of artistic genius that privilege the stroke of inspiration over the minute assembly of a mosaic. Shelley's and Benjamin's differing evaluations of the mosaic thus indicate a difference not of conception but of priorities: Shelley aspires to be a poet writing 'unpremeditated song'; Benjamin, a philosophical critic carefully assembling *Denkbruchstücke*.

'A Poet participates in the eternal, the infinite, and the one,' Shelley asserts in the 'Defence'.[18] The term 'participate' translates the Greek μετέχω ('partake of, share in'), which is the verb that Plato uses to describe the relation between phenomena and noumena: 'All other things are beautiful through a participation of it,' Diotima says of Beauty, adding 'that although they [things] are subject to production and decay, it [Beauty] never becomes more or less, or endures any change. When any one, ascending from a correct system of Love, begins to contemplate this supreme beauty, he already touches the consummation of his labour.'[19] While Diotima here describes the philosopher's work of loving wisdom, Shelley transfers her insights to the sphere of poetic composition. In the 'Defence', he echoes her description of the steps that lead the philosopher from corporeal love towards the contemplation of 'supreme beauty in itself'[20] when he offers an example from literary history:

> The Provençal Trouveurs, or inventors, preceded Petrarch, whose verses are as spells, which unseal the inmost enchanted fountains of the delight which is in the grief of Love. It is impossible to feel them

without *becoming a portion of that beauty which we contemplate*: it were superfluous to explain how the gentleness and the elevation of mind connected with these sacred emotions can render men more amiable, more generous, and wise, and *lift them out of the dull vapours of the little world of self*. Dante understood the secret things of love even more than Petrarch. . . . His apotheosis of Beatrice in Paradise, and the *gradations of his own love and her loveliness, by which as by steps he feigns himself to have ascended to the throne of the Supreme Cause*, is the most glorious imagination of modern poetry.[21]

In escaping the realm of selfish appetites and allowing us to ascend, as by steps (*Sinnstufen* in Benjamin's term), towards Beauty, and moreover in enabling us to partake in the Beauty which we contemplate, poetry achieves the very ends that Diotima ascribes to philosophy.

C. E. Pulos has suggested that while 'Plato ascends progressively from particular beauties to Beauty, Shelley tends to reverse this process and to seek Beauty in its earthly manifestations.'[22] This seems to fundamentally misconstrue the relation between phenomenal and noumenal, earthly and ideal Beauty. This relation is not a one-way street – neither from object to Idea (the view Pulos ascribes to Plato) nor from Idea to object (the view he ascribes to Shelley) – but participatory. The notion of participation secures the continuity between the sensuous beauty of bodily forms, the civic beauty of political institutions and the intellectual beauty of philosophical doctrines that underwrites the political aspect of Shelley's poetics – all are good insofar as they participate in the Idea of Beauty and Truth. 'Language, colour, form, and religious and civil habits of action are all the instruments and materials of poetry; they may be called poetry by that figure of speech which considers the effect as a synonime of the cause,' Shelley concludes.[23] As it happens, this is the very figure of speech used by Diotima to explain why, if the desire for the good manifested in love is universal, we do not say that everyone loves at all times. Her example is poetry:

> Poetry; which is a general name signifying every cause whereby anything proceeds from that which is not, into that which is; so that the exercise of every inventive art is poetry, and all such artists poets. Yet they are not called poets, but distinguished by other names; and one portion or species of poetry, that which has a relation to music and rhythm, is divided from all others, and known by the name belonging to all. For this alone is properly called poetry, and those who exercise the art of this species of poetry, poets. So,

with respect to Love. Love is indeed universally all that earnest desire for the possession of happiness and that which is good; the greatest and the subtlest love, and that which inhabits the heart of every human being; but those who seek this object through the acquirement of wealth, or the exercise of the gymnastic arts, or philosophy, are not said to love, nor are called lovers[.][24]

Poetry is the proper name of all making (ποίησις) and love is the name of all desire towards happiness, so that all beneficial practices may be called poetry and love if we consider them as effects synonymous with their cause. Building a beautiful social order is therefore not essentially different from writing a beautiful poem; the two are but different modalities of participation in Beauty itself.

According to Benjamin, phenomenal thoughts 'participate' in noumenal Ideas through the concept (*Begriff*). 'Through their mediating role concepts enable phenomena to participate in the existence of ideas. It is the same mediating role which fits them for the other equally basic task of philosophy, the representation of ideas.'[25] This representation is not mimetic: that is, the concept does not resemble an Idea (again, it is not a copy of an original); rather, if we imagine the Idea as a mosaic, then each concept is akin to one of its constituent pieces. Ideas are represented through the relations between concepts just as the motif depicted on a mosaic emerges from the relations between tiny pieces that – each on its own – have no relation to the image represented by the whole. 'For ideas are not represented in themselves, but solely and exclusively in an arrangement of concrete elements in the concept: as the configuration of these elements.'[26]

The distinction between individual piece and mosaic helps Benjamin resolve the tension between the world of things and the world of Ideas. Concepts are derived from empirical observations in the world of things; such observations are necessarily fragmentary – mosaic-pieces. Yet when properly ordered, their arrangement manages to convey something that transcends the individual observations. The Idea. 'The set of concepts which assist in the representation of an idea makes it present as such a configuration. For phenomena are not incorporated in ideas. They are not contained in them. Ideas are, rather, their objective, virtual arrangement, their objective interpretation.'[27] This also means that – for the same reason that one word is not enough to evoke prosodic measure – one concept is never enough to represent an Idea: both require the harmonious interaction of different parts. Offering another image to explain his reasoning, Benjamin asserts that 'Ideas are to objects as constellations [*Sternbilder*] are to stars.'[28] The stars in a constellation are light years apart and have little relation to one another beyond that represented by the constellation, which is projected onto them by the earthbound stargazer. In the same manner, empirical observations lead to concepts, which are then arranged so that an Idea can be read into them. In other words, concepts are not copies of Ideas, but they can participate in Ideas by being arranged in such a way that the Idea becomes visible in their interrelations – and, in German, a constellation (*Sternbild*) is quite literally a picture (*Bild*), like a mosaic made of stars (*Sternen*).

The *Symposium*'s third discourse on love is delivered by Eryximachus, a physician. He begins by positing that love 'is different in a sane and in a diseased body' and that 'he is the most skilful physician who can trace in those operations the good and evil love' so as to restore a balance of 'mutual love'.[29] This balance is not unique to the healthy body, but pervades everything in its proper state, from 'the gymnastic arts and agriculture' to music and even 'the constitution of the seasons of the year'.[30] All of these fields can only flourish when brought into a harmonious order, which Eryximachus illustrates with a citation from Heraclitus, 'One thought apparently differing, yet so agrees with itself, as the harmony of a lyre and a bow.' Eryximachus unpacks Heraclitus' idea as follows:

> It is great absurdity to say that an harmony differs, and can exist between things whilst they are dissimilar; but probably [Heraclitus] meant that from sounds which first differed, like the grave and the acute, and which afterwards agreed, harmony was produced according to musical art. For no harmony can arise from the grave and the acute whilst yet they differ. But harmony is symphony: symphony is, as it were, concord. But it is impossible that concord should subsist between things that differ, so long as they differ. Between things which are discordant and dissimilar there is then no harmony. A rhythm is produced from that which is quick, and that which is slow, first being distinguished and opposed to each other, and then made accordant; so does medicine, no less than music, establish a concord between the objects of its art, producing love and agreement between adverse things.[31]

Love is Eryximachus' name for the careful arrangement of discordant sounds into euphonic structures whereby harmony and rhythm are produced. We could think of it as a sonic mosaic. This ordering principle applies equally to the human body as in poetry and politics – music is just the paradigmatic example of the harmonious rhythm that structures anything good, beautiful and true.

Shelley adapts Eryximachus' discourse on love in the 'Defence', where it serves both to confirm the supremacy of poetry, defined as measured – that is, rhythmic and harmonious – language, and to establish the continuity between the work of poetry and other aspects of social organisation. 'In the youth of the world, men dance and sing and imitate natural objects, observing in these actions, as in all others, a certain rhythm or order,' he writes at the outset, and in the course of his argument he makes clear that 'an approximation to this order' not only regulates dance, song and the mimetic arts, but also governs social life.[32] Shelley's assertion that the 'true Poetry of Rome lived in its institutions; for whatever of beautiful, true and majestic they contained could have sprung only from the faculty which creates the order in which they consist' is therefore not a metaphor.[33] Insofar as these institutions are beautifully ordered creations, they are poems.

A thing's participation in the Idea of Beauty is phenomenologically perceptible as the 'certain rhythm or order' most appropriate to that thing. Rhythm is, moreover, distinguished by an ability to balance opposites: it encompasses not only the unpremeditated stream of song but also the pauses that interrupt it. This is part of the reason why Benjamin was interested in the concept: sudden stops arrest the musical movement but, even in so doing, they add to the total rhythm of the piece as a whole. Hölderlin explored this question in the notes to his translation of Sophocles' *Oedipus*. In 'The Task of the Translator', Benjamin commends Hölderlin's Greek translations, and he turns to Hölderlin once more when contemplating how beauty may be represented in words. In a passage cited by Benjamin, Hölderlin writes:

> For the tragic transport is actually empty, and the least restrained. – Thereby, in the rhythmic sequence of the representations wherein the transport presents itself, there becomes necessary what in syllabic measure [*Sylbenmaasse*] is called caesura, the pure word, the counter-rhythmic rupture – namely, in order to meet the onrushing [*reißenden*] charge of representations at its highest point, in such a manner that not the change of representations but the representation itself very soon appears.[34]

A caesura may interrupt the poetic metre, but this very interruption completes the poem's overall rhythm. While Benjamin on the one hand insists on reading the caesura as a violent interruption that destroys the rhythmic order of the line, he also emphasises that, in the exact moment that the caesura shatters the line, it arranges the shattered fragments into a harmonious order around itself. Just as importantly, the momentary pause in the metre differentiates poetically measured language from quotidian speech. Hölderlin, and Benjamin in his wake, expands this prosodic principle to apply to a tragedy as a whole. At the height of a tragic drama, when the risk of being carried away by its emotional momentum is the greatest, the interruption arrests the transport, pierces the illusion, reminds us that we are seeing a representation. In other words, it alerts us to its 'infra-thin' separation from life. For Hölderlin, this is a question of sobriety (*Nüchternheit*), which Benjamin reads as 'another name for that caesura, in which, along with harmony, every expression simultaneously comes to a standstill,' – with Mallarmé, one could say that expression is 'stilled, in the blanks' – 'in order to give free reign to an expressionless power [*ausdruckslosen Gewalt*] inside all artistic media'.[35] In this act of naming, Benjamin links the expressionless to his own specular name (manifested in the resonance between 'Walter' and *Gewalt*) as well as Mallarmé's notion of 'a total rhythm, which would be the poem, stilled'.[36]

In the course of his discussion of Beauty, Benjamin assimilates Hölderlin's idea of the caesura as a counter-rhythmic rupture to the contrapuntal dynamic that he sets up between the expressionless and semblance (*Schein*). When Benjamin comes to writing a poetics of criticism in the 'Epistemo-Critical Prologue', the caesura is translated into sentence breaks. It is the peculiar characteristic of philosophical prose, Benjamin observes in the 'Prologue', that 'the writer must stop and restart with every new sentence'.[37] This is a continually repeated interruption that mirrors the intermittent rhythm of contemplation embodied in the treatise's mosaic form:

> The contemplative mode of representation must follow writing closer than any other. For this kind of representation does not aim to carry the reader along in its onrush [*mitzureißen*] and inspired momentum. Only when it forces the reader to stop in stages of contemplation is the representation assured of itself. The larger its object, the more discontinuous must it be. Its prosaic sobriety [*Nüchternheit*] remains . . . the only mode of writing that befits philosophical investigation.[38]

And so the rhythm of philosophical writing becomes indispensable to its content, just as the form of a literary work is. The stop–start movement of the treatise is the most appropriate form for representing truth in language because only this rhythm is capable of capturing what Benjamin's translator John Osborne, in a felicitous formulation, terms the truth that is 'bodied forth in the dance of represented ideas'.[39] Far from attempting to translate Ideas into words, as copies, the treatise employs a form that rhythmically evokes the structure of their interrelations; its language is dancing truth.

Imagine it as a syncopated rhythm, for instance, such as might arise from Shelley's suspension of any distinction between poetry and philosophy. Rather than representing these as two separate spheres of intellectual creativity, Shelley ascribes a 'two-fold' function to the 'poetical faculty': 'by one it creates new materials of knowledge, and power and pleasure; by the other it engenders in the mind a desire to reproduce and arrange them according to a certain rhythm and order which may be called the beautiful and the good'.[40] The poet–philosopher apprehends new relations between things *and* arranges these relations in accordance with the rhythm and order of Beauty. This duality is of course also present in Shelley's reading of Plato himself. In a draft Preface to his *Symposium* translation, he remarked that 'Plato exhibits the rare union of close and subtle logic, with the Pythian enthusiasm of poetry, melted by the splendour and harmony of his periods into one irresistible stream of musical impressions, which hurry the persuasions onward, as in a breathless career.'[41] The fusion of 'close and subtle logic' and poetry hinges on the caesurae of Plato's periods: they arrest the onrushing (*mitreißende*) transport of his sentences, but in so doing they propel the reader along the measured flows of his prose. Breathlessly, not senselessly.

Shelley's interpretation of Plato's prose form as a rhythm that encompasses its own interruptions, which he here refers to as 'pauses', is explored at greater length in the 'Defence':

> He rejected the measure of the epic, dramatic, and lyrical forms, because he sought to kindle a harmony in thoughts divested of shape and action, and he forbore to invent any regular plan of rhythm which would include, under determinate forms, the varied pauses of his style. . . . His language has a sweet and majestic rhythm, which satisfies the sense, no less than the almost superhuman wisdom of his philosophy satisfies the intellect; it is a

> strain which distends, and then bursts the circumference of the hearer's mind, and pours itself forth together with it into the universal element with which it has perpetual sympathy.[42]

Commenting on this passage, Ross Wilson notes that 'Shelley specifies quite clearly that Plato is a poet thanks to his splendid imagery and, perhaps more significantly, the intensity of his linguistic melody, which, though it eschewed the metrical forms of particular poetic genres, is nevertheless strikingly rhythmical.'[43] Although generating philosophical ideas and shaping language into poetic forms might seem to be separate activities, one is ineffective without the other – capturing the true rhythm is essential in all areas of human invention, philosophy no less than poetry or politics:

> All the authors of revolutions in opinion are not only necessarily poets as they are inventors, nor even as their words unveil the permanent analogy of things by images which participate in the life of truth; but as their periods are harmonious and rhythmical and contain in themselves the elements of verse; being the echo of the eternal music.[44]

For Shelley, as for Benjamin, writing represents the Idea of Truth not by copying it, but by rhythmically bodying forth 'the dance of represented ideas'. This dance is carried out to the measure of 'eternal music', an allusion to the Pythagorean concept of the harmony of the spheres, *musica universalis*, that emanates from the movement of celestial bodies across the skies. Benjamin also evokes this concept at the close of his discussion of Plato's doctrine of Ideas:

> Just as the harmony of the spheres depends on the orbits of stars which do not come into contact with each other, so the existence of the *mundus intelligibilis* depends on the unbridgeable distance between pure essences. Every idea is a sun and is related to other ideas just as suns are related to each other. The harmonious relationship between such essences is what constitutes truth.[45]

And truth is, of course, both beautiful and good. Its harmony manifests itself in the rhythm of a dance or in the social order of a historical era, in the measure of a poem or in the mosaic arrangement of paragraphs. By attending to this rhythm, critical writing, too, can participate in the Idea of Beauty.

Notes

1. 'Goethe's *Elective Affinities*', *SW1*, p. 353; *GS1*, p. 197; *Origin*, p. 27; *GS1*, p. 207.
2. *Origin*, p. 28; *GS1*, pp. 207–8.
3. While the 'Prologue' is concerned with defining the form of the philosophical treatise – and does not mention literary criticism – *The Origin of German Tragic Drama* itself is a study of German baroque plays. Benjamin is here suspending the distinction between philosophy and literary history and criticism.
4. Letter to Gershom Scholem, 22 December 1924, in *Correspondence*, p. 256, translation emended; *Briefe 1*, p. 366.
5. *Origin*, p. 28, translation emended; *GS1*, p. 208.
6. Letter to Gershom Scholem, 22 December 1924, in *Correspondence*, p. 256, translation emended; *Briefe 1*, p. 366.
7. 'The Task of the Translator', *SW1*, p. 255; *GS4*, p. 12.
8. 'The Task of the Translator', *SW1*, p. 255; *GS4*, p. 12.
9. *Origin*, p. 28, translation emended; *GS1*, p. 208.
10. *Origin*, p. 28; *GS1*, p. 208.
11. 'The Task of the Translator', *SW1*, p. 260; *GS4*, p. 18.
12. To Max Rychner, 7 March 1931, *Correspondence*, p. 372; *Briefe 1*, p. 524.
13. Mallarmé, 'Crisis of Verse', pp. 208–9.
14. 'A Defence of Poetry', *SPP*, p. 532.
15. 'A Defence of Poetry', *SPP*, p. 532.
16. 'A Defence of Poetry', *SPP*, p. 531.
17. Carl Grabo, *A Newton Among Poets: Shelley's Use of Science in* Prometheus Unbound (Chapel Hill, NC: University of North Carolina Press, 1930), p. vii.
18. 'A Defence of Poetry', *SPP*, p. 513.
19. 'The Symposium', *SoL*, p. 158. Tracy Ware has also made the link between Shelley's 'participates' and Plato's μετέχω in 'Shelley's Platonism in A Defence of Poetry', *SEL*, 23.4 (1983), 549–66 (p. 563).
20. 'The Symposium', *SoL*, p. 159.
21. 'A Defence of Poetry', *SPP*, p. 525; emphasis added.
22. C. E. Pulos, *The Deep Truth: A Study of Shelley's Scepticism* (Lincoln, NE: University of Nebraska Press, 1962), pp. 77–8.
23. 'A Defence of Poetry', *SPP*, p. 513.
24. 'The Symposium', *SoL*, p. 152.
25. *Origin*, p. 34; *GS1*, p. 214. Benjamin's phrase, which is here rendered as 'participate in', is *leihen . . . Anteil*, a German equivalent of μετέχω.
26. *Origin*, p. 34; *GS1*, p. 214.
27. *Origin*, p. 34, translation emended; *GS1*, p. 214.
28. *Origin*, p. 34; *GS1*, p. 214.
29. 'The Symposium', *SoL*, pp. 130–1.
30. 'The Symposium', *SoL*, pp. 131–2.
31. 'The Symposium', *SoL*, p. 131.
32. 'A Defence of Poetry', *SPP*, pp. 511–12.
33. 'A Defence of Poetry', *SPP*, p. 523.
34. Hölderlin, 'Annotations to Oedipus'; cited in 'Goethe's *Elective Affinities*', *SW1*, pp. 340–1, translation emended; *GS1*, pp. 181–2.
35. 'Goethe's *Elective Affinities*', *SW1*, p. 341; *GS1*, p. 182.
36. Mallarmé, 'Crisis of Verse', p. 209.
37. *Origin*, p. 29; *GS1*, p. 209.
38. *GS1*, p. 209; my translation. Compare *Origin*, p. 29.
39. *Origin*, p. 29; *GS1*, p. 209. The German reads 'Die Wahrheit, vergegenwärtigt im Reigen der dargestellten Ideen . . . '
40. 'A Defence of Poetry', *SPP*, p. 531.
41. 'On the Symposium, or Preface to the Banquet of Plato', *SoL*, p. 113.

42 'A Defence of Poetry', *SPP*, pp. 514–15.
43 Ross Wilson, 'Shelley's Plato', in *The Routledge Handbook of Translation and Philosophy*, ed. by J. Piers Rawling and Philip Wilson (London: Routledge, 2018), pp. 345–57 (p. 348).
44 'A Defence of Poetry', *SPP*, p. 515.
45 *Origin*, p. 37; *GS1*, pp. 217–18.

6
Love

Socrates is ugly. This is clear from references in any of the Platonic dialogues, but in the case of the *Symposium*, Socrates' ugliness is essential to what Mary Shelley described as the 'whole mechanism of the drama'.[1] Shelley undertook the translation at least in part for her sake. 'I am employed just now having little better to do,' he wrote to their friends John and Maria Gisborne, 'in translating into my fainting & inefficient periods the divine eloquence of Plato's Symposium – only as an exercise or perhaps to give Mary some idea of the manners & feelings of the Athenians – so different on many subjects from that of any other community that ever existed.'[2] Shelley's translation is the first time the work was rendered into English in its entirety, praise of homosexuality and all, and seems to have had a dual motive – to illuminate his wife about the sexual politics of ancient Athens and to practise transferring the harmonies of Plato's prose into his own English periods, however 'fainting & inefficient' their rhythm might be. This latter aim also includes mastering the *Symposium*'s dramatic mechanism. Michael O'Neill clarifies that the term had 'a quasi-technical significance in literary criticism of the time; it means something like the "adaptation of the parts" to the demands of a work's structure, or . . . "the mode of operation of [the work's] process"'.[3] In other words, 'mechanism' refers to the supplementary arrangement of different elements that, taken together, generate the transport of a dramatic work. This is a lesson in choreography that Shelley will incorporate into his own dramatic writing.

The *Symposium*'s main action is contained within an account by Apollodorus to an unnamed companion. Apollodorus himself had it from Aristodemus, who had been present at a feast given by Agathon to celebrate his winning the first prize at the tragedy contest. At this party, Eryximachus proposes that each person present should give what 'is called ερωτικος or a discussion upon Love'.[4] The proposition is accepted, and discourses are delivered by Phaedrus, Pausanias, Eryximachus, Aristophanes, Agathon and finally Socrates, the bulk of whose speech is given over to recounting his dialogue with the prophetess Diotima. Diotima had taught Socrates about the steps by which the aspiring philosopher ascends to contemplation of the Idea of Beauty. While this might appear to be the dialogue's climax, it is not – no sooner has Socrates stopped speaking than Alcibiades arrives: young, beautiful, noble and drunk. When invited to deliver his own ερωτικος, Alcibiades declares that 'should I praise in his [Socrates'] presence, be it God or man, any other beside himself, he would not keep his hands off me'[5] and therefore launches into a panegyric on Socrates, in the course of which it becomes clear that Alcibiades is the living embodiment of the ideal philosopher-lover described by Diotima.

Socrates and Alcibiades are therefore point and counterpoint in the *Symposium*'s dramatic structure. The differences between them in age, appearance and social situation place them on distinct stages in the ascent from physical to ideal Beauty. A beautiful body is the outer manifestation of a beautiful soul (Alcibiades), yet a soul only attains to a view of true Beauty when it learns to look beyond superficial bodily phenomena to the intellectual spirit that can reside even in an ugly body (Socrates). 'I will begin the praise of Socrates by comparing him to a certain statue,' Alcibiades says. 'Socrates is exactly like those Sileniuses that sit in the sculptors' shops, and which are carved holding flutes or pipes, but which, when divided in two, are found to contain withinside the images of the Gods.'[6] As he goes on, it becomes clear that what is found inside Socrates is equivalent to the Ideas that the philosopher desires to contemplate:

> [I]f you open him, you will find within admirable temperance and wisdom. For he cares not for mere beauty, and despises more than any one can imagine all external possessions, whether it be beauty or wealth, or glory, or any other thing for which the multitude felicitates the possessor. He esteems these things and us who honour them, as nothing, and lives among men, making all the objects of their admiration the playthings of his irony. But I know not if any one of you have ever seen the divine images which are within, when he has been opened and is serious. I have seen them, and they are so supremely beautiful, so golden, so divine, and wonderful, that everything which Socrates commands surely ought to be obeyed, even like the voice of a God.[7]

The physical person of Socrates is like an inverted reflection of the ascent sketched out by Diotima: despite his exterior ugliness, whoever manages to crack him open will be able to contemplate true Beauty itself.

But for all that Socrates contains true Beauty within him and scorns the 'mere' beauty of outward appearances, Alcibiades also notes 'how passionately Socrates affects the intimacy of those who are beautiful' – a point proven by the circle assembled at Agathon's house in the *Symposium*. However, even as he surrounds himself with beautiful young men, Socrates resists the customary erotic interactions with them. Alcibiades confesses that he had 'imagined that Socrates was in love with me on account of my beauty, and was determined to seize so favourable an opportunity, by conceding to him all that he require, of learning from him all that he knew';[8] this is the kind of exchange of a young man's desirable body for the superior attractions of an older man's mind endorsed by Diotima. Yet Socrates refuses to live up to the customary terms of the bargain: what begins as a conventional exchange of sexual for intellectual favours soon turns into a story of the lover spurned.

What follows is a very honest and explicit description of the various tricks with which Alcibiades tried to seduce Socrates, from private conversation, to gymnastic exercises, dinner and outright declaration, succeeded by sleeping together under one garment: 'I lay the whole night with my arms around this truly divine and wonderful being' and yet 'awoke and arose from as unimpassioned an embrace as if I had slept with my father or my elder brother!'[9] The incestuous connotation merely veils the real scandal of Alcibiades' confession: his interactions with Socrates break with the established conventions of Greek love – it is the older lover who should seek out and seduce a young beloved, not the other way around. Nonetheless, it gradually becomes clear that all the young men in the company have been in erotic pursuit of Socrates, and all have similarly failed to seduce him. When, at the end of Alcibiades' discourse, 'the whole party burst into laughter at the frankness with which he seemed to confess that he was still in love with Socrates',[10] this is not a laughter of scorn at someone who has sexually embarrassed themselves, but a laughter of recognition with someone who has shared the experience. Alcibiades is 'like one bitten by a viper, who they say will not tell his misfortune to any, but those who are bitten in the same manner, since they alone knowing what it is, will pardon him for whatever he dares to do or say under the mitigation of his pain'.[11] The dramatic mechanism of the dialogue thus hinges on the opposition between the old, ragged, ill-mannered and often distracted Socrates, who 'is always talking about great market-asses, and brass-founders, and leather-cutters and skin-dressers', and the young beautiful men who love him.[12]

'What is most barbaric about the figure of Socrates', Benjamin writes in an essay of 1916, 'is that this man estranged from the Muses constitutes the erotic centre of relationships in the circle around Plato.'[13] Written in the same year as 'On Language as Such and on the Language of Man', Benjamin's essay 'Socrates' brings his thought on language in relation to love. In the former, Benjamin had suggested that the Fall of Man had also brought about a Fall of Language – into communication, in German *Mitteilung*. This word contains a split (*mit-teilen*; lit. 'with-dividing'), which Benjamin maps onto the interior rift in language as human words separate from the divine λογος in which they originated. By and large, communication is a negative term in Benjamin's thought: it is profane and vacuous information destined to die in the moment of its birth. Yet in 'Socrates' and a number of other related essays that all draw on Benjamin's early reading of Plato, *Mitteilung* can be rendered differently: *mit-teilen* (lit. 'with-sharing'). 'True Love in this differs from gold and clay,' Shelley wrote in his Platonic mode, 'That to divide is not to take away.'[14] Sharing the love (*die Liebe teilen*) makes it grow.

This is the subject of 'Conversation on Love', a dialogue written around 1913 that appears to be Benjamin's continuation of the *Symposium*. It opens *in medias res* with a question from Agathon, who shares a name with the *Symposium*'s host, to Sophia, whose name is of course identical with σοφία, the wisdom that philosophers love:

> *Agathon*: You were saying recently, Sophia, that there is only *one* love. How am I to understand this, since there's love of one's spouse, love of one's friend, love of children – not to mention the others! Are these all various forms of the same basic matter? Or isn't it perhaps the case that love is already in itself something manifold, and our poor language has to rest content with *one* word for a diversity of things?
>
> *Vincent*: There is only one love, Agathon. Spouses love each other with the same love as friends, as mother and son. Where differences become apparent here, something else has entered the picture: marriage – friendship – motherhood. It's not in their love that spouses, friends or parents are differentiated – only in that other, supervening factor.
>
> *Sophia*: And what seems to us differing expressions of love are just expressions of something that goes together with love or in its train. Sexual will is not love, any more than motherhood is love.[15]

In the course of the conversation, Vincent and Sophia seek to convince Agathon that love is 'something eternal and invariable' in which 'there are only degrees, not differences'.[16] Different types of love (parental, romantic, friendly) are not differing in essence but only in the degree to which they participate in eternal and unchangeable Love, much as all beautiful things to a lesser or greater degree participate in the Idea of Beauty.

The conversation moves beyond the Platonic framework by placing an emphasis on how love is being expressed. Sophia says:

> Here, I believe, we must first of all speak of what is properly the sole right of love: expression [*die Äußerung*]. There is no love that would not be constantly impelled to become visible. Other influences may for the moment act as a hindrance – but love always seeks to reveal itself to the beloved.[17]

When love is denied expression, it is perverted into jealousy. 'The silence that is not animated – the constrained, impressed silence – engenders distrust. "If you really love me, open your arms and your heart!" . . . But the lover stands there obstinately, with folded arms.'[18] As Alcibiades makes clear in his ερωτικος, Socrates is precisely such an obstinate lover, who refuses to either speak or show his love. For Sophia, this is an example of *frevelnde Willkür* ('wanton self-will'), terms that Benjamin will repeat in his denunciation of what is 'most barbaric about the figure of Socrates': 'But if his love lacks the general power of communicating itself [*sich mitzuteilen*], if it lacks art, how does he sustain it? By means of will [*Willen*]. Socrates forces *eros* to serve his purposes. This outrage [*Frevel*] is reflected in the castratedness of his person.'[19] Socrates' inability to communicate his love, his castratedness, shatters the union between lovers, but it also offers an early instance of the tension between expression and its stifling that will later reappear as the conflict between semblance and the expressionless that shatters the work of art.

The radical nature of Shelley, in 1818, presenting the first complete and uncensored translation of the *Symposium* can be brought into relief by Benjamin's polemical cry for a reform of classical education in secondary schools written almost a century later:

> The classical Greek world, in this secondary school, will not be a fabulous realm of 'harmonies' and 'ideals' but that woman-despising

> and man-loving Greece of Pericles, aristocratic, with slavery, with the dark myths of Aeschylus. Our humanistic secondary school should look these things in the face. . . . Now, in our reading hours, we have aestheticism without aesthetic education. Chatter about *sōphrosunē* ['prudence, temperance'] without an inkling of the immoderateness of ancient Asia. Platonic dialogues without a reading of the *Symposium* (in its entirety, gentlemen, in its entirety!).[20]

Shelley, too, believed that the *Symposium* should be read in its entirety. His translation was a gift of love to his wife, Mary, to give her access to a world of Greek philosophy otherwise reserved to expensively educated men. It was also accompanied by a draft for an introduction, 'A Discourse on the Manners of the Ancient Greeks Relative to the Subject of Love', which defended the need for an uncensored translation while trying to navigate the delicate task of contextualising homosexual practices for his contemporaries. 'There is no book which shows the Greeks precisely as they were,' Shelley complains; they have all been censored so that

> no practice or sentiment, highly inconsistent with our present manners, should be mentioned, lest those manners should receive outrage and violation. But there are many to whom the Greek language is inaccessible, who ought not to be excluded by this prudery to possess an exact and comprehensive conception of the history of man; for there is no knowledge concerning what man has been and may be, from partaking of which a person can depart, without becoming in some degree more philosophical, tolerant, and just.[21]

There is no way of determining the extent to which Shelley's strictures on Greek love were genuinely held beliefs or just strategic attempts to ingratiate himself with a prudish audience – and it may well be that reading the *Symposium* had made him more 'philosophical, tolerant, and just' towards homosexuality than he had been previously; in either case, in the 'Discourse' Shelley represents Greek homosexual practices as ills arising from the gendered inequalities of Greek society.

While Shelley generally tends to idealise Greece, in the 'Discourse' he admits that its cultural achievements were marred by two major imperfections: firstly, the existence of slavery – which Shelley passes over quite quickly – and, secondly, 'the regulations and the sentiments respecting sexual intercourse'.[22] This latter issue will bring Shelley to the limit of what he can formulate in philosophical prose: 'We are not exactly aware, – and the laws of modern composition scarcely permit a modest writer to investigate the subject with philosophical accuracy, – what that action was by which the Greeks expressed this passion.'[23] Since he cannot bring himself to name the act he is taking about, Shelley's argument threatens to disintegrate whenever it touches on those sexual practices it sets out to explain. In Benjamin's terms, homosexual sex is the expressionless power, *ausdruckslose Gewalt*, that ruptures Shelley's 'Discourse'. Yet, it is precisely his inability to write about sex that turns the 'Discourse' into such a perfect expression of the Romantic era's understanding of the sexual side of love: 'It is impossible', he asserts, 'that a lover could usually have subjected the object of his attachment to so detestable a violation or have consented to associate his own remembrance in the beloved mind with images of pain and horror.'[24] While these images of pain and horror are here associated specifically with anal sex (perhaps masking traumatic memories from his own time at Eton), as he goes on Shelley rejects all physical intimacy. Instead, his ideal sexuality manifests itself as disembodied mental masturbation:

> If we consider the facility with which certain phenomena connected with sleep, at the age of puberty, associate themselves with those images which are the objects of our waking desires; and even that in some persons of an exalted state of sensibility, that a similar process may take place in reverie, it will not be difficult to conceive the almost involuntary consequences of a state of abandonment in the society of a person of surpassing attractions, when the sexual connection cannot exist, to be such as to preclude the necessity of so operose and diabolical a machination as that usually described.[25]

This disgust at physical contact leads Shelley so far as to consider the hypothesis that a Greek man would have sex with 'his wife or his slave' so as to only engage in beautiful reverie ('lofty thoughts and feelings') together with his lover. This is pure intellectual sex.

Yet, beneath the squeamishness, Shelley makes a much more sophisticated argument against homosexual love on account of it being an expression of a false balance between the sexes. In a line of reasoning that echoes the work of Mary Wollstonecraft (who was always a presence in Shelley's statements on women's rights), Shelley argues that while Greek men 'received the highest cultivation and refinement', Greek women 'were educated as slaves and were raised but few degrees in all that related to moral or intellectual excellence above the condition of savages'.[26] Women, slaves and savages. It is self-evident that no refined man would ever be attracted to such. Possessing 'the habits and qualities of slaves', Shelley continues, Greek women 'were probably not extremely beautiful' since beauty is incompatible with the absence of intellectual refinement:

> They were certainly devoid of that moral and intellectual loveliness with which the acquisition of knowledge and the cultivation of sentiment animates, as with another life of overpowering grace, the lineaments and the gestures of every form which it inhabits. Their eyes could not have been deep and intricate from the workings of the mind, and could have entangled no heart in soul-enwoven labyrinths.[27]

To clinch his point, Shelley adds that the word καλος ('beautiful') is more frequently used to describe men than women.[28] Nonetheless, all men must love. Being 'deprived of its legitimate object', woman, this universal imperative to love seeks another outlet, and this is why Greek men had to turn to other men. Homosexual practices among the ancients were thus the expression of a natural propensity towards love, perverted by the sociocultural subjugation of women – and there is little doubt that Shelley considers this to be a perversion that has been corrected in the course of time. 'In modern Europe', he concludes, 'the sexual and intellectual claims of love, by the more equal cultivation of the two sexes, so far converge towards one point, as to produce, in the attempt to unite them, no gross violation in the established nature of man.'[29]

But even this is but a midway point. Ultimately, it is not only homosexual sex, but in fact all physical love-making, that is to be overcome with time. The more 'civilization and refinement' are advancing, the less of a part does 'the gratification of the senses' have to play in 'the sexual connection. It soon becomes a very small part of that profound and complicated sentiment, which we call Love, which is rather the universal thirst for a communion not only of the senses, but of our whole nature, intellectual, imaginative and sensitive.'[30] Shadowing the steps on Diotima's ladder, erotic desire is at first physical and gradually becomes more and more ideal: 'the perfection of intercourse consisting, not perhaps in a total annihilation of the instinctive sense [i.e. sexual desire], but in the reducing it to as minute a proportion as possible, compared with those higher faculties of our nature, from which it derives a value'.[31] At last we reach a state of heightened sexlessness where we can say, with Shelley, that 'The act itself is nothing'.[32] And yet, and yet. Much as he abjures the body, Shelley falls into the same trap as Socrates: claiming that intellectual beauty matters more than physical beauty, he nonetheless prefers to surround himself with beautiful young women. So we find him insisting that 'the person selected as the subject of this [sexual] gratification should be as perfect and beautiful as possible, both in body and in mind; so that all sympathies may be harmoniously blended'.[33] Ugly bodies cannot make beautiful love.

The Shelleyan ἔρως ascends from the 'operose and diabolical' mechanics of sex to the essentially sexless consummation of intellectual love. This ascent can be mapped onto the life of an individual or onto different social groups within a society (libertines vs. philosophers), and also onto social development over time. As a result, anything to do with the physical aspect of love becomes relegated to earlier and more primitive stages of society: 'represent this passion as you will,' Shelley writes of sex, 'there is something totally irreconcilable in its cultivation to the beautiful order of social life'.[34] For all its good intentions, the perverse asceticism of this position can be brought into relief by contrasting it with the uses that Audre Lorde makes of the erotic. Like Shelley, Lorde opposes the conflation between eroticism and pornography (or what Shelley would call 'prostitution' and 'libertinism'), but rather than discarding both, she invites us – especially Black women – to reclaim the erotic in all aspects of life and work, to unlearn the cultural history that has taught us 'to separate the erotic demand from most vital areas of our lives other than sex'.[35]

Oppression operates by corrupting or distorting the pleasure and satisfaction that we take from ourselves and our actions in the world, Lorde argues. Tapping into the erotic is a way of undoing centuries of denying 'the power of our unexpressed and unrecognised feeling'.[36] When we embrace the erotic, 'not only do we touch our most profoundly creative source, but we do that which is female and self-affirming in the face of a racist, patriarchal, and anti-erotic society'.[37] If it loves wisdom, philosophy should not try to transcend the body, but should on the contrary affirm it – even in its ugliness and messy humanity. And the same is also true of literary criticism: if it is to be more than a barren practice of 'reading two books to write a third', as one wit had it, it must embrace the intimacy of our encounter with the text. The writer's words forming in your eyes, your mind, your lips, and your offering of your own words in return.

Shelley's discussion of sex is at once quaintly prudish and centuries ahead of his time. Starting from the premise that 'all human beings have an indefeasible claim' to participation in social life, Shelley attacks 'the Greek arrangement' for excluding the female 'half of the human race'. But the root of the problem is not just the Greek gender roles that place women in a subordinate position, it lies in the notion of gender as such: 'This invidious distinction of human kind, as a class of beings of intellectual nature, into two sexes, is a remnant of savage barbarism which we have less excuse than they for not having totally abolished.'[38] Since intellect is sexless, our intellectual nature knows no sexes – and so our society is advancing towards a utopian horizon where sex (both gender and intercourse) is reduced to being a relic of the past.

In his youth, Benjamin saw himself as living in such a future, representing male and female as two Ideas in which people of both sexes participate. In a 1913 letter to his friend Herbert Belmore, he explains:

> And, as you so nicely put it, 'the man must be gentle, must become feminine, if the woman becomes masculine.' I have felt this way for a long time. . . . you should understand that I consider the types 'man'/ 'woman' as somewhat primitive in the thought of civilized humanity. Why do we usually stop short at this division (as conceptual principles? Fine!). But if you mean something concrete, then the atomization has to go much further, even down to the last single individual. Europe consists of individuals (in whom there are both masculine and feminine elements), not of men and women.[39]

Benjamin's reflections on gender smack of an essentialism that has not aged much better than Shelley's comments on homosexuality: he associates masculinity with productive speech and femininity with receptive silence. In 'The Metaphysics of Youth', for example, Benjamin considers the rhythm of a conversation: 'Silence is the inner frontier of conversation,' he states.[40] 'The woman is the guardian of the conversations.'[41] The text reads a bit like the self-justifications of a mansplainer – its paradigmatic conversation takes place between a male genius and a female prostitute, who emerges as the ideal silent listener: 'She rescues the conversation from triviality; greatness has no claim upon her, for greatness comes to an end in her presence. Already in her presence every manhood has had its day, and now the stream of words flows away into her nights.'[42] Feminine silence swallows words as darkness swallows light.

This strong association between femininity and silence makes it impossible to even conceptualise the idea of speech in a female community, and soon we find Benjamin wondering in all earnestness:

> How did Sappho and her women friends talk among themselves? Language is veiled like the past, futural like silence. The speaker summons the past in it; veiled by language, he receives his womanly past in conversation. – But the women remain silent. What they listen for are the unspoken words. They bring their bodies close and caress one another. Their conversation has freed itself from the subject and from language. Nonetheless it has marked out a terrain. For only among them, and because they are together, has the conversation itself passed and come to rest.[43]

Sapphic conversation brings language to a standstill. As such, it is the counterpoint to Socratic castratedness: if Sappho caresses without words, Socrates babbles without caresses. But Sappho among her female friends shrouded in the darkest night and Socrates surrounded by his male disciples lit by the glare of reason are only the two extremes – Benjamin himself aims at something in between, a creative release that comes when the two, feminine silence and masculine speech, are counterpoised: when the dark night itself kindles and begins to shine (an English word fortuitously homophonous with *Schein*).

In the second part of the essay on 'Socrates', Benjamin illustrates the idea with Grünewald's altar piece:

> Grünewald painted the saints with such grandeur that their halos emerged from the greenest black. The radiant is true only where it is refracted in the nocturnal; only there is it great, only there is it expressionless [*ausdruckslos*], only there is it asexual and yet of supramundane sexuality. The one who radiates in this manner is the genius. He confirms, he guarantees its asexuality. In a society of men, there would be no genius; genius lives through the existence of the feminine.[44]

The division into masculine and feminine can therefore be seen as a provisional step in identifying the essentially sexless nature of genius: purely masculine creation is 'something evil, dead', purely feminine creation is 'flat and weak and does not break through the night', yet in the coexistence of both principles, at the asexual point of indifference between them, there 'true creativity' takes shape.[45] Does this sound like nonsense? Benjamin calls it 'the greatest mystery. Human beings have not been able to solve it. For them genius is still not the expressionless one [*der Ausdruckslose*] who breaks out of the night, but rather an expressive one [*ein Ausdrücklicher*] who hovers and vibrates in the light.'[46] This great mystery is a seed that will

LOVE

eventually grow into Benjamin's theorisation of the interplay between *Schein* and *das Ausdruckslose*, as well as the associated *Idee der Unenthüllbarkeit* that 'is the idea of art criticism'.[47] The concepts that govern Benjamin's theory of criticism originated in a consideration of masculine and feminine speech and sexuality; what is expressed, what is stifled.

'In the *Symposium*, Socrates celebrates the love between men and youths and acclaims it as the medium of the creative spirit,' Benjamin writes in 'Socrates'.[48] His negative assessment of homosexuality is, like Shelley's, qualified by his understanding of the social relations between the sexes in classical Athens: both perform a seamless transition between sexual and cultural aberration. But whereas Shelley attacks the miseducation of Greek women, Benjamin takes issue with the Socratic understanding of creativity, which ultimately boils down to an understanding of how art is created: that is, the work of ποίησις. 'According to his teaching, the knower is pregnant with knowledge,' Benjamin writes, referring to Diotima's analogy between giving birth to philosophical or artistic works and bearing children: 'all human beings are alike pregnant with their future progeny, and when we arrive at a certain age, our nature impels us to bring forth and propagate'.[49] Diotima goes on to explain that the exact nature of how we propagate depends on the person:

> Those whose bodies alone are pregnant with this principle of immortality are attracted by women, seeking through the production of children what they imagine to be happiness and immortality and an enduring remembrance; but they whose souls are far more pregnant than their bodies, conceive and produce that which is more suitable to the soul. What is suitable to the soul? Intelligence, and every other power and excellence of the mind, of which all poets, and all other artists who are creative and inventive, are the authors.[50]

Whereas, for Diotima, creating art is superior to having babies just as loving Ideas is superior to desiring beautiful bodies, for Benjamin such an admixture of the bodily and the artistic violates the separation between divine creations (*Geschöpfe*) and artistic artifacts (*Gebilde*), and he draws on theological concepts to refute the *Symposium*'s metaphors of pregnancy. 'Just as, for the woman, immaculate conception is the exalted idea of purity, so conception without pregnancy is the most profound spiritual manifestation of male genius. This manifestation, for its part, is a radiance. Socrates extinguishes it.'[51]

Nonetheless, Benjamin must have been drawn to Diotima's comments on propagation because of the implications they have for the life (and afterlife) of artworks. She introduces the metaphor of pregnancy to explain the association between Love and the human desire for immortality: 'we must desire immortality together with what is good, since Love is the desire that good be forever present to us. Of necessity Love must also be the desire of immortality,' Diotima says.[52] Furthermore, mortal beings can only attain immortality through generation: Diotima represents it as a process of replacement that 'forever leaves another new in place of the old' – be it a new strand of hair in place of one that has been cut off, a new thought in place of a forgotten one or a child in place of their parent.[53] 'By this contrivance, O Socrates, does what is mortal, the body and all other things, partake of immortality,' Diotima concludes.[54] Literary works can also be said to partake of immortality; their potentially eternal afterlife consists of being reread, adapted, translated and criticised by future generations of readers. Each such act leaves a new interpretation of the text in place of the old. In Diotima's terms, we can think of these textual interventions as expressions of love – a love of the original text, but also a love of that which is generated by the act of interpretation: the adaptation, the translation, the critical reading. 'Wonder not, then, if every thing by nature cherishes that which was produced from itself, for this earnest Love is a tendency towards eternity.'[55] We are bound to love our progeny because they allow us to live on, both through the body and in remembrance. By the same logic, the critic is bound to love their reading, the translator their translation and so on. This is how our work merges with the literary text, partaking of its immortal afterlife.

Let's linger on this idea of criticism as a form of love. If criticism is the art of splitting, let's say that criticism is a love of cracking open the work. But, as is also clear from the preceding, it is not the case that any work can be split open and have its truth revealed once and for all. As its own distinct species of intellectual ἔρως, criticism too aims towards the kind of generation that 'is something eternal and immortal in mortality'.[56] This kind of generation takes place in the relation between the historical moment of critical interpretation and the achronological temporality in which the literary work subsists over time. Criticism mediates between the two, as the Platonic ἔρως mediates between bodies and Ideas. Diotima, for this reason, calls Love 'A great Daemon' because 'every thing daemoniacal holds an intermediate place between what is divine and what is mortal'.[57] Criticism is daemonical in this very sense: it anchors timeless artworks in historically situated readings.

Benjamin represents literature's relation to its own atemporality in an oft-cited image from the opening of his essay on Goethe's *Elective Affinities*:

> If, to use a simile, one views the growing work as a burning funeral pyre, then the commentator stands before it like a chemist, the critic like an alchemist. Whereas, for the former, wood and ash remain the sole objects of his analysis, for the latter only the flame itself preserves an enigma: that of what is alive. Thus, the critic inquires into the truth, whose living flame continues to burn over the heavy logs of what is past, and the light ashes of what has been experienced.[58]

The difference between the material logs and the immaterial flame emanating from them is the difference between what Benjamin terms the truth content, *Wahrheitsgehalt*, as opposed to the material content, *Sachgehalt*, in a work of art: 'Critique seeks the truth content [*Wahrheitsgehalt*] of a work of art; commentary its material content [*Sachgehalt*].'[59] Shelley illustrates this difference with a variant on his familiar image of a veil:

> But a poet considers the vices of his contemporaries as a temporary dress in which his creations must be arrayed, and which cover without concealing the eternal proportions of their beauty. An epic or dramatic personage is understood to wear them around his soul, as he may the ancient armour or the modern uniform around his body; whilst it is easy to conceive a dress more graceful than either. The beauty of the internal nature cannot be so far concealed by its accidental vesture, but that the spirit of its form shall communicate itself to the very disguise, and indicate the shape it hides from the manner in which it is worn. A majestic form and graceful motions will express themselves through the most barbarous and tasteless costume. Few poets of the highest class have chosen to exhibit the beauty of their conceptions in its naked truth and splendour; and it is doubtful whether the alloy of costume, habit, etc., be not necessary to temper this planetary music [*musica universalis*] for mortal ears.[60]

The 'temporary dress', 'accidental vesture', 'alloy of costume, habit, etc.' are other names for the *Sachgehalt* in which a particular work's *Wahrheitsgehalt* is veiled. If this dress is necessary to 'temper' the beauty of the truth contained in a work, it also gives the work a historical time stamp: ancient armour as well as modern uniform distinguish not only a soldier but also the epoch in which he lives. And much as the proportions of a human body remain the same while once-fashionable costumes come to appear barbarous and tasteless, so the historically determined *Sachgehalt* of a work, over time, becomes disjointed from its eternal *Wahrheitsgehalt*. This is how Benjamin describes their interaction:

> The relation between the two is determined by that basic law of literature according to which the more significant the work, the more inconspicuously [*unscheinbarer*] and intimately its truth content [*Wahrheitsgehalt*] is bound up with its material content [*Sachgehalt*]. If, therefore, the works that prove enduring are precisely those whose truth is most deeply sunken in their material content, then, in the course of this duration, the concrete realities rise up before the eyes of the beholder all the more distinctly the more they die out in the world. With this, however, to judge by appearances [*der Erscheinung nach*], the material content and the truth content, united at the beginning of a work's history, set themselves apart from each other in the course of its duration, because the truth content always remains to the same extent hidden as the material content comes to the fore.[61]

Sachgehalt is that quaint, foreign, even barbaric, out-of-date feel that literary works acquire over time without, for that reason, becoming obsolete. Both Shelley and Benjamin took issue with the *Sachgehalt* of the *Symposium*'s sexual politics while still being able to embrace its vision of truth. But since truth of necessity appears dressed in contemporary prejudice, the tasks of commentary and critique cannot be so neatly separated as Benjamin's metaphor of chemist and alchemist would have it: no flame without wood and ashes, no reading without a moral element determined by its time. Not only the time when a work is written, but also the time in which it is being read.

Notes

1 Mary Shelley, 'Preface', *Essays, Letters from Abroad, Translations and Fragments by Percy Bysshe Shelley*, 2 vols (London: Moxon, 1840), i, pp. v–xxviii (p. ix). In a draft Preface to his *Symposium* translation, Shelley calls it a 'drama (for so the lively distinction of characters and the various and well-wrought circumstances of the story almost entitle it to be called)' ('On the Symposium, or Preface to the Banquet of Plato', *SoL*, p. 114).
2 To John and Maria Gisborne, 10 July 1818, *Letters 2*, p. 20.
3 Michael O'Neill, 'Emulating Plato: Shelley as Translator and Prose Poet', in *Shelleyan Reimaginings and Influence: New Relations* (Oxford: Oxford University Press, 2019), pp. 28–44 (p. 36).
4 The phrase is from Shelley's draft Preface to the translation. 'On the Symposium, or Preface to the Banquet of Plato', *SoL*, p. 114.

5 'The Symposium', *SoL*, p. 162.
6 'The Symposium', *SoL*, p. 163.
7 'The Symposium', *SoL*, pp. 164–5.
8 'The Symposium', *SoL*, p. 165.
9 'The Symposium', *SoL*, p. 167.
10 'The Symposium', *SoL*, p. 171.
11 'The Symposium', *SoL*, p. 166.
12 'The Symposium', *SoL*, p. 170.
13 'Socrates', *EW*, p. 233; *GS2*, p. 129.
14 *Epipsychidion*, ll. 160–1.
15 'Conversation on Love', *EW*, p. 139; *GS7*, pp. 15–16.
16 'Conversation on Love', *EW*, p. 140; *GS7*, p. 16.
17 'Conversation on Love', *EW*, pp. 140–1; *GS7*, p. 17.
18 'Conversation on Love', *EW*, p. 141; *GS7*, p. 17.
19 'Socrates', *EW*, p. 233; *GS2*, p. 129.
20 'Teaching and Valuation', *EW*, pp. 96–7; *GS2*, pp. 40–1.
21 'A Discourse on the Manners of the Ancient Greeks Relative to the Subject of Love', *SoL*, p. 105.
22 'A Discourse on the Manners of the Ancient Greeks Relative to the Subject of Love', *SoL*, p. 105.
23 'A Discourse on the Manners of the Ancient Greeks Relative to the Subject of Love', *SoL*, pp. 109–10.
24 'A Discourse on the Manners of the Ancient Greeks Relative to the Subject of Love', *SoL*, p. 110.
25 'A Discourse on the Manners of the Ancient Greeks Relative to the Subject of Love', *SoL*, p. 110.
26 'A Discourse on the Manners of the Ancient Greeks Relative to the Subject of Love', *SoL*, p. 107.
27 'A Discourse on the Manners of the Ancient Greeks Relative to the Subject of Love', *SoL*, p. 106.
28 'A Discourse on the Manners of the Ancient Greeks Relative to the Subject of Love', *SoL*, p. 108.
29 'A Discourse on the Manners of the Ancient Greeks Relative to the Subject of Love', *SoL*, pp. 107–8.
30 'A Discourse on the Manners of the Ancient Greeks Relative to the Subject of Love', *SoL*, p. 106.
31 'A Discourse on the Manners of the Ancient Greeks Relative to the Subject of Love', *SoL*, p. 109.
32 'A Discourse on the Manners of the Ancient Greeks Relative to the Subject of Love', *SoL*, p. 109.
33 'A Discourse on the Manners of the Ancient Greeks Relative to the Subject of Love', *SoL*, p. 109.
34 'A Discourse on the Manners of the Ancient Greeks Relative to the Subject of Love', *SoL*, p. 111.
35 Audre Lorde, 'Uses of the Erotic: The Erotic as Power', in *Your Silence Will Not Protect You* (London: Silver Press, 2017), pp. 22–30 (p. 24).
36 Lorde, 'Uses of the Erotic', p. 22.
37 Lorde, 'Uses of the Erotic', p. 30.
38 'A Discourse on the Manners of the Ancient Greeks Relative to the Subject of Love', *SoL*, p. 111.
39 To Herbert Belmore, 23 June 1913, *Correspondence*, p. 34; *Briefe 1*, p. 65.
40 'The Metaphysics of Youth', *EW*, p. 145; *GS2*, p. 92.
41 'The Metaphysics of Youth', *EW*, p. 148; *GS2*, p. 94.
42 'The Metaphysics of Youth', *EW*, p. 147; *GS2*, p. 93.
43 'The Metaphysics of Youth', *EW*, p. 149; *GS2*, p. 95.
44 'Socrates', *EW*, p. 234; *GS2*, p. 130.
45 'Socrates', *EW*, p. 234; *GS2*, p. 130.
46 'Socrates', *EW*, p. 234; *GS2*, p. 130.
47 'Goethe's *Elective Affinities*', *SW1*, p. 351, translation emended; *GS1*, p. 195.
48 'Socrates', *EW*, p. 234; *GS2*, p. 131.
49 'Socrates', *EW*, p. 234; *GS2*, p. 131; 'The Symposium', *SoL*, p. 153.
50 'The Symposium', *SoL*, p. 156.
51 'Socrates', *EW*, pp. 234–5; *GS2*, p. 131.
52 'The Symposium', *SoL*, p. 154.
53 'The Symposium', *SoL*, p. 154.
54 'The Symposium', *SoL*, p. 155.
55 'The Symposium', *SoL*, p. 155.
56 'The Symposium', *SoL*, p. 154.
57 'The Symposium', *SoL*, p. 149.
58 'Goethe's *Elective Affinities*', *SW1*, p. 298; *GS1*, p. 126.
59 'Goethe's *Elective Affinities*', *SW1*, p. 298; *GS1*, p. 125.
60 'A Defence of Poetry', *SPP*, pp. 516–17.
61 'Goethe's *Elective Affinities*', *SW1*, p. 297; *GS1*, p. 125.

III
Legacies of Violence

7
Guilt

'The Socratic dialogue needs to be studied in relation to myth,' Benjamin writes in the 1816 'Socrates' essay. 'What did Plato intend with it? Socrates: this is the figure in which Plato has annihilated the old myth and received it. Socrates: this is the offering of philosophy to the gods of myth, who demand human sacrifice.'[1] Benjamin did not pursue this line of inquiry with regards to the Socratic dialogues, but he did continue to explore and reformulate his conception of myth, which remained part of his theoretical armature until the very end of his career. He sometimes associates it with a prehistoric or classical past; sometimes with literary texts, such as the works of Franz Kafka; and at other times with contemporary phenomena, such as capitalism. *What he never considers is the extent to which his theorisation of myth resonates with the process of racialisation that underpins global capitalism.* In the notes towards his last major achievement, the posthumously published *On the Concept of History*, Benjamin offers his final definition of myth: 'The fundamental conception of myth is the world as punishment – a punishment which actually engenders those to whom punishment is due.'[2]

This is the world in which Shelley's tragedy of *The Cenci* is set, *based on true historical events that he found in a manuscript 'copied from the archives of the Cenci Palace',*[3] *the play's action takes place in Rome at the end of the sixteenth century, a time when the transatlantic slave trade was just getting underway,* and, in what follows, I will study this drama in relation to Benjamin's theorisation of myth *as well as the practices and legacies of transatlantic slavery. Although Shelley had much to say about liberty, and allegedly did not take slave-produced sugar in his tea, he never directly addressed the situation of enslaved Africans in his writing. The subject of anti-Black racism does not appear to have interested Benjamin either (unlike his friend Theodor Adorno, who took an embarrassingly dim view of jazz, or Hannah Arendt, who offered no less embarrassing views on segregation in the US South).*[4]

Nonetheless, in this part, I will use these interlinear insertions, counter-rhythmic interruptions in the flow of my argument, to sketch out how Shelley's tragedy and Benjamin's ideas about myth can be related to the afterlife of racial slavery – not because slavery is implicitly or explicitly present in their writings, but because its legacy is impossible to ignore in the present of my reading. Addressing this subject is thus an ethical task, set to me by the historical moment that I am living through, a moral element determined by my time, but which first grew from a reading of ancient tragedy. Benjamin argued that it was 'in tragedy that the head of genius lifted itself for the first time from the mist of guilt, for in tragedy demonic fate is breached'.[5] The key terms here are 'guilt' and 'fate'. In the world of myth, the two are one. 'Fate shows itself', Benjamin further explains, 'in the view of life, as condemned, as having essentially first been condemned and then become guilty.'[6] 'What have I done?' Beatrice, the heroine of Shelley's tragedy, demands after being raped by her father, the powerful count Francesco Cenci:

> Am I not innocent? Is it my crime
> That one with white hair, and imperious brow,
> Who tortured me from my forgotten years,
> As parents only dare, should call himself
> My father, yet should be![7]

The incestuous rape is but the culmination of a lifelong campaign of mental and physical abuse that Beatrice interprets as punishment. Like Benjamin's tragic hero, she is born condemned – condemned to being her father's child, yet it is her very suffering at the hands of her father that engenders the crime, parricide, that will retrospectively justify the torture that her father had inflicted on her. For Beatrice sentences her father to death. 'Mighty death! | Thou double-visaged shadow! Only judge! | Rightfullest arbiter!'[8] In other words, it is Beatrice's fate of being born a Cenci that provokes the parricide that she will be guilty of – and turns

Beatrice herself into a parricide worthy of her fate.[9] Shortly after the deed is done, the Pope's legate Savella arrives with a papal order for the arrest and execution of Count Cenci. The assassination is uncovered and Beatrice is arrested together with her accomplices: her stepmother Lucretia, brother Giacomo and two hired assassins. The drama ends with their trial and execution.

'I have endured a wrong, | Which though it be expressionless, is such | As asks atonement,' says Beatrice,[10] thereby designating her crime with a word whose German equivalent – *ausdruckslos* or, as noun, *das Ausdruckslose* – appears at key junctures in Benjamin's thought. In part, the crime is 'expressionless' due to practical considerations: it would have been impossible to have an incestuous rape openly spoken about or enacted on a London stage in 1819; but the historical account is summarised in the Preface and Shelley did not attempt to hide the inexpressible act that generates the action – on the contrary, the impossibility of naming the crime is crucial for generating the moral dilemma at the heart of the play.

'In the expressionless, the sublime violence [*Gewalt*] of the true appears as that which determines the language of the real world according to the laws of the moral world,' Benjamin writes about Goethe's *Elective Affinities*, an observation that also holds true of Shelley's *The Cenci*.[11] In both works, speech fails in the face of a higher moral law. This indicates the ethical dimension of the expressionless: it does not merely provide an aesthetic counterpoint to *Schein* but, in its very speechlessness, opens the work towards a higher truth. In this regard, too, Benjamin draws inspiration from Hölderlin, suggesting that the 'expressionless power . . . has rarely become clearer than in Greek tragedy, on the one hand, and in Hölderlin's hymnic poetry, on the other. Perceptible in tragedy as the falling silent of the hero, and in the rhythm of the hymn as objection [*Einspruch im Rhythmus*].'[12] In the hero's reticence or in the metric interruption of a caesura, expression gives room to the expressionless, the not-said slides into what cannot-be-said simply because language has neither sound nor concept for it. This sonic absence, this *not*, is what relates the prosodic periods in Hölderlin's metre to the silence of the tragic hero.

The *not* transforms mere silence into ethical judgment: 'in tragedy pagan man becomes aware that he is better than his god, but the realization robs him of speech, remains unspoken'.[13] This is the cause of Beatrice's silence at the end of her trial, *but there is also a silence that comes from becoming aware that one is worse than one's ideals. This is a*

GUILT   99

silence that surrounds much literary criticism, with critics politely looking away from the iniquitous contexts in which many of the works they study were composed: in the vast critical literature on The Cenci, no one has paused to consider Shelley's dubious ethics in turning this true tragic story, 'sad reality' as he calls it in the Preface, into a salacious drama to amuse his audience and establish himself as a dramatic poet. The tragic transport of The Cenci is carried onward by Beatrice's growing awareness that she is better than her God. The 'expressionless' violence that she suffers propels her insight into her position outside the law; like enslaved persons who were subject to violations that remained expressionless within the legal code of the British Empire insofar as the law viewed them as chattel, not humans but property, and their testimony was not admitted in any court, she realises that 'in this mortal world | There is no vindication and no law | Which can adjudge and execute the doom | Of that through which I suffer'.[14] The oppressed and excluded have to make their own laws; therefore, Beatrice must take the atonement that her wrong requires into her own hands.

During her arrest and throughout her trial, she not once stoops to defend herself by offering mitigating circumstances for her crime. Rather her defence, initially fuelled by her faith in God, takes the form of a challenge to a legal system that fails to offer a name and thus an avenue of redress for crimes that demand atonement. 'Unless | The crimes which mortal tongue dare never name | God therefore scruples to avenge.'[15] For Beatrice, this is inconceivable, and her faith remains unshaken even in the face of the Christian analogy between her own violent father and God the Father. 'I have borne much, and kissed the sacred hand | Which crushed us to the earth, and thought its stroke | Was perhaps some paternal chastisement!' she says of her father in the first act.[16] 'Paternal chastisement' was also how many enslaved Africans were invited to view their lot, their black skin marking them out as the inheritors of the curse of Ham, whose skin was blackened in punishment for seeing his father, Noah, 'drunken' and 'uncovered'.[17]

In the second act, Beatrice still insists that Cenci's depravity is not enough to make her implicate the 'great God, | Whose image upon earth a father is' in her own father's crimes.[18] The rape is a turning point. Since Ham's punishment so far outweighs the alleged crime, it may be that the biblical phrasing 'saw the nakedness of his father' contains a veiled reference to an incestuous, sexual transgression.[19] After the rape, she can no longer conceive of Cenci's violence against her as 'paternal chastisement', but neither can she accuse God for not curbing Cenci. Thus, for her, the rape annuls Cenci's paternal rights. 'I have no father,' Beatrice says afterwards, but adds that not even this atrocity suffices to destroy her faith in God:

'Many might doubt there were a God above | Who sees and permits evil, and so die: | That faith no agony shall obscure in me.'[20] However, this is precisely what happens in the course of the play, which traces the gradual destruction of Beatrice's faith, culminating in her final realisation that not God but her father was 'alone omnipotent | On Earth, and ever present'.[21]

Only in the final act, when it is no longer possibly to deny that God will not deliver her from her predicament, does Beatrice begin to question divine justice. To the Judge's final question, 'Art thou not guilty of thy father's death?', she answers:

> Or wilt thou rather tax high-judging God
> That he permitted such an act as that
> Which I have suffered, and which he beheld;
> Made it unutterable, and took from it
> All refuge, all revenge, all consequence,
> But that which thou hast called my father's death?[22]

Her accusation of God marks the limit of Beatrice's faith: realising that her God is not just, she renounces not only the theological order that she has been brought up in but even the very language in which she is being tried – not forgetting that language is originally God's gift to man. Referring to the parricide as what her Judge 'hast called my father's death', she says that it

> is or is not what men call a crime,
> Which either I have done, or have not done;
> Say what ye will. I shall deny no more.
> If ye desire it thus, thus let it be.
> And so an end of all. Now do your will[.][23]

This speech is a retraction of speech. Beatrice refuses to place her actions within the terms that her Judges employ – not only does the law embodied by her God and His Church render the wrong she suffered expressionless, the atonement it required is likewise impossible to express within its legal framework: it 'is or is not what men call a crime'. This is the moment in which Beatrice, tragic heroine that she is, realises that she is better than her God, 'but the realization robs [her] of speech, remains unspoken'.[24] Beatrice's expressionless wrong tears open the judicial system of papal Rome, intimating the prospect of a truer justice beyond it.

It is the expressionless nature of the crime, its position outside the law, that justifies an extrajudicial response and thus generates the conflict between individual and social norms that constitutes *The Cenci*'s moral lesson. It also indicates the possibility of a different social contract. Benjamin notes that the 'hero, who scorns to justify himself before the gods, *as Beatrice scorns to justify herself before her judges,* reaches agreement with them in a, so to speak, contractual process of atonement which, in its dual significance, is designed not only to bring about the restoration but above all the undermining of an ancient body of laws in the linguistic constitution of a new community'.[25] *The abolition of slavery, and later decolonisation, are examples of processes that repeal a set of unjust laws while inaugurating new communities of free human beings or independent states. But, in both cases, the process misfired. Rather than gaining freedom, the formerly enslaved were locked into exploitative relations with their former enslavers such that the inequalities are still felt decades and even centuries later.*

At the same time, in service to newly gained liberty, the past was put aside along with any notion that the enslavers should pay back any of the wealth they had extracted. As Ariella Aïsha Azoulay puts it: 'Decolonization without reparations relegated colonial violence to a temporal realm beyond accountability, a past that is sealed off in museums and archives.'[26] *A past that can be found in an archive and made the subject of a tragic story but not of an actual living debt. And yet the crime 'though it be expressionless, is such | As asks atonement'.*[27] As a violated woman outside the patriarchal law, Beatrice can be said to establish a new moral code, according to which incestuous rape is punishable by death. While most readers would probably (hopefully) disagree with capital punishment in reality, within the allegorical climate of the drama, the death penalty seems appropriate, and there is a long tradition of criticism that asserts Beatrice's essential innocence despite her obvious crime.

This was exactly Shelley's intention. He sought to make it impossible to accept either Beatrice's guilt or her innocence – in the Preface he explains that it 'is in the restless and anatomizing casuistry with which men seek the justification of Beatrice, yet feel that she has done what needs justification; it is in the superstitious horror with which they contemplate alike her wrongs and their revenge, that the dramatic character of what she did and suffered, consists'.[28] The real drama takes place not on the stage but in the audience's hearts and minds; as Michael Scrivener notes, their 'moral capacities undergo an educational experience'.[29] This is in line with the pedagogic function that Shelley accords to drama overall. 'The highest moral purpose aimed at in the highest species of the drama, is the teaching of the human heart, through its sympathies and antipathies, the knowledge of itself,' he writes in the Preface.[30]

Shelley's evocation of the 'highest moral purpose' of 'the highest species of the drama' serves to distinguish *The Cenci* from the gothic thrills a contemporary audience would have been accustomed to seeing on a London stage. However horrid *The Cenci* may be, it teaches a lesson associated with the highest form of art. A few years later, Shelley develops the idea in the 'Defence': 'In a drama of the highest order there is little food for censure or hatred; it teaches rather self-knowledge and self-respect.'[31] Like a Platonic dialogue, *The Cenci* teaches knowledge, 'in proportion to the possession of which knowledge, every human being is wise, just, sincere, tolerant, and kind'.[32] In this way, studying the drama directly contributes to a happy life. But its moral lessons are also subject to Benjamin's condition about making ethical judgments based on literary works. Dividing creation into artistic *Gebilde* and divine *Geschöpfe*, Benjamin writes:

> And indeed the artist is less the primal ground or creator [*Schöpfer*] than the origin or form giver [*Bildner*], and certainly his work is not at any price his creature [*Geschöpf*] but rather his form [*Gebilde*]. To be sure, the form [*Gebilde*], too, and not only the creature [*Geschöpf*] has life. But the basis of the decisive difference between the two is this: only the life of the creature [*des Geschöpfes*], never that of the formed structure [*des Gebildeten*], partakes, unreservedly, of the intention of redemption.[33]

This means that ethical judgments drawn from reading are unlike those drawn from life: whereas each person is to be judged – and forgiven – as an individual before God, fictional characters are to be judged through their interactions. 'And what is crucial in the case of fictional characters is not to make ethical findings but rather to understand morally what happens' in the choreography of relations between them.[34]

The critic's task is therefore not to pass judgment on individual characters or attempt to determine if they were good or bad, guilty or innocent, *which, to a certain extent, also holds true with regards to historical persons and events. Passing moral judgment on a long dead person – say, by arguing that Shelley and/or Benjamin were racist, sexist, homophobic – is of little interest and will not do anything towards atoning for all the suffering at the bloodied roots of our prosperity (full disclaimer: I write this as an academic working for an institution, funded by a charitable trust, and within an intellectual tradition, all of which have materially benefited from enslaved Black labour and colonialism*) rather, it is the choreography governing the interactions between the different characters that determines the mechanism of the drama, and therefore forms the basis for any critical evaluation of its action. The individual characters may be regarded like pieces in a mosaic, or like stars who, circling one another, contribute to the aesthetic harmony of the whole. *Likewise with history: rather than distributing personal guilt among the long-dead, it is more crucial to understand the social relations that enabled such violence to be wielded systemically against racialised bodies back then, and how these relations live on into our present. Study the past to rescue the living.*

Most critics begin their reading of *The Cenci* by noting Beatrice's entrapment in a society governed by a patriarchal 'triple entente' of Father, Pope and God.[35] The Pope is complicit with the patriarchal order; as Cardinal Camillo explains, he 'holds it of most dangerous example | In aught to weaken the paternal power, | Being, as 't were, the shadow of his own'.[36] He therefore refuses to intervene in a conflict between a father and his children. This leaves Beatrice with a choice that is really not one: she can either do nothing and remain subject to her father's sexual violence, or she can draw upon herself the guilt of parricide. It is this impossible position that characterises the mythic nature of her predicament, stuck in what Benjamin describes as 'an order whose sole intrinsic concepts are misfortune [*Unglück*] and guilt [*Schuld*], and within which there is no conceivable path of liberation (for insofar as something is fate, it is misfortune and guilt)'.[37]

A moral code whose only constitutive concepts are *Unglück* (misfortune) and *Schuld* (guilt) leaves no room for justice, *Gerechtigkeit*. 'Another sphere must therefore be sought in which misfortune and guilt alone carry weight, a balance on which bliss and innocence are found too light and float upward. This balance is the scale of law [*Recht*].'[38] Benjamin thus sets up an opposition between divine justice, *Gerechtigkeit*, and mythic law, *Recht*. Where the former forgives, the latter condemns. Furthermore: 'Law [*Das Recht*] condemns not to punishment but to guilt.'[39] It is the tragic hero's fate to find themselves trapped in circumstances where every choice leads to guilt. For Benjamin, divine violence enters and shatters this world view: 'Just as in all spheres God opposes myth, mythic violence is confronted by the divine.'[40] In *The Cenci*, however, it is precisely God – enshrined in the figure of the Pope and the institution of the Church – who represents the mythic violence that needs to be overcome in the name of justice.

'That matter of the murder is hushed up | If you consent to yield his Holiness | Your fief that lies beyond the Pincian gate,' are the first words spoken in the play, by Cardinal Camillo to Count Cenci.[41] As Linda Brigham notes, the drama 'begins with Cardinal Camillo's complaint that Count Cenci has reached his credit limit with the Church'.[42] The statement echoes the play's Preface, where Shelley informs us that the Pope's motive in ordering Beatrice's execution is not justice, but revenge for depriving the Church of the financial benefit of selling indulgences to Cenci:

> The old man [Cenci] had, during his life, repeatedly bought his pardon from the Pope for capital crimes of the most enormous and unspeakable kind, at the price of a hundred thousand crowns; the death therefore of his victims can scarcely be accounted for by the love of justice. The Pope, among other motives for severity, probably felt that whoever killed the Count Cenci deprived his treasury of a certain and copious source of revenue.[43]

Cenci's ability to purchase absolution for his transgressions points to the nature of money, which provides a measure that makes incommensurable things commensurable, *or fungible, an economic term sometimes used to describe the commodification of Black bodies under slavery. As Shannon Winnubst puts it, 'the bodies of the enslaved are abstracted into the metrics of property and capital. They are then fed as measurable units of cargo into the economic machine of risk/profit calculation. The bodies themselves and the differences between them are measured by a single metric: fungibility.'*[44]

This choice of words, so close to my own, stuns me. Can I speak of metrics in poetry without evoking the inhuman abstraction inherent in all measures? 'To be fungible, in both its economic and legal meanings, is to have all distinctive characteristics and contents hollowed-out. It is a relationship of equity that requires a purely formal semblance. In economic terms, fungibility refers to those goods and products on the market that are substitutable for one another: a bushel of wheat from Kazakhstan is fungible with a bushel of wheat from Nebraska, assuming the quality and grade of wheat is the same.'[45] *So one metric foot is fungible with any other, assuming it slots into the poem's measure; one slave is fungible with any other, assuming their age and state of health are the same.* **By opening with the price of murder in papal Rome, Shelley sets the standard against which Beatrice's act is to be measured but he also indicates the dynamics that structure male relations within the play. Camillo continues:**

> [The Pope] said that you
> Bought perilous impunity with your gold;
> That crimes like yours if once or twice compounded
> Enriched the Church, and respited from hell
> An erring soul which might repent and live;
> But that the glory and the interest
> Of the high throne he fills, little consist
> With making it a daily mart of guilt[46]

While Camillo sees no conflict in equating 'enriching the Church' and 'respiting souls from hell', Cenci does: 'Respited me from Hell!' he responds; 'So may the Devil | Respite their souls from Heaven.'[47] 'The cash nexus', Scrivener comments on this dialogue, 'is so obviously the most essential component in Camillo's speech that one admires Cenci's honesty.'[48] Cenci's only virtue may be his exposure of the Pope's 'daily mart of guilt', openly acknowledging that his own sins 'are the stewards' of the Pope's revenue.[49] Within the choreography of the play, Cenci's role is to reveal how the Catholic Church converts guilt into money.

While the sale of indulgences is at the root of the Reformation, *The Cenci* is not a Protestant critique of Catholicism, but a moral denunciation of the entanglements between religion and capitalism: a world in which divine providence manifests itself as the invisible hand of the market. Shelley may even be deliberately punning on the two senses of the German word *Schuld* in his representation of the papal economy as a daily mart in which moral guilt (*Schuld*) is converted into monetary debt (*Schuld*). *The fiat of the transatlantic slave system is the creation of an economy where moral guilt is evacuated. Atrocities committed against enslaved persons were rarely, if ever, punishable, and whoever became rich enough by exploiting and torturing others would be able to return 'home' to Britain and retire in luxury, all past sins washed away by the cleansing properties of wealth.* In this regard, Shelley's drama anticipates Karl Marx's analysis of money, which makes human qualities and material things fungible:

> I am ugly, but I can buy myself the most beautiful women. Consequently I am not ugly, for the effect of ugliness, its power of repulsion, is annulled by money. . . . I am a wicked, dishonest man without conscience or intellect, but money is honoured and so also is its possessor. Money is the highest good and so its possessor is good.[50]

By enabling its possessor to acquire anything they might desire – be it intelligence, skills or goods – money degrades the value of desirable things. And because money 'confounds and exchanges all things', Marx goes on, 'it is the universal confusion and exchange of all things, the inverted world'.[51] The world of Babel, one might say, in which the confusion of the tongues is only a local symptom of a universal disordering and debasement of value.

At the close of the first act, Cenci throws a banquet to celebrate the deaths of his sons. While this serves to show his depravity, there is also a very rational reason behind his joy: his sons 'will need no food or raiment more: | The tapers that did light them the dark way | Are their last cost,' Cenci brags and invites his guests to 'Rejoice with me – my heart is wondrous glad.'[52] Money also governs Cenci's conflict with his remaining son, Giacomo. In his first appearance on stage, we find Giacomo complaining that his father has deprived him of money, and, like his brothers before him, he plans to petition the Pope to obtain provision for his needs. 'There is an obsolete and doubtful law | By which you might obtain a bare provision | Of food and clothing,' Camillo promises him, but Giacomo wants more: 'Nothing more? Alas! | Bare must be the provision which strict law | Awards, and agèd, sullen avarice pays.'[53] Giacomo's woes began when Cenci borrowed his wife's dowry and then refused to return it. When Giacomo accused Cenci, 'he coined | A brief yet specious tale, how I had wasted | The sum in secret riot'.[54] Giacomo's wife believes the tale that Cenci *coins*, and her consequent accusations make Giacomo's home a hell. 'And to that hell will I return no more | Until mine enemy has rendered up | Atonement,' he exclaims.[55] While Giacomo is not yet aware of the rape, his words echo Beatrice's demand for atonement spoken just before he arrives on the scene.

As the scene unfolds, Shelley's staging emphasises parallels between the two siblings. Just as Beatrice has asserted that she has no father, Giacomo says of Cenci that 'We | Are now no more, as once, parent and child, | But man to man; the oppressor to the oppressed.'[56] The turn of phrase not only echoes Beatrice but also uses a formulation, 'the oppressor and the oppressed', that Beatrice will herself repeat during her trial.[57] The atonement that Giacomo seeks likewise perfectly matches Beatrice's: 'That word parricide, | Although I am resolved, haunts me like fear,' he confesses to Orsino.[58] Orsino assures him that 'what you devise | Is, as it were, accomplished', explaining that 'Cenci has done an outrage to his daughter' that already constitutes his death warrant.[59] 'My doubts are well appeased,' Giacomo replies. 'There is a higher reason for the act | Than mine; there is a holier judge than me, | A more unblamed avenger.'[60] While learning of Cenci's rape of Beatrice appeases Giacomo's fear of parricide, he was resolved to commit it independently of the rape, in vengeance for his father's having deprived him of money. 'O heart, I ask no more | Justification!' Giacomo exclaims at the close of the scene.[61]

The scene establishes that both siblings are victims of Cenci's wickedness, both believe that Cenci has forfeited his paternal rights, both demand atonement by death. However, these parallels also highlight the differences in their respective situations: the daughter wants to avenge an expressionless sexual crime, whereas the son wants retribution for a financial one. Giacomo rounds off his demand for atonement with the suggestive lines that 'as he gave life to me | I will, reversing nature's law —'.[62] However, the law that Giacomo reverses is not the law of nature, but that of the Church. Whereas the Pope absolves capital crime by accepting gold, Giacomo will demand repayment of his gold through a capital crime. In his response to Giacomo, Orsino suitably equivocates between financial repayment and moral retribution: 'Trust me, | The compensation which thou seekest here | Will be denied'.[63] Giacomo will not get his money back, nor will he get revenge.

Orsino's pun on the two meanings of the word 'compensation' could be translated into German as *Vergeltung*, a key term in Benjamin's thoughts on 'the economy of the moral universe'.[64] The German word *Vergeltung* ('retribution') is etymologically related to *Geld* ('money') and echoes it phonetically.[65] *Vergeltung* is retribution in terms of payback. Against this, Benjamin sets *Vergebung* ('forgiveness'), which is etymologically rooted in *Gabe* ('gift') and therefore connotes a giving away, or writing off, of debts. The terms are used to differentiate two types of violence, forgiving versus retributive: 'we know from older forms of law that the power of retribution [*vergeltende Gewalt*] was able to extend its sway to succeeding, increasingly distant generations'.[66] Such vengefulness is typified by God in Numbers 14:18, where He is described as 'by no means clearing the guilty, visiting the iniquity of the fathers upon the children unto the third and fourth generation'.

But multi-generational debt is also a feature of secular political economy. *Partus sequitur ventrem is the name of the legal doctrine, first passed in Virginia in 1662, that dictates that the condition of a child follows that of the mother. Many children born to enslaved women were fathered through rape by free white men; the* partus sequitur ventrem *doctrine served to clarify their status by legislating that they too were enslaved. This reversed the patriarchal structure of inheritance typical of Western economies. As*

Jennifer Morgan explains, 'the logic of the paternal link formally unravelled as hereditary racial slavery congealed'.[67] *At the same time, it strengthened the connection between being Black and being enslaved until Blackness itself came to signify 'enslavability'.*[68] *Under the 'one-drop rule', this iniquity was visited upon the children unto the sixteenth generation.* The national debt is an example of a present expenditure that will tax future generations. Shelley analyses this problem in 'A Philosophical View of Reform', the trip 'over the sandy desert of politics' that he commenced after finishing *The Cenci*.[69] He argues that the national debt is instrumental in binding together the rich and the rulers: when the government is indebted to the rich, they get to dictate policy; at the same time, the rich have an interest in the government's preservation in order to ensure that they get their money back.

While the national debt serves to consolidate the sovereign power of the rich, it is financed by taxes and hence repaid by the whole of society. If the national debt were to be paid off at once, as Shelley advocates, '[i]t would be a mere transfer among persons of property', but since both debtors and creditors belong to the same elite, they all stand to gain by 'abstain[ing] from demanding the principal which they must all unite to pay, for the sake of receiving an enormous interest' accrued over time.[70] That is, by postponing repayment, the rich and the powerful ensure that they will receive interest on the money lent, enriching themselves by passing on their debts into an indefinite future: 'They would both shift to the labor of the present and of all succeeding generations the payment of the interest on their own debt.'[71] *Shelley's foray into national economics is prophetic. When slavery was abolished in the British Empire in 1833, the British government agreed to pay former slave owners (many of whom sat in Parliament) a compensation for loss of property that amounted to £20 million or 40% of the national budget at the time. In 2015, the Treasury released a self-congratulatory tweet that this debt had finally been paid off. Many British taxpayers were dismayed to discover that their taxes had gone towards paying off debts incurred to compensate slave owners. Needless to say, the formerly enslaved received nothing but their freedom, and barely even that as slavery was initially replaced by enforced, unpaid labour under an apprenticeship system. In contrast, the sheer thought of Britain or former slave owners paying reparations to Caribbean countries remains a utopian vision.* The national debt is a national inheritance, which is to say a hereditary debt (*Schuld*) owed by generations of ordinary British people to the wealthy elites.

'Fate is the guilt context [*Schuldzusammenhang*] of the living,' Benjamin writes.[72] The term *Zusammenhang* is a favourite with him; however, as Anthony Phelan has explained, it 'presents a problem for translation', not least because '*Zusammenhang* is not really an abstract noun at all: the associated verb *zusammenhängen* means to be joined to or related to something – literally, to hang together'.[73] For instance, as lengths of twine may be tied together to form a net. In tragedy, guilt forms such a net that captures the protagonist. But keeping in mind the other meaning of the word *Schuld*, 'debt', we can following Shelley read the national debt as quite literally the *Schuldzusammenhang* of the British. The future becomes indentured to the past as each generation has to pay for the expenditure of their predecessors. Robert Mitchell argues that Shelley 'recognized that the conservative temporal structure of institutions such as paper money and the national debt – their tendency to locate the active source of events in past debts – directly opposed the expansion of time consciousness that his poetry sought to encourage'.[74] The national debt chains the present to the past and the future to the present – thereby precluding the possibility of true liberation.

For Benjamin, liberation from the past can only come through destruction, the work of divine violence. Although, in the Bible, it is God himself who is said to visit the iniquity of the fathers upon the children, Benjamin nonetheless contrasts this generational *vergeltende Gewalt* with what he terms divine violence, which is characterised by being forgiving, *vergebend*. Tracy McNulty suggests that Benjamin's opposition between mythic retributive violence and divine forgiving violence pits the God who gives the commandments (the written law) against the arbitrarily punishing God of the earlier parts of the Old Testament. 'In this respect, one might even argue that the first "mythic violence" opposed by the written law is the mythic violence of God himself.'[75] Thus, in giving the law, the violence of God turns in on its own lawlessness. If such violence destroys, it is to wipe away all guilt: Benjamin describes it as 'the hand that obliterates the traces of his misdeeds, even if it must lay waste to the world in the process. As the purifying hurricane speeds ahead of the thunder and lightning, God's fury roars through history in the storm of forgiveness, in order to sweep away everything that would be consumed forever in the lightning bolts of divine wrath.'[76] Destroying creation itself with the force of its forgiveness, divine violence annihilates even the time that has served as a medium to transmit hereditary guilt, bringing history to a standstill.

In the opening scene, Cenci challenges himself to a crime that might break through the perverse entanglement of capitalism and religion that characterises the moral economy he lives in. 'But much yet remains | To which they show no title,' he says of the Pope and his nephews.[77] A crime to which the Pope shows no title is a crime that stands outside of the jurisdiction of the Catholic Church, its guilt economy. In 'Critique of Violence', Benjamin addresses how the monopolisation of violence is necessary to institutions that preserve the law, such as the Catholic Church in *The Cenci*, and invites us to consider the possibility 'that violence [*Gewalt*], when not in the hands of the law, threatens it not by the ends that it may pursue but by its mere existence outside the law [*Recht*]'.[78] That is, extrajudicial exercise of violence is not problematic because of the consequences in any particular situation but because, in existing outside the law, it undercuts the law's authority and therefore risks destabilising the entire social and judicial order upheld by it. So Benjamin concludes that 'law [*Recht*] sees violence [*Gewalt*] in the hands of individuals as a danger undermining the legal system'.[79]

Cenci's violent outbursts threaten the legal system represented by the Church, but the indulgences that he pays in absolution for his crimes signal his ultimate submission to its superior authority. In this way, his violence is contained by the Pope's 'daily mart of guilt' where spiritual guilt (*Schuld*) is converted into monetary debt (*Schuld*). As long as Cenci pays for his disobedience, the papal order is secure, *a dynamic of containment that also structured relations between the European powers and their colonies. Take the Haitian Revolution, for example. In 1791, inspired by the ideals of the French Revolution, the enslaved people of the French Caribbean island of Saint Domingue rose to throw off their so-called 'owners'. Even though Britain, the Netherlands and Spain were at war with Revolutionary France in Europe, they sent troops to quench the uprising, fearing the example a successful Black revolution could set for the enslaved on their own neighbouring 'Sugar Islands'. Only in 1804 did Haiti become the first free Black republic in the Americas. Despite the military victory, the fledgling state was soon forced into submission by economic means. In this way, the European colonial order in the Caribbean remained secure.*

An important pivot in the play, and a detail not present in Shelley's source manuscript, is the arrival, moments after Cenci's death, of the papal legate Savella with an order for Cenci's execution. Stuart Sperry reads it as 'a single crux of such importance that it crystallizes in itself the vital interpretive problems' of the play.[80] And indeed interpretations of this scene have been radically different: at one extreme Savella's arrival has been read as a vindication of the papal justice system – had Beatrice shown a little bit more patience, the Pope would have rescued her – and at the other extreme it confirms the irrational and arbitrary ways of the Church, as there is no immediately apparent reason for the Pope to order Cenci's execution. This reason is, however, uncovered in Brigham's reading of the play's financial motifs: she locates the pivotal moment in the banquet scene where Cenci celebrates the accidental death of his sons. 'God, | I thank thee! In one night didst thou perform, | By ways inscrutable, the thing I sought. | My disobedient and rebellious sons | Are dead!'[81]

One of his sons, 'Rocco | Was kneeling at the mass, with sixteen others, | When the church fell and crushed him to a mummy; | The rest escaped unhurt'.[82] His other son, 'Cristofano | Was stabbed in error by a jealous man, | Whilst she he loved was sleeping with his rival'.[83] Since this takes place 'in the self-same hour of the same night', Cenci infers a divine intervention, adding that God's 'most favoring Providence was shown | Even in the manner of their deaths. . . . Which shows that Heaven has special care of me.'[84] 'Not only does Cenci exempt himself from the Church's credit control,' Brigham writes; 'he threatens the very units of its control, its monopoly on the representation of God.'[85] It is by publicly usurping the Church's claim on an immediate relation to God that Cenci signs his own death warrant – and Savella is dispatched with an order for his arrest and execution soon after. Which is to say that it is not by killing or torturing or stealing from this or that person that Cenci breaks his contract with the Church; it is by claiming God's favour, the very foundation of the Church's power, that Cenci commits the unpardonable crime.

Since the relationship between Cenci and his children is framed by the Christian analogy between father, Pope and God, Beatrice's parricide is, symbolically speaking, a deicide; but it is also important to remember that the deicide is triggered by Cenci's own actions – he himself initiates the chain of events that will lead to his death. That is, with the incestuous rape, he hits upon a crime that is beyond the limit of the papal legal order (which will neither persecute a rapist nor indict a father) but that nonetheless requires atonement – a crime, therefore, that will force Beatrice to take the law into her own hands. By raping his daughter, Cenci challenges her to attack God's image in himself, and in this way consummate his defiance of the patriarchal order of Christianity. Beatrice follows her father's cue in flouting the Church's judicial authority. Her exclamation after the rape, 'Oh! in this mortal world | There is no vindication and no law | Which can adjudge and execute the doom | Of that through which I suffer,' suggests that the Church's legal system (which is to say God's law on earth) cannot accommodate the 'atonement' that her wrong requires.[86] This authorises a different kind of hearing:

> I have prayed
> To God, and I have talked with my own heart,
> And have unravelled my entangled will,
> And have at length determined what is right.[87]

While Beatrice will come to claim divine sanction for the decision that her father must die, there is no evidence that her prayer has been answered – not even such as provided by the 'miraculous deaths' of her brothers. On the contrary, as she explicitly puts it in this speech, Beatrice has 'unravelled [her] entangled will' and 'determined what is right'. With or without divine intervention, it is her will that determines the right, or *Recht*, according to which Cenci's atonement requires his death. The Catholic Church executes her less for killing Cenci (after all, the Pope had already issued a death warrant for him) than for the crime of usurping its God-given right to set the law.

Notes

1. 'Socrates', *EW*, pp. 233–4; *GS1*, pp. 129–30.
2. 'Paralipomena to "On the Concept of History"', *SW4*, p. 403, translation emended; *GS1*, p. 1234.
3. Preface to *The Cenci*, *PS2*, p. 727. Mary Shelley translated the account as 'A Relation of the Death of the Cenci Family' for publication alongside the play.
4. I am referring to Adorno's 1936 essay 'On Jazz' and Hannah Arendt's 1959 'Reflections on Little Rock'. On the latter, see Kathryn T. Gines, *Hannah Arendt and the Negro Question* (Bloomington, IN: Indiana University Press, 2014).
5. 'Fate and Character', *SW1*, p. 203; *GS2*, pp. 174–5. The statement is first made in the essay 'Fate and Character', then Benjamin cites the complete paragraph in *Origin*, pp. 109–10; *GS1*, pp. 288–9.
6. 'Fate and Character', *SW1*, p. 204; *GS2*, p. 175.
7. *The Cenci*, III.i.69–74.
8. *The Cenci*, III.i.177–9.
9. It is a peculiarity of the English language that the person committing a parricide becomes a parricide, as if individuality is expended in the crime. Cf. *OED*, parricide, n.[1] and [2]. Derrida notes a similar peculiarity in the French word *parjure*: 'The same word, *parjure*, in French means both the act of perjuring, the crime of perjury, in sum, and the author of the perjury, the guilty one, the perjurer.' '"Le Parjure," Perhaps: Storytelling and Lying ("abrupt breaches of syntax"),' in *Acts of Narrative*, ed. by Carol Jacobs and Henry Sussman (Stanford, CA: Stanford University Press, 2003), pp. 195–234 (p. 196, cf. p. 212).
10. *The Cenci*, III.i.213–15.
11. 'Goethe's *Elective Affinities*', *SW1*, p. 340; *GS1*, p. 181.
12. 'Goethe's *Elective Affinities*', *SW1*, p. 341; *GS1*, p. 182.
13. 'Fate and Character', *SW1*, p. 203; *GS2*, pp. 174–5.
14. *The Cenci*, III.i.134–7.

15. *The Cenci*, IV.iv.123–5.
16. *The Cenci*, I.iii.111–3.
17. Genesis, 9:21.
18. *The Cenci*, II.i.16–7.
19. Genesis, 9:22.
20. *The Cenci*, III.i.40, III.i.100–2.
21. *The Cenci*, V.iv.68–9.
22. *The Cenci*, V.iii.77–83.
23. *The Cenci*, V.iii.84–8.
24. The citation is from Benjamin's description of the tragic hero in 'Fate and Character', *SW1*, p. 203; *GS2*, p. 175.
25. *Origin*, p. 115; *GS1*, p. 294.
26. Ariella Aïsha Azoulay, *Potential History: Unlearning Imperialism* (London: Verso, 2019), p. 77.
27. *The Cenci*, III.i.214–15.
28. Preface to *The Cenci*, *PS2*, p. 731.
29. Michael Scrivener, *Radical Shelley: The Philosophical Anarchism and Utopian Thought of Percy Bysshe Shelley* (Princeton, NJ: Princeton University Press, 1982), p. 188.
30. Preface to *The Cenci*, *PS2*, p. 730.
31. 'A Defence of Poetry', *SPP*, p. 520.
32. Preface to *The Cenci*, *PS2*, p. 730.
33. 'Goethe's *Elective Affinities*', *SW1*, pp. 323–4; *GS1*, p. 159. The word 'partakes' here translates *hat Anteil*, the same word that Benjamin uses to describe how phenomena participate in noumenal Ideas.
34. 'Goethe's *Elective Affinities*', *SW1*, p. 304; *GS1*, p. 133.
35. James Rieger, *The Mutiny Within: The Heresies of Percy Bysshe Shelley* (New York, NY: George Braziller, 1967), p. 114. The analogy appears in various guises throughout criticism on the play; see, e.g., Scrivener, pp. 193–4, Young-Ok An, 'Beatrice's Gaze Revisited: Anatomizing "The Cenci"', *Criticism*, 38 (1996), p. 55, Stuart Curran, *Shelley's Cenci: Scorpions Ringed with Fire* (Princeton, NJ: Princeton University Press, 1970), p. 134. However, see Michael Kohler, 'Shelley in Chancery: The Reimagination of the Paternalist State in "The Cenci"', *Studies in Romanticism*, 37.4 (1998), 545–89 for a refutation.
36. *The Cenci*, II.ii.54–6.
37. 'Fate and Character', *SW1*, p. 203; *GS2*, p. 174.
38. 'Fate and Character', *SW1*, p. 203; *GS2*, p. 174.
39. 'Fate and Character', *SW1*, p. 204; *GS2*, p. 175.
40. 'Critique of Violence', *SW1*, p. 249; *GS2*, p. 199.
41. *The Cenci*, I.i.1–3.
42. Linda C. Brigham, 'Count Cenci's Abysmal Credit', *Texas Studies in Literature and Language*, 38 (1996), 340–58 (p. 342).
43. Preface to *The Cenci*, *PS2*, p. 728.
44. Shannon Winnubst, 'The Many Lives of Fungibility: Anti-Blackness in Neoliberal Times', *Journal of Gender Studies*, 29.1 (2020), 101–12 (p. 104).
45. Winnubst, 'The Many Lives of Fungibility', p. 104.
46. *The Cenci*, I.i.5–12.
47. *The Cenci*, I.i.26–7.
48. Scrivener, *Radical Shelley*, p. 190.
49. *The Cenci*, I.i.32.
50. Karl Marx, 'On Money', in *Karl Marx: Selected Writings*, ed. by David McLellan, 2nd edn (Oxford: Oxford University Press, 2000), pp. 118–21 (p. 118).
51. Marx, 'On Money', p. 119.
52. *The Cenci*, I.iii.46–8, I.iii.50.
53. *The Cenci*, II.ii.1–3, II.ii.3–5.
54. *The Cenci*, III.i.318–20.
55. *The Cenci*, III.i. 331–3.
56. *The Cenci*, III.i.281–3; cf. III.i.40.
57. *The Cenci*, V.iii.88.
58. *The Cenci*, III.i.340–1.
59. *The Cenci*, III.i.345–6, III.i.348.
60. *The Cenci*, III.i.362–5.

61 *The Cenci*, III.i.372–3.
62 *The Cenci*, III.i.333–4.
63 *The Cenci*, III.i.334–6.
64 'The Meaning of Time in the Moral Universe', *SW1*, p. 287; *GS6*, p. 98.
65 Jochen Hörisch comments on this etymological connection in *Kopf oder Zahl: Die Poesie des Geldes* (Frankfurt am Main: Suhrkamp, 1996), p. 17.
66 'The Meaning of Time in the Moral Universe', *SW1*, p. 286; *GS6*, p. 97.
67 Jennifer L. Morgan, *Reckoning with Slavery: Gender, Kinship, and Capitalism in the Early Black Atlantic* (Durham, NC: Duke University Press, 2021), p. 1.
68 Morgan, *Reckoning with Slavery*, p. 10.
69 Letter to John and Maria Gisborne, 6 November 1819, in *Letters 2*, p. 150.
70 'A Philosophical View of Reform', *Prose*, pp. 249–50.
71 'A Philosophical View of Reform', *Prose*, p. 250.
72 'Fate and Character', *SW1*, p. 204; *GS2*, p. 175.
73 Anthony Phelan, '*Fortgang* und *Zusammenhang*: Walter Benjamin and the Romantic Novel', in *Walter Benjamin and Romanticism*, ed. by Andrew Benjamin and Beatrice Hanssen (London: Continuum, 2002), pp. 69–82 (p. 72).
74 Robert Mitchell, *Sympathy and the State in the Romantic Era: Systems, State Finance, and the Shadows of Futurity* (New York, NY: Routledge, 2007), p. 164.
75 Tracy McNulty, 'The Commandment against the Law: Writing and Divine Justice in Walter Benjamin's "Critique of Violence"', *Diacritics*, 37 (2007), 34–60 (p. 50).
76 'The Meaning of Time in the Moral Universe', *SW1*, p. 287; *GS6*, p. 98.
77 *The Cenci*, I.i.33–4.
78 'Critique of Violence', *SW1*, p. 239; *GS2*, p. 183.
79 'Critique of Violence', *SW1*, p. 238; *GS2*, p. 183.
80 Stuart Sperry, 'The Ethical Politics of Shelley's "The Cenci"', *Studies in Romanticism*, 25 (1986), 411–427 (p. 416).
81 *The Cenci*, I.iii.40–4.
82 *The Cenci*, I.iii.58–61.
83 *The Cenci*, I.iii.61–3.
84 *The Cenci*, I.iii.64, I.iii.57–65.
85 Brigham, 'Count Cenci's Abysmal Credit', p. 350.
86 *The Cenci*, III.i.134–7, III.i.215.
87 *The Cenci*, III.i.218–21.

8
Atonement

Tragedy starts with transgression and ends in atonement. In its course, the beholder is invited to pass judgment not only on the character who transgresses or the mosaic of their social relations, but also on the moral scale on which transgression and atonement are measured. For Benjamin, tragedy marks the limit of this scale in the ancient world; it was 'in tragedy that the head of genius lifted itself for the first time from the mist of guilt' as 'pagan man becomes aware that he is better than his god'.[1] Neither Francesco nor Beatrice Cenci manage to break free from their fate, and Shelley consistently uses cloudy imagery – mist, fogs, clouds and vapours – to figure the Cenci family's moral corruption. Cenci is the first to evoke this cloud when he curses his daughter, promising that 'she shall grope through a bewildering mist | Of horror'.[2] This mist comes from within Cenci, yet unfolds to encompass his daughter's whole universe:

> I bear a darker, deadlier gloom
> Than the earth's shade, or interlunar air,
> Or constellations quenched in murkiest cloud,
> In which I walk secure and unbeheld[3]

Beatrice's first speech after the rape echoes Cenci's climatic imagery: 'The sunshine on the floor is black! The air | Is changed to vapours such as the dead breathe | In charnel pits! Pah! I am choked!'[4] The sunshine turns black as Beatrice breathes in the 'darker, deadlier gloom' or 'murkiest cloud' in which Cenci has styled himself.

The Cencian cloud again forms around Beatrice as she decides for the parricide: 'All must be suddenly resolved and done. | What is this undistinguishable mist | Of thoughts, which rise, like shadow after shadow, | Darkening each other?' she asks herself shortly before retiring to unravel her will and determine that Cenci must die.[5] This means that Beatrice's decision to kill her father is taken out of the mists that his gloom has enveloped her in, mists that, on her own testimony, form the fateful circumstances that entrap her: 'I, | Though wrapt in a strange cloud of crime and shame, | Lived ever holy and unstained', she says in the final scene.[6] It is also the idea of being enveloped in her father's spirit that informs Beatrice's vision when she, for the first time, begins to doubt her faith in God:

> If there should be
> No God, no Heaven, no Earth in the void world;
> The wide, grey, lampless, deep, unpeopled world!
> If all things then should be – my father's spirit,
> His eye, his voice, his touch, surrounding me;
> The atmosphere and breath of my dead life![7]

The Cencian 'atmosphere' quenches all divine light and is another variation on the 'darker, deadlier gloom' in which Cenci envelops himself to confound light and darkness, the 'undistinguishable mist' out of which Beatrice's decision to kill her father is taken, and the 'strange cloud of crime and shame' in which she lived her life.

All this cloudy imagery blurs the moral distinctions between father and daughter: shrouded in a mist of guilt, they essentially become one – a form of atonement 'in the radical etymological sense' noted by Geoffrey Hill: 'an act of at-one-ment, a setting at one, a bringing into concord, a reconciling, a uniting in harmony'.[8] As Hill defines it, at-one-ment is another name for the measure of a literary work, the scale on which its different elements (sound, sense, rhythm, rhyme) are carefully counterbalanced: he cites W. B. Yeats's remark that 'a poem comes right with a click like a closing box' to illustrate the point. One might also think of it as putting in the final piece of a puzzle (or, indeed, a mosaic). In drama, at-one-ment is another name for the choreography that governs the relations between the various characters.

Hill is not only concerned with technical perfection but also with the ethical dimension of poetry, and literature more widely: atonement in its theological sense. 'When the poem "comes right with a click like a closing box", what is there effected is the atonement of aesthetics with the rectitude of judgment.'[9] *Such at-one-ment is also required in the sphere of history. 'Still today, it is not obvious to the eyes of all that the enslaving of the Negroes and colonial atrocities are part of our world memory; even less that this memory, as common, is not the property of the sole peoples that suffered these events, but of humanity as a whole,' Achille Mbembe has noted.*[10] *When addressing European history – and this is as true of literary as of political history – atonement can only begin with the acknowledgment that the histories of White freedom and Black enslavement are one.* The mist in which Francesco and Beatrice Cenci are enveloped is the figure of their at-one-ment, the moral dilemma of the play in which they attempt, yet fail, to break free from their entrapment in fate. *Not unlike how Britain, today, remains trapped in the delusions spun by its imperial past.*

From the outset it is clear that Beatrice is unlike anyone whom Cenci has ever encountered. In the first act, Cenci tells us that there is nothing to check him – 'I have no remorse and little fear, | Which are, I think, the checks of other men.'[11] The word 'check' echoes throughout the play. 'Will none among this noble company | Check the abandoned villain?' one of Cenci's guests exclaims at the banquet, but no one does.[12] Camillo reports to Beatrice that he has 'urged [the Pope] then to check | Your father's cruel hand' but the Pope professes to keep a 'blameless neutrality' in 'the great war between the old and young' and refuses to intervene.[13] Instead, it is Beatrice who 'alone stood up, and with strong words | Checked his [Cenci's] unnatural pride', as Lucretia says of the banquet scene.[14] This scene offers the play's first direct exchange between father and daughter:

> *Cenci*
> Retire to your chamber, insolent girl!
> *Beatrice*
> Retire thou impious man! Aye, hide thyself
> Where never eye can look upon thee more![15]

Beatrice's first words to her father echo his command to 'retire', setting up the battle of wills between them that is the catalyst for the action. Not only does she interrupt Cenci's festivities, she attempts to send him to his room like a petulant child.

Cenci keeps up appearances long enough to dismiss the assembled company, but as soon as Beatrice is offstage he admits that their encounter has unsettled him: 'I feel my spirits fail | With thinking what I have decreed to do,' he confesses.[16] Beatrice has managed to do something that no one else has: check him. This is an insult that he will not let pass without having his vengeance. 'I know a charm shall make thee meek and tame, | Now get thee from my sight!' he retorts to Beatrice's command that he retire.[17] The charm referred to is the intended rape, a word whose German equivalent, *Vergewaltigung*, points to what is at stake here. The word is related to *Gewalt* ('violence, power'), which Benjamin places at the foundation of the mythic law. Having successfully outmanoeuvred all other forms of authority, Cenci's *Vergewaltigung* of his daughter is a bid to assert his will over its last check – Beatrice. 'A rebel to her father and her God', Cenci calls her, conveniently forgetting that he himself is no less of a rebel to his God – 'He does his will, I mine!' Cenci exclaims a few lines later, '*Leaping up, and throwing his right hand towards Heaven*'.[18] The rape is therefore purely about power (*Gewalt*). Cenci wants to extort Beatrice's submission to his will – a submission the more powerful because she is his equal in rebellious defiance.

Despite being a man notable for brief transitions from word to deed, Cenci remains remarkably indecisive with regards to the rape. Act I ends with his assertion: 'It must be done; it shall be done, I swear!'[19] but when the next act opens the deed is still undone. Act II is set the following morning. Beatrice appears 'disordered' by the events of the preceding night, but she also makes clear that Cenci has done no more than threaten her with 'one word . . . one little word; | One look, one smile. . . . He said, he looked, he did, – nothing at all | Beyond his wont, yet it disordered me'.[20] Even unbeknownst to herself, she has in fact checked Cenci again – he failed to commit the rape that he set out to do. When he appears on stage soon after, he confronts Beatrice with new determination:

> Why, yesternight you dared to look
> With disobedient insolence upon me, . . .
> Then it was I whose inarticulate words
> Fell from my lips, and who with tottering steps
> Fled from your presence, as you now from mine. . . .
> Never again, . . .
> Shalt thou strike dumb the meanest of mankind;
> Me least of all.[21]

Stuart Curran explains that 'Beatrice commits the unforgivable sin. She overpowers her father',[22] to which it is also important to add that she overpowers his power of expression: Beatrice strikes Cenci dumb and simultaneously foils his attempt to commit the crime that she will later designate as 'expressionless'. The rape brings both father and daughter to the limit of what can be said. Here, too, the staging creates parallels between the characters: with 'inarticulate words' and 'tottering steps' is precisely how Beatrice had appeared on stage shortly before her father's arrival. Cenci's description of himself can just as well be applied to his daughter's demeanour.

The rape does not work the charm that Cenci expects of it. In his first appearance after the rape, Cenci frets that 'so to leave undone | What I most seek! No, 'tis her stubborn will, | Which, by its own consent, shall stoop as low | As that which drags it down'.[23] Although he has already raped her, the greater aim of bending Beatrice's will is still not achieved, which is to say that she was *vergewaltigt*, but does not yield to the force of Cenci's *Gewalt*. So Cenci vows to himself that 'For Beatrice, worse terrors are in store, | To bend her to my will'.[24] But he fails. Instead of bending to her father's will, Beatrice decides to trump his crime. Her response is to do

> something which shall make
> The thing that I have suffered but a shadow
> In the dread lightning which avenges it;
> Brief, rapid, irreversible, destroying
> The consequence of what it cannot cure.[25]

Parricide is a crime so heinous that incestuous rape fades into insignificance in comparison. In other words, Beatrice outdoes Cenci at his own violent game.

Cenci attacks Beatrice not because she is a defenceless girl, but because he recognises her as his equal, as becomes evident from the terms with which he curses his daughter:

> God!
> Hear me! If this most specious mass of flesh,
> Which thou hast made my daughter; this my blood,
> This particle of my divided being;
> Or rather, this my bane and my disease,
> Whose sight infects and poisons me[26]

Beatrice is a particle of Cenci's divided being, his blood, his flesh. If she can check his *Gewalt*, she does so as part of his own being: in her, his violence turns in upon itself, and so Cenci claims to be infected and poisoned by his daughter. Beatrice, for her part, draws on the same language of fleshly contamination to represent her situation. After the rape she describes herself as follows:

> There creeps
> A clinging, black, contaminating mist
> About me – 'tis substantial, heavy, thick;
> I cannot pluck it from me, for it glues
> My fingers and my limbs to one another,
> And eats into my sinews, and dissolves
> My flesh to a pollution, poisoning
> The subtle, pure, and inmost spirit of life![27]

The mist that dissolves Beatrice's flesh is that same 'bewildering mist | Of horror' that Cenci has evoked earlier. As Beatrice outlines how this mist dissolves her flesh into one polluted mass, she anticipates the terms of Cenci's curse in which he refers to her as a 'most specious mass of flesh', 'my blood' that is a 'bane' and a 'disease' which 'infects and poisons' him: 'Oh blood,' Beatrice exclaims, 'which art my father's blood, | Circling through these contaminated veins'.[28] Father and daughter acknowledge their at-one-ment and, to use a biological metaphor, they react with autoimmunity: mutually allergic, attacking each other as poisons although they are in fact particles of one being, one flesh.

In assaulting Beatrice, Cenci directs his violence against the image of himself that he recognises in his child (not forgetting that, in the tragedy's Christian worldview, the image of the father is an image of the God against whom the Cencis are rebelling). This is brought to the fore at the climax of his curse:

> That if she ever have a child – and thou,
> Quick Nature! I adjure thee by thy God,
> That thou be fruitful in her, and increase
> And multiply, fulfilling his command,
> And my deep imprecation! – may it be
> A hideous likeness of herself; that, as
> From a distorting mirror, she may see
> Her image mixed with what she most abhors,
> Smiling upon her from her nursing breast.[29]

Cenci curses Beatrice to give birth to a child which is 'a hideous likeness of herself', a 'distorting mirror' in which she finds her own face 'mixed with what she most abhors' – which is himself. This is a child that will be the image of the same father whose image its mother is. Cenci's revenge for checking him is thus to father a child that will be to Beatrice exactly what she is to Cenci. Since this incestuous trinity of father, daughter/mother and child are all part of one divided being, Cenci's destruction of Beatrice is best understood as a form of self-destruction. *The quip that 'it is easier to imagine the end of the world than the end of capitalism' is a leftie cliché,*[30] *yet it can also be read as Cenci's mantra: to dismantle the moral economy where blood is exchanged for gold, gold for blood, he is ready to destroy his whole world, including the progeny through whom he would have lived on past his death.* Such self-destruction is like that divine violence that 'obliterates the traces of his misdeeds, even if it must lay waste to the world in the process'.[31]

In the *Symposium*, Diotima speaks of children and artworks as examples of 'generation in the beautiful' through which we can achieve 'something eternal and immortal in mortality'.[32] Cenci's treatment of his daughter is like a dark parody of this idea, a generation in the horrible that takes aim at immortality through destruction. Planning his legacy in front of his wife Lucretia, Cenci first congratulates himself on the deaths of his two sons and the plotted ruination of Giacomo and Beatrice. Then he continues:

> When all is done, out in the wide Campagna
> I will pile up my silver and my gold;
> My costly robes, paintings, and tapestries;
> My parchments and all records of my wealth;
> And make a bonfire in my joy, and leave
> Of my possessions nothing but my name[33]

Cenci begrudges every penny that his sons spend, only to destroy all his accumulated wealth, thereby reducing his legacy to nothing but a name, which he vows 'shall be an inheritance to strip | Its wearer bare as infamy'.[34] *The name is one of the first things that Africans were stripped of as they were transformed into chattel: repackaged as nameless cargo for the Middle Passage, then renamed with debased European or classical names for the plantation. Like the* partus sequitur ventrem *doctrine, this inverts the Western patriarchal economy according to which both property and names are passed down on the paternal line. 'The mother's mark, not the father's name, determined your fate,' as Saidiya Hartman writes in her meditation on the legacies of the transatlantic slave trade.*[35] *This may help explain the pride that her own father took in the family name, despite the fact that it was inherited from a man who once owned her ancestors: 'The Hartman name, according to my father, was our anchor in the world. It was our sole inheritance; we possessed no wealth but it. So when my grandfather's white cousins tried to buy back the family name from the brown ones in an attempt to erase a history of owners and property they feared would be mistaken for kinship, our clan doggedly held on to it.'*[36] *This, too, can be read as an example of what Geoffrey Hartman called the 'Romance of Being Named'.* **By immolating all his earthly possessions, Cenci signals his withdrawal from the Pope's 'daily mart of guilt' and moves into another economy, one whose primary currency is the name, which is to say language and therefore, ultimately, poetry.**

Beatrice is the only one of the Cenci children to understand the true value of a name. She explains her predicament in a dialogue with her lover Orsino, shortly after the rape:

> *Orsino*
> Accuse him of the deed, and let the law
> Avenge thee.
> *Beatrice*
>   Oh, ice-hearted counsellor!
> If I could find a word that might make known
> The crime of my destroyer; and that done,
> My tongue should. . .
>   lay all bare,
> So that my unpolluted fame should be
> With vilest gossips a stale-mouthed story;
> A mock, a byword, an astonishment.[37]

This introduces a continued preoccupation with her reputation which suggests that, for Beatrice, the rape is as much a crime against her public image as it is one against her body. 'Do you know,' she says to her stepmother Lucretia after the rape, 'I thought I was that wretched Beatrice | Men speak of'.[38] The loss of her sense of self is coupled with a loss of her future fame: 'Oh, what am I? | What name, what place, what memory shall be mine? |

What retrospects, outliving even despair?'[39] At the scene of her arrest, Beatrice pleads with the officers to let her go in the name of her reputation:

> And yet, if you arrest me,
> You are the judge and executioner
> Of that which is the life of life: the breath
> Of accusation kills an innocent name,
> And leaves for lame acquittal the poor life
> Which is a mask without it.[40]

An innocent name is for Beatrice the 'life of life' and thus she is concerned with protecting the purity of hers. 'Think, I adjure you, what it is to slay | The reverence living in the minds of men | Towards our ancient house, and stainless fame!', she demands of Marzio, the assassin whom she'd hired to kill her father, during their trial.[41] It is also in the name of Cenci that she accuses Lucretia and Giacomo for having confessed (under torture) to their crime:

> Ignoble hearts!
> For some brief spasms of pain, which are at least
> As mortal as the limbs through which they pass,
> Are centuries of high splendour laid in dust?
> And that eternal honour which should live
> Sun-like, above the reek of mortal fame,
> Changed to a mockery and a byword? What![42]

Her concern about the posterity of the Cenci name also informs Beatrice's final words to her brother Bernardo at the end of the play: 'Ill tongues shall wound me, and our common name | Be as a mark stamped on thine innocent brow'.[43] Boiling down to their shared name, Beatrice's bequest to her brother exactly corresponds to Cenci's will that left him 'nothing but my name; | Which shall be an inheritance to strip | Its wearer bare as infamy'.[44]

The play's tragic irony is that Beatrice acts to protect the 'eternal honour' of her name until the very end, yet it is her own actions that guarantee its immortal infamy. Thus, even in killing her father, Beatrice fulfils his wish– she renders their family history fit for dramatic treatment: *The Cenci* 'comes to Shelley's hands, already made and played', as James Chandler puts it.[45] Yet it does take Shelley's poetic intervention to turn one family's tragic fate into a literary work that has come to live on among future readers (or would you have known of the Cenci family were it not for Shelley's drama?). His own writing fulfils the desire for immortal fame that he puts into the mouths of his tragic protagonists. Does this apotheosis into art compensate, or indeed atone, for the suffering of the historical Beatrice Cenci? Diotima would say yes: on her account 'all men are ready to engage in any dangers, and expend their fortunes, and submit to any labours and incur any death' for the sake of 'the immortal memory of their actions'.[46] It is likely that Shelley would agree too, whose own tragic death has become an important component in the story of his afterlife. A more level-headed reader might, however, be sceptical about appropriating the suffering of others to make our own work 'come right with a click like a closing box'. *And this is as true of the suffering of the millions of Africans shipped across the Atlantic as it is of one noble family in late sixteenth-century Rome.*

Notes

1. 'Fate and Character', *SW1*, p. 203; *GS2*, pp. 174–5.
2. *The Cenci*, II.i.184–5.
3. *The Cenci*, II.i.189–92.
4. *The Cenci*, III.i.14–16.
5. *The Cenci*, III.i.169–72.
6. *The Cenci*, V.iv.147–9.
7. *The Cenci*, V.iv.57–62.
8. Geoffrey Hill, 'Poetry as "Menace" and "Atonement"', in *Poetry in Theory: An Anthology 1900–2000*, ed. by Jon Cook (Malden, MA: Blackwell Publishing, 2004), pp. 464–73 (p. 466).
9. Hill, 'Poetry as "Menace" and "Atonement"', p. 472.
10. Achille Mbembe, *Necropolitics*, trans. by Steven Corcoran (Durham, NC: Duke University Press, 2019), p. 126.
11. *The Cenci*, I.i.84–5.
12. *The Cenci*, I.iii.91–2.
13. *The Cenci*, II.ii.30–1, II.ii.38–40.
14. *The Cenci*, II.i.43–4.
15. *The Cenci*, I.iii.145–7.
16. *The Cenci*, I.iii.171–2.
17. *The Cenci*, I.iii.167–8.
18. *The Cenci*, IV.i.90, IV.i.139, and stage direction.
19. *The Cenci*, I.iii.178.
20. *The Cenci*, II.i.63–77.
21. *The Cenci*, II.i.106–20.
22. Stuart Curran, *Shelley's Cenci: Scorpions Ringed with Fire* (Princeton, NJ: Princeton University Press, 1970), p. 85.
23. *The Cenci*, IV.i.9–12.
24. *The Cenci*, IV.i.75–6.
25. *The Cenci*, III.i.87–91.
26. *The Cenci*, IV.i.114–9.
27. *The Cenci*, III.i.16–23.
28. *The Cenci*, III.i.95–6.
29. *The Cenci*, IV.i.141–9.
30. See Matthew Beaumont, 'Imagining the End Times: Ideology, the Contemporary Disaster Movie, *Contagion*', in *Žižek and Media Studies*, ed. by Matthew Flisfeder and Louis-Paul Willis (New York, NY: Palgrave Macmillan, 2014), pp. 79–89.
31. 'The Meaning of Time in the Moral Universe', *SW1*, p. 287; *GS6*, p. 98.

32 'The Symposium', *SoL*, p. 154.
33 *The Cenci*, IV.i.55–60.
34 *The Cenci*, IV.i.61–2.
35 Saidiya V. Hartman, *Lose Your Mother: A Journey Along the Atlantic Slave Route* (New York, NY: Farrar, Straus and Giroux, 2007), p. 80.
36 Hartman, *Lose Your Mother*, p. 82.
37 *The Cenci*, III.i.152–60.
38 *The Cenci*, III.i.42–4.
39 *The Cenci*, III.i.74–6.
40 *The Cenci*, IV.iv.135–40.
41 *The Cenci*, V.ii.144–7.
42 *The Cenci*, V.iii.27–33.
43 *The Cenci*, V.iv.150–1.
44 *The Cenci*, IV.i.60–2.
45 James Chandler, *England in 1819: The Politics of Literary Culture and the Case of Romantic Historicism* (Chicago, IL: University of Chicago Press, 1998), p. 503.
46 'The Symposium', *SoL*, p. 155.

9
Forgiveness

Shelley wrote *The Cenci* in an interlude between writing the first three acts and the fourth (and final) act of *Prometheus Unbound*. This means that there is a relation between the two dramas that matches the choreography of relations within them. Both are concerned with incalculable wrongs and the measure of forgiveness, and both explore these themes in the shadow of Shelley's reading of Milton's *Paradise Lost*. In the Preface to *Prometheus Unbound*, Shelley writes:

> The only imaginary being resembling in any degree Prometheus, is Satan; and Prometheus is, in my judgment, a more poetical character than Satan, because, in addition to courage, and majesty, and firm and patient opposition to omnipotent force, he is susceptible of being described as exempt from the taints of ambition, envy, revenge, and a desire for personal aggrandisement, which, in the Hero of Paradise Lost, interfere with the interest. The character of Satan engenders in the mind a pernicious casuistry which leads us to weigh his faults with his wrongs, and to excuse the former because the latter exceed all measure.[1]

Shelley might have avoided this pernicious casuistry in his representation of Prometheus, but he indulged it in his Beatrice: as he explains in the

Preface to *The Cenci*, he is drawn to her story on account of 'the restless and anatomizing casuistry' that it engenders in the spectator.[2] Beatrice has been wronged by her father and her God, and being, like Satan, not 'exempt from the taints of ambition, envy, revenge, and a desire for personal aggrandisement', she decides to take action to defend the purity of her reputation, her spotless name, in the face of a patriarchal order that does nothing to protect her.

Beatrice's exercise of violence has a superficial similarity to what Benjamin terms the divine violence that destroys mythic *Recht* – except that divine violence is forgiving whereas Beatrice's exercise of violence, like that of her father, is vindictive and self-serving. This does not take away from the fact that the Cenci rebellion against authority is justified to a certain extent – we can admire Cenci's defiance of the Pope's 'daily mart of guilt' or Beatrice's need, as a violated woman outside the law, to pursue the atonement that her wrong requires herself. On Benjamin's model, the violence exerted by the Cencis can be identified with a violence of a third kind – neither divine nor mythic. The exemplar of such violence is Prometheus, who 'challenges fate with dignified courage, fights it with varying fortunes, and is not left by the legend without hope of one day bringing a new law [*Recht*] to men'.[3] What may be termed Promethean violence is a refusal to submit to the mythic 'fate, which in all cases underlies legal violence'.[4]

In *The Cenci*, mythic fate is represented by the divine authority vested in the Catholic Church. Both father and daughter seek to impose their own will over God's *Recht* to set the law; however, since this kind of resistance still adheres to the same violent means, it cannot truly break free of the mythic guilt economy. Nonetheless, we may sympathise with the ambition to defy fate: it is the Promethean 'hero and the legal violence of the myth native to him that the public tries to picture even now in admiring the miscreant', Benjamin writes,[5] pinpointing the exact reason why Shelley admires Milton's Satan:

> Milton's Devil as a moral being is as far superior to his God as one who perseveres in some purpose which he has conceived to be excellent, in spite of adversity and torture, is to one who in the cold security of undoubted triumph inflicts the most horrible revenge upon his enemy – not from any mistaken notion of bringing him to repent of a perseverance in enmity but with the open and alleged design of exasperating him to deserve new torments.[6]

In this scenario, siding with Satan against God is the Christian thing to do, as is siding with Beatrice against her rapist father, or with Cenci against the corrupt Pope's daily mart of guilt, *but while such ethical nuance sounds very well in fiction, it does not help us deal with the legacy of historical injustices in practice. The archival record contains scores of self-pitying and self-justified complaints by colonisers, slave traders, sailors, plantation owners and managers: the slaves are lazy, devious, disloyal; the climate is hot, unwholesome, dangerous; the landscape is hostile, threatening, poisonous. The suffering of these men was real and undeserved insofar as they perceived it, yet their direct and active part in facilitating the slave economy puts them well beyond the reach of moral sympathy.*

Benjamin's early essays speak of the Fall of Language as a fall into communication, *Mitteilung*; when he addresses the internal split of language in the context of myth, he uses the term *dämonische Zweideutigkeit* ('demonic ambiguity'). This is no longer the Platonic daemon that mediates between human and divine; it is the biblical sweet-talker who uses language to entrap mankind. The German word *Zweideutigkeit* is formed from *zwei Deutungen* ('two interpretations'), so it too harbours an internal split, and could very literally be rendered as 'two-interpretation-ness'. This interpretative doubling assails mythic language. 'There is no truth, for there is no unequivocalness [*Eindeutigkeit*, lit. "one-interpretation-ness"] – and hence not even error – in myth,' Benjamin asserts in the essay on Goethe's *Elective Affinities*.[7] He picks up this thread in *The Origin of German Tragic Drama* where he describes tragedy as a confrontation with a 'demonic world-order': 'The tragic is to the demonic what the paradox is to ambiguity [*Zweideutigkeit*]. In all the paradoxes of tragedy . . . ambiguity [*Zweideutigkeit*], the stigma of the demon, is in decline.'[8] Just as Benjamin does not direct the translator towards a restitution of the Adamic language, so he is not expecting an act of atonement through which the tragedian will fuse *Zweideutigkeit* back into *Eindeutigkeit*. Instead his task is to resolve ambiguities into paradoxes. This resolution is achieved through the hero's silence. Beyond tragedy, Benjamin locates the paradigm of such resolution in the figure of Viennese satirist Karl Kraus. 'The dark background from which Kraus's image detaches itself is not formed by his contemporaries, but is the primeval world, or the world of the demon [*Dämon*].'[9] This is the world of myth, mapped onto Benjamin's present.

Benjamin interprets Kraus's work, especially the satirical journal *Die Fackel* ('The Torch'), which Kraus edited from 1899 to 1936, as a kind of quixotic war: 'In ancient armour, wrathfully grinning, a Chinese idol, brandishing a drawn sword in each hand, he dances a war-dance before the burial vault of the German language.'[10] *Note the casual Orientalism.* More specifically, Kraus is on a crusade against the language of journalism, a language as empty and vacuous as the hypocritical pieties of the Catholic Church in *The Cenci*. As in Shelley's drama, it is capitalism that has emptied out value. For Kraus, Benjamin claims, journalism is 'the expression of the changed function of language in the world of high capitalism. The empty phrase of the kind so relentlessly pursued by Kraus is the commodity sign [*Warenzeichen*] that makes a thought marketable, the way flowery language, as ornament, gives a thought value for the connoisseur.'[11] The compound *Warenzeichen* is a nod to Marx's critique of the commodity (*Ware*) as well as to the bourgeois view of language as *bloßes Zeichen* ('mere sign') that Benjamin dismissed in his essay 'On Language'. With journalism, language has undergone a second Fall – from communication into commodification.

In addition, Kraus has something Satanic about him: 'if he breaks off in lamentation [*Klage*], it is only to file a complaint [*Anklage*] at the Last Judgment'.[12] The pun on *Klage* ('lament') and *Anklage* ('legal complaint, accusation') alludes to the Book of Job, which is the first instance in the Hebrew Bible when Satan is named (in Genesis there is only talk of a Serpent). Job opens on 'a day when the sons of God came to present themselves before the Lord, and Satan came also among them. And the Lord said unto Satan, Whence comest thou? *'Where are you from?' This is a question that besets all Black and Brown people in Europe. The question that reminds you that even if you were born here and have never lived anywhere else, you are not from here, you do not belong here. The question that demands that you render up account of yourself, presuming that whoever poses it has a right to know what you – with your dark skin and exotic features – are doing here, on their ancestral lands. The question that erases the fact that we – Black and Brown people – are here because Europeans went there, to that 'dark', 'barbarian', 'primitive' place that we come from.* Then Satan answered the Lord, and said, From going to and fro in the earth, and from walking up and down in it.'[13] After a brief discussion, God gives Satan permission to afflict the righteous and devout Job as a way of testing his faith – admittedly an unfair act. Job's *Klage* ('lament') can therefore be read as an *Anklage* ('accusation') against divine justice: God lets him be afflicted even though he has done nothing wrong.[14]

By suggesting that Kraus files a complaint (*Anklage*) at the Last Judgment, Benjamin however does not liken him to the afflicted Job but to Satan, whose God-given task is to accuse humanity. As Shelley glosses Job in his satirical 'Essay on the Devil, and Devils':

> The Devil is Διάβολος, an Accuser. In this character he presented himself among the other Sons of God before his Father's throne to request to be allowed to tempt Job by tormenting him so that God might damn him. . . . In this view he [the Devil] is at once the informer, the attorney general, and the jailor of the celestial tribunal. It is not good policy, or at least cannot be considered as constitutional practice, to unite these characters. The Devil must have a great interest to exert himself to procure a sentence of guilty from the judge; for I suppose there will be no jury at the resurrection – at least if there is it will be so overawed by the bench, and the counsel for the Crown as to ensure whatever verdict the court shall please to recommend.[15]

The Hebrew *Satan*, the Greek Διάβολος, the German *Ankläger* and the English *Accuser* all translate into one another – a name defined by Satan's role in the administration of divine justice. Rather than being God's adversary, he is his emissary.

Benjamin reads *Die Fackel* as a secular equivalent to God's celestial court where Kraus as Satanic *Ankläger* appears to indict the language of man. Or more precisely, the language of modern man manifested in the newspaper – hypocritical, vapid and disposable. Rather than expressing anything, this is a language designed to fill an issue to be printed and sold at set times of the day, a language puffed up by empty phrases, a language in which euphemistic platitudes cover political horrors. *But I worry that any attempt to write the suffering of others risks turning into such opportunistic and self-serving platitude. Who am I to veil myself in moral righteousness and talk of slavery? Growing up, one of only a handful of family legends transmitted to me had to do with an ancestor who had hidden in the bushes from slave hunters. I could see their feet through the leaves, feel the vibrations of their feet padding the dry ground, not breathing lest the least sound would betray me. This intrepid ancestor saved the family line from the shame of slavery – a shame that attaches to the victim more than the perpetrator.*

The language of accusation is rendered inoperative in *Prometheus Unbound*. This does not, however, mean that Prometheus retracts his original curse of Jupiter, the reason why he was chained to a rock in the Caucasus. For Shelley, the 'moral interest' of the Promethean myth 'would be annihilated if we could conceive of him as unsaying his high language' – that is, apologising before Jupiter and begging to be released.[16] 'For thine own sake unsay those dreadful words. | When high God grants, he punishes such prayers,' Lucretia warns Cenci when she hears his will.[17] The trope of 'unsaying' connects Cenci's curse of his children and Prometheus' curse of Jupiter *and it also hints at a relation between Shelley's dramas and M. NourbeSe Philip's 'un-telling' of the story of the Zong.*[18] *Like The Cenci, Philip's poem is based on an archival document: a court report detailing the trial that took place after the slave ship captain Luke Collingwood threw 150 Africans overboard to claim insurance for lost 'cargo', but the insurers refused to pay up. Not on account of the wanton mass murder, but because the insured goods had been wilfully destroyed. The story is too horrible for telling, yet it must be told. So Philip takes the words of the court report – the sole witnesses to the event – and breaks them down: sentence by sentence, syllable by syllable, letting the resulting fragments of language flow over her pages before finally sinking into their depths. In the process, Philip offers new names to the murdered whose names have been lost, forgotten by history, an act of spectral naming that underwrites the bottom margins of her pages.* But, of course, Cenci does not unsay his high language – instead he compels his children to kill him in revenge.

Contrast this to Prometheus, who already in his opening monologue discovers a way of annulling his curse without unsaying his language: 'I speak in grief, | Not exultation, for I hate no more | As then, ere misery made me wise. The curse | Once breathed on thee I would recall.'[19] Carol Jacobs has unpacked the triple sense of 'recall' at stake in this scene. Prometheus has to remember, repeat and revoke the words he spoke:

> For *recall* . . . suggests a calling back to memory and even more a general summoning back, a restoration, a making present once again. How to reconcile this with its sense as revoking or annulling the purport of a text – and this again with its sense as 're-call,' to call again, a second time?[20]

Shelley's drama suspends the three meanings of the word 'recall', capturing the word in a state of not being one. *Similar to Zong!, this is an attempt to release language from the violent history that this language has made possible.* Prometheus does not, in fact, speak his curse again; he makes it present by summoning the Phantasm of Jupiter, his adversary. As the Phantasm appears, the curse is displaced onto its figure: 'I see the curse on gestures proud and cold, | And looks of firm defiance, and calm hate, | And such despair as mocks itself with smiles, | Written as on a scroll', Prometheus says as he faces the Phantasm.[21] While the Phantasm does speak the curse, words are no longer necessary because the

Phantasm itself embodies the identity of Prometheus' violent words and Jupiter's violent reign. This displacement allows Prometheus to abnegate his curse without the need of saying, or calling, it again. In this sense, the Promethean recall is a renunciation not only of spoken language but also of memory – even as he sees his curse, Prometheus does not, in fact, recall (remember) it. 'Were these my words, O Parent?' is his first response to hearing the curse.[22]

With Benjamin's adaptation of the Prometheus legend in mind, one can say that Shelley's Prometheus renounces precisely his Promethean violence: he no longer seeks to rebel against Jupiter, but to forgive him. 'It doth repent me: words are quick and vain,' Prometheus says after seeing and hearing the phantom; 'I wish no living thing to suffer pain.'[23] The force of Promethean forgiveness is stronger than all Jupiter's violence, and it is the recall of the curse that sets in motion the chain of events leading to Jupiter's overthrow and the new millennium of Act IV. *This is the scale of forgiveness demanded of the descendants of the enslaved and the colonised, yet the demand can only be met in the moment when racial justice is realised. In other words: in a future that for now remains a utopian wish only.* Alexander Freer has noted that Promethean forgiveness also places a demand on us, Shelley's belated readers, to forgive him. Forgive Shelley for not being better than his time. In the 'Defence', Shelley stated that 'a poet considers the vices of his contemporaries as a temporary dress in which his creations must be arrayed', which is of course also true of his own work.[24] *These vices are never more apparent than when Shelley addresses the question of slavery; for instance, his assertion that the 'abolition of personal slavery is the basis of the highest political hope that it can enter into the mind of man to conceive' is not a call for an end to racialised chattel slavery in his present – on the contrary, it is part of a retrospective celebration of how modern Europeans have overcome the vices of the Ancient Greeks.*[25] *In Shelley's historiography, the 'abolition of personal and domestic slavery, and the emancipation of women from a great part of the degrading restraints of antiquity' are both attributed to the progress of poetry, signs of how the present is superior to the past.*[26]

The rub is that 'personal and domestic slavery' were not abolished in Shelley's lifetime. While the British Parliament outlawed the slave trade in 1807, slavery itself remained legal until 1833 – and the intervening years were riven by debates between abolitionists and the pro-slavery 'West India Interest'.[27] *Shelley directly encountered these questions when he witnessed the will of his fellow-author and Caribbean plantation owner Matthew 'Monk' Lewis, in which Lewis freed his slaves – but only on his death. There is no doubt that Shelley was aware of the existence of chattel slavery, but he completely disregarded it in his construction of literary history, according to which poetry had produced the abolition of slavery by the time of the Provençal troubadours. In this gesture, he effectively writes Black people in the British Empire out of history.* In Freer's words, our forgiveness manifests itself in 'a mournful but resolute kind of critical reading, tracing the graceful motions that exist alongside, but remain inseparable from, barbarity.'[28] The beauty of poetry is not a consolation for the horrors of history, not a veil covering them up, but a light that emerges even out of 'the greenest black'.[29] In elucidating these specks of light, criticism must neither forget nor be choked by the surrounding darkness.

The Promethean recall is a particular kind of citation. The word is derived from the Latin *citāre*, which the *Oxford English Dictionary* defines as 'to move, to excite, to summon, to quote (an author or text)'. This means that, aside from lending authority to a critical interpretation, the act of citation has a juridical undertone, heard in its first listed meaning: 'To summon formally to appear, either as a principal or a witness, in a court of law, or to attend some comparable judicial or quasi-judicial hearing.'[30] In a literary or critical text, past words are cited so that we may pass judgment on them in the present. But, for the same reason that we cannot step into the same river twice, words spoken in the past and recalled in the present are never quite the same words. The passage of time has rent them in two. The cited phrase is therefore internally fractured by the temporal lapse between the original *Zusammenhang* ('context') in which it first appeared and the *Zusammenhang* in which it is cited.

Benjamin places this temporal fracture at the heart of his historiographical method: 'To write history thus means to *cite* history. It belongs to the concept of citation, however, that the historical object in each case is torn from its context [*Zusammenhang*].'[31] As Ian Balfour explains, 'It is not just that our knowledge of history is mediated by reading and citation: it is *structured* as they are, as the encounter of a determinate present with a determinate past'; in this way, Benjamin orients our 'attention to the temporality of the relation separating the moment of the text from the moment of reading'.[32] The way in which a citation brings the past into the present inspired Benjamin's famous conception of the 'dialectical image': 'It's not that what is past casts its light on what is present, or what is present its light on what is past; rather, image is that wherein what has been comes together in a flash with the now to form a constellation.'[33] The dialectical image or constellation is inherently discontinuous – a moment torn from the past is cited in what

Benjamin terms the *Jetzt der Erkennbarkeit* ('now of recognizability') in which it becomes legible for its future present.

Take my citations from Shelley's dramas, for example: historical to us, they are themselves citations of historical texts already at their moment of composition: *The Cenci* is inspired by a manuscript 'copied from the archives of the Cenci Palace at Rome',[34] while *Prometheus Unbound* is a kind of adaptation of Aeschylus' lost *Prometheus Unbound*. The relation between Shelley's texts and their historical precedents can be understood through Tom Phillips's reading of Shelley's 'Hymn to Mercury' and the classical allusions in his 'Ode to Liberty':

> both translation and allusion disclose morally and intellectually significant aspects of ancient texts that are only subject to recognition by being situated as antecedents of the particular futurity that Shelley's own poetry realizes. Such dialogues respond to the anachronistically unstable nature of translation and literary history by linking his own age to antiquity and by allowing the ancient world to be understood as harbouring potentialities that render it untimely in relation to itself.[35]

In other words: latent potentialities in the original work only become recognisable within the translation, allusion or citation. These new works participate in the original work's afterlife as 'particles of its divided being', to borrow a phrase from *The Cenci*. This does not presuppose a linear process through which the past unfolds into the present – it is not simply a question of finding that place in, say, the surviving fragments of Aeschylus' *Prometheus* trilogy where a process was set in motion that, automatically as it were, led to Shelley's *Prometheus Unbound*. Rather, past and present are co-constitutive: the original work is altered by each new addition to its afterlife – so Shelley's reworking of Aeschylus generates elements within the ancient text that speak to the concerns of the historical moment in which he is writing, *and I identify elements in* The Cenci *and Benjamin's thought on tragedy that speak to the concerns of my own historical moment even if these elements were not yet imagined at the time of composition.*

In the Preface to *Prometheus Unbound*, Shelley is direct about the fact that he has not 'attempted to restore the lost drama of Aeschylus' because of his aversion to 'a catastrophe so feeble as that of reconciling the Champion with the Oppressor of mankind'.[36] Whereas in the myth, Prometheus recants and apologises to Zeus, Shelley's Prometheus recalls his curse without unsaying his language. In this way, Shelley's *Prometheus*

Unbound marks a moment in which the mythic conflict between man and divine authority manifested in Aeschylus' dramas attains a new legibility for a generation born during the French Revolution and believing itself to be on the brink of a new revolution. That revolution did not come. But while the fears and hopes of Shelley's historical moment have passed into history, his works continue to disclose potentialities that unfold in our present of citing them.

Whereas Hölderlin and Mallarmé offered Benjamin an ideal of translation, Kraus represents the paradigm of citation: 'From within the linguistic sphere of the name, and only from within it, can we discern Kraus's basic polemical procedure: citation. To cite a word is to call it by its name.'[37] To call a word by its name is to recall its origin in the divine λόγος, and thus to perform an act of at-one-ment that is at once poetical and political. This is how citation, and what Benjamin calls citability (*Zitierbarkeit*), slots into his linguistic schema, according to which language is fallen, words internally divided from their origin in the Name. In the (Krausian) citation, Benjamin argues, the recalled Name appears 'sonorously, congruously, in the structure of a new text. As rhyme it gathers the similar into its aura; as name, it stands alone and expressionless.'[38] As sonic repetition, rhyme marks the similarity between how words sound; as verbal repetition, citation marks the conceptual resonance between passages of text, even when the sound or the citation have been torn from their original contexts.

Benjamin's metaphor of 'the linguistic sphere of the name' also recalls the *musica universalis* that informed his interpretation of Platonic Ideas (which he also related to the Adamic language of Names). In other words, Benjamin's reading of Kraus is marked by his prior reading of the *Symposium*; Kraus's praxis, according to Benjamin, partakes in the philosopher's ἔρως-driven ascent from sensuous experience to disembodied ideals.

> Language has never been more perfectly distinguished from spirit, never more intimately bound to eros, than by Kraus in the observation, 'The more closely you look at a word, the more distantly it looks back.' This is a Platonic love of language. The only closeness from which the word cannot escape, however, is the rhyme. So the primal erotic relationship between nearness and distance is, in his language, given voice as rhyme and name.[39]

To illustrate how Kraus generates simultaneous nearness and distance (a phenomenon that Benjamin elsewhere discusses under the heading of 'aura'), Benjamin cites the 2 August 1916 issue of *Die Fackel* in which Kraus includes a short notice from 'our Brussels correspondent'.[40] The correspondent relates of a Belgian soldier who stood guard one night. While the heavy shelling shook the ground beneath his feet, all night long he heard a nightingale singing, unmindful of the warfare all around. To this report, Kraus appends a line from Shakespeare's *Romeo and Juliet*. It is taken from a scene set at the break of dawn when Juliet tries to convince Romeo to stay a bit longer:

> Wilt thou be gone? it is not yet near day:
> It was the nightingale, and not the lark,
> That pierced the fearful hollow of thine ear;
> Nightly she sings on yon pomegranate-tree:
> Believe me, love, it was the nightingale.[41]

By tearing Juliet's words from their original context in a tragic love drama and placing them in the real-life context of the Western Front, the citation undergoes a transformation comparable to what happens to one of Duchamp's 'readymades': the words may be identical, but nonetheless they do 'differ from each other by an infra-thin value of separation'.[42] Benjamin is particularly taken by the slight adjustment that Kraus makes to the found citation:

> He transports it to his own sphere, and the empty phrase is suddenly forced to recognize that even in the deepest dregs of the journals it is not safe from the voice that swoops on the wings of the word to drag it from its darkness. How wonderful if this voice approaches not to punish but to save, as it does on the Shakespearean wings of the lines in which, before the town of Arras, someone sends word home of how in the early morning, on the last blasted tree beside the fortifications, a lark began to sing. A single line, and not even one of his, is enough to enable Kraus to descend, as saviour, into this inferno, and insert a single italicization [*Sperrung*]: 'It was a nightingale and not a lark which sat there on the pome*granate* tree and sang.'[43]

As the editorial note informs us: '*Granat* means "pomegranate"; *Granate*, "grenade" or "shell."'[44] Kraus's added emphasis brings out a shell not previously present in Shakespeare's pomegranate tree. However, the word *Sperrung*, which Edmund Jephcott translates as 'italicization', in

FORGIVENESS   137

fact means something else – in line with German orthography at the time, Kraus does not use italics for emphasis, but spacing: 'G r a n a t baum'.[45] The word is visually fragmented. By splitting it up from within, Kraus highlights its two separate meanings. Benjamin enthusiastically greets this ploy as a special kind of synthesis between name and rhyme. 'It summons the word by its name, wrenches it destructively from its context [*Zusammenhang*], but precisely thereby calls it back to its origin.'[46] An origin that seems to confirm the hypothesis that the biblical tree of knowledge was a pomegranate.

Kraus wrenches the *Granate*-shell from Shakespeare, Benjamin from Kraus, and I, in my turn, from Benjamin: in this citation, I call the name of Shelley, and at the same time recall that originary moment in classical legend when Hermes fashions a shell into a lyre and invents lyric poetry. To relate the Homeric shell to a *Granate* is to emphasise the violence that underlies the lyric art: 'I know you will sing sweetly when you're dead,' Shelley's Mercury gleefully croaks to the tortoise whom he's about to kill so as to fashion a lyre from its shell.[47] Similarly, the violence in which the historical Cenci family were mired forms the basis of Shelley's drama, *while the violence of European colonial history interrupts, and in so doing adds nuance to, my critical reading.* Kraus's *Granate*-shell is deliberately placed here, at the end of the book, to counterbalance the lyric shell in its opening; 'motifs of the same type balance each other, stabilizing each other at a distance', to once more evoke Mallarmé's words.[48] *But the very final shell in my mosaic is a* fotuto, *a 'flute-like device made from a conch shell' and associated with maroons, that is, communities of escaped slaves in the Caribbean.*[49] *It was blown during festivities or to warn of approaching danger. In other words, the music of the* fotuto *shell sounds a note of freedom resonant with the 'mighty music' loosened from the 'many-folded shell' blown by The Spirit of the Earth in the final act of* Prometheus Unbound *which I discussed at the outset. Citing this image again at the close of the book, I want to suggest that the music of the shell, which is to say poetry, celebrates a recall of mythic violence: at once remembering and revoking past wrongs, though not yet, not quite, amounting to justice.*

Notes

1 Preface to *Prometheus Unbound*, *PS2*, p. 472.
2 Preface to *The Cenci*, *PS2*, p. 731.
3 'Critique of Violence', *SW1*, p. 248; *GS2*, p. 197.

4 'Critique of Violence', *SW1*, p. 248; *GS2*, p. 197.
5 'Critique of Violence', *SW1*, p. 248; *GS2*, p. 197.
6 'Essay on the Devil and Devils', *Prose*, p. 267.
7 'Goethe's *Elective Affinities*', *SW1*, p. 326; *GS1*, p. 162.
8 *Origin*, p. 109, translation emended; *GS1*, p. 288.
9 'Karl Kraus', *SW2*, p. 441; *GS2*, p. 345.
10 'Monument to a Warrior', in *One-Way Street*, *SW1*, p. 469; *GS4*, p. 121.
11 'Karl Kraus', *SW2*, p. 435, translation emended; *GS2*, p. 337.
12 'Karl Kraus', *SW2*, p. 443; *GS2*, p. 349.
13 Job 1:6–7.
14 This aspect is emphasised in the translation and commentary on Job that Gershom Scholem was working on between August 1918 and August 1919, a period that he spent with Benjamin in Switzerland. See Gershom Scholem, *Tagebücher nebst Aufsätzen und Entwürfen bis 1923*, ed. by Karlfried Gründer, Herbert Kopp-Oberstebrink and Friedrich Niewöhner, 2 vols (Frankfurt am Main: Jüdischer Verlag, 2000), II, pp. 315–91.
15 'Essay on the Devil and Devils', *Prose*, pp. 268–9.
16 Preface to *Prometheus Unbound*, *PS2*, p. 472.
17 *The Cenci*, IV.i.137–8.
18 Philip, *Zong!*, p. 199.
19 *Prometheus Unbound*, I.56–9.
20 Carol Jacobs, *Uncontainable Romanticism: Shelley, Brontë, Kleist* (Baltimore, MD: Johns Hopkins University Press, 1989), p. 25.
21 *Prometheus Unbound*, I.258–61.
22 *Prometheus Unbound*, I.302.
23 *Prometheus Unbound*, I.303, l.305.
24 'A Defence of Poetry', *SPP*, p. 516.
25 'A Defence of Poetry', *SPP*, p. 525.
26 'A Defence of Poetry', *SPP*, p. 525.
27 See Michael Taylor, *The Interest: How the British Establishment Resisted the Abolition of Slavery* (London: Vintage, 2021).
28 Alexander Freer, 'Unbinding Forgiveness: *Prometheus Unbound*', *European Romantic Review*, 33.5 (2022), 697–711 (p. 708).
29 The phrase is Benjamin's depiction of Grünewald's halos in 'Socrates', *EW*, p. 234; *GS2*, p. 130.
30 *OED*, cite, *v*., 1.a.
31 [N11, 3], *AP*, p. 476; *GS5*, p. 595.
32 Ian Balfour, 'Reversal, Quotation (Benjamin's History)', *MLN*, 106.3 (1991), 622–47 (p. 636, p. 635).
33 [N2a,3], *AP*, p. 462; *GS5*, p. 576; cited verbatim in [N3,1], *AP*, p. 463; *GS5*, p. 578.
34 Preface to *The Cenci*, *PS2*, p. 727.
35 Phillips, 'Unapprehended Relations', p. 109.
36 Preface to *Prometheus Unbound*, *PS2*, p. 472.
37 'Karl Kraus', *SW2*, p. 453, translation emended; *GS2*, p. 362.
38 'Karl Kraus', *SW2*, p. 454. *GS2*, p. 363.
39 'Karl Kraus', *SW2*, p. 453, translation emended; *GS2*, p. 362.
40 Karl Kraus, 'Es war die Nachtigall und nicht die Lerche', *Die Fackel*, 2 August 1916, p. 24 , my translation.
41 William Shakespeare, *Romeo and Juliet*, III.v.2098–102.
42 Duchamp, 'Inframince', p. 290; cited in Malt, 'The Space-Time of the Surrealist Object', p. 92.
43 'Karl Kraus', *SW2*, pp. 453–4; *GS2*, p. 363.
44 'Karl Kraus', *SW2*, p. 458, n. 12.
45 Kraus, 'Es war die Nachtigall und nicht die Lerche', p. 24; cited in *GS2*, p. 363.
46 'Karl Kraus', *SW2*, p. 454. *GS2*, p. 363.
47 'Hymn to Mercury', l. 44.
48 Mallarmé, 'Crisis of Verse', pp. 208–9.
49 Theresa Ann Singleton, 'Archaeology of Marronage in the Caribbean Antilles', *Revista do Museu de Arqueologia e Etnologia*, 35 (2020), 1–13 (p. 10).

Coda

Benjamin cites Shelley thrice. In the summer of 1938, when Europe was already sliding off the brink of catastrophe, Benjamin visited his friend Bertolt Brecht, then living in exile in Skovsbostrand outside of Svendborg, a small town in southern Denmark. Benjamin hoped to finish a draft of his book *Charles Baudelaire: A Lyric Poet in the Era of High Capitalism*, while Brecht, together with Margarethe Steffin, was at work on a translation of two poems by Shelley, *The Mask of Anarchy* and *Peter Bell the Third*. Benjamin cites Shelley in Brecht's translation and by and large in line with Brecht's interpretation.[1] But while Benjamin's assessment of Shelley is enthusiastic, it has less to say about Shelley than about what Baudelaire is *not*. Here is his longest remark in full:

> On the flight of images in allegory. It often cheated Baudelaire out of part of the return on his allegorical imagery. One thing in particular is missing in Baudelaire's employment of allegory. This we can recognize if we call to mind Shelley's great allegory of the city of London: the third part of 'Peter Bell the Third,' in which London is presented to the reader as hell. The incisive effect of this poem depends, for the most part, on the fact that Shelley's *grasp* of allegory makes itself felt. It is this grasp that is missing in Baudelaire. This grasp, which makes palpable the distance of the modern poet from allegory, is precisely

what enables allegory to incorporate into itself the most immediate realities. With what directness this can happen is best shown by Shelley's poem, in which bailiffs, parliamentarians, stock-jobbers, and many other types figure. The allegory, in its emphatically antique character, gives them all a sure footing, such as, for example, the businessmen in Baudelaire's 'Crépuscule du soir' do not have. – Shelley rules over allegory, whereas Baudelaire is ruled by it.[2]

The comparison between Shelley and Baudelaire hinges on the relation between the modern poet and allegory. Shelley's grasp on the form 'makes palpable the distance of the modern poet from allegory', a formulation that recalls the formula that Benjamin cites from Kraus: 'The more closely you look at a word, the more distantly it looks back.' The more closely you grasp allegory, the more distant it appears – and the separation is here a historical one. Grasping allegory has to do with maintaining the right distance between the classical contexts, *Zusammenhänge*, of allegory and the modern contexts, *Zusammenhänge*, of the city. The dynamic resembles that of a citation which becomes the more distant from its original context the more tightly it is woven into a new text.

Calibrating correspondences between past and present is a central concern in Benjamin's interpretation of Baudelaire. 'The modern is a principal accent of his poetry,' he writes. 'But precisely modernity is always citing primal history.'[3] Or, in another formulation: 'And in fact, with Baudelaire, modernity is nothing other than the "newest antiquity."'[4] And furthermore: 'The correspondence between antiquity and modernity is the sole constructive conception of history in Baudelaire. With its rigid armature, it excludes every dialectical conception.'[5] This suggests that Baudelaire cites antiquity in the wrong way. His figures bring the past into the present, but they are not dialectical images. Rather than maintaining the tension arising from the temporal distance that opens up in every citation of old materials, Baudelaire's allegorical gaze turns antiquities into ornamental trinkets. His Paris is a shopping arcade, always open, its commodities winking at you seven days a week. But the dynamic of consumerism means that even just to touch is already to lose interest, to begin desiring the next novelty. Benjamin equates this consumerist drive with the Christian doctrine that eternal punishment must be endlessly varied lest the agonies of damnation become, to borrow a phrase from Shelley, 'blunted by reiteration': 'the torments of hell figure as the latest novelty of all time, as "pains eternal and always new"'.[6] For Baudelaire, the allegorical object cited from antiquity is merely one such novelty, no sooner taken up than discarded.

In *The Origin of German Tragic Drama*, Benjamin had argued that the allegorical gaze petrifies its object. More precisely, it is brooding on objects that turns them to stone: Albrecht Dürer's *Melencolia I* (1514) is the patron saint of Benjaminian allegory, pensively contemplating the scatter of things around her. Importantly, she contemplates without touching, keeping the physical distance even as her thoughts engulf the object. This take on melancholy owes something to the Platonic philosopher, who likewise contemplates Ideas without touching them, even as his mind fully participates in them. Moreover, the intellectual intimacy is enabled by a gradual distancing from the physical: although the love of wisdom is sensuous at first, we only attain to contemplation of Ideas in their purity once we have transcended the senses. Thinking entails forgetting that the body exists. Such forgetting cannot be maintained in the capitalist metropolis where the senses are ever-overwhelmed by new impressions.

'No one ever felt less at home in Paris than Baudelaire,' Benjamin writes, because no one was less prepared to handle this onslaught of sensuous stimuli. Benjamin's Baudelaire has a fundamentally allegorical intention, an intention that comes alive in the asceticism of philosophical contemplation, which ponders the object without touching it. This intention is everywhere undercut by the city crowding in on the poet. Benjamin figures this tumult as a form of erotic violence (*Gewalt*):

> Every intimacy with things is alien to [Baudelaire's] allegorical intention. To touch on things means, for it, to violate [*vergewaltigen*] them. To recognize things means, for it, to see through them. Wherever the allegorical intention prevails, no habits of any kind can be formed. Hardly has a thing been taken up than allegory has dispensed with the situation. Thing and situation become obsolete for allegory more quickly than a new pattern for the milliner.[7]

Shelley does not maintain any physical distance from the city either, but the effect is different. Shelley's intention is not mediative but interventionist; his allegory not classical but political. His focus, accordingly, is less on the things in themselves than on how things are embedded in social relations. Benjamin cites *Peter Bell the Third*, Shelley's parody on the conversion story in Wordsworth's *Peter Bell*. Whereas Wordsworth's Peter Bell finds God, Shelley's goes to Hell, a fate for which he is predestined by both his name and his complexion:

> Thy name is Peter Bell;
> Thy skin is of a brimstone hue;
> Alive or dead – aye, sick or well –
> The one God made to rhyme with hell;
> The other, I think, rhymes with you.[8]

So say Peter's pious friends. It is Shelley's representation of Peter's sojourn in Hell that Benjamin compares to Baudelaire's Paris. (In passing, one may note the similarity between the German words *Hölle*, 'hell', and *Hülle*, 'veil' or 'shell'.) But contrary to Benjamin's gloss 'in which London is presented to the reader as hell', Shelley does not present London as Hell: 'Hell *is* a city just like London.'[9]

The move naturalises the supernatural, and presents hell in 'this world which is', a modern metropolis that is 'Thrusting, toiling, wailing, moiling' with 'German soldiers – camps – confusion – | Tumults – lotteries – rage – delusion – | Gin – suicide – and Methodism'.[10] Commodities and sights are interspersed with various character types: 'Lawyers – judges – old hobnobbers | Are there – Bailiffs – Chancellors – | Bishops – great and little robbers – | Rhymesters – pamphleteers – stock-jobbers', who all meet and mingle

> At conversazioni – balls –
>   Conventicles and drawing-rooms –
> Courts of law – committees – calls
> Of a morning – clubs – book stalls –
>   Churches – masquerades and tombs.
>
> And this is Hell – and in this smother
>   All are damnable and damned;
> Each one damning, damns the other;
> They are damned by one another,
>   By none other are they damned.[11]

Damned, and too busy to even notice that they are damned. Syntax breaks down in the sheer profusion of things, what Eric Lindstrom has called the poem's 'farrago style',[12] so that the metric beat becomes the only thing that holds together the capitalist phantasmagoria of Hell. This whirlwind is what allows Shelley to make the distance from allegory felt: it is the accelerated banality of everyday life in the early capitalist metropolis that is Hell and that distinguishes it from the ordered rhythms of classical allegory.

The treatment of the urban masses is, for Benjamin, the main difference between Shelley and Baudelaire: 'It is rare in French poetry that the big city is evoked through nothing but the immediate presentation of its inhabitants. This occurs with unsurpassable power in Shelley's poem on London,' he writes in the Baudelaire convolute of *The Arcades Project*.[13] He develops this point further in 'The Paris of the Second Empire in Baudelaire', while discussing the poet's handling of the Parisian crowds:

> The deepest fascination of this spectacle lay in the fact that, even as it intoxicated him [Baudelaire], it did not blind him to the horrible social reality. He remained conscious of it, though only in the way in which intoxicated people are 'still' conscious of reality. This is why in Baudelaire the big city almost never finds its expression through a direct presentation of its inhabitants. The directness and harshness with which Shelley captured London through the depiction of its people could not benefit Baudelaire's Paris.[14]

This is followed by a citation of the first five lines of *Peter Bell the Third*'s 'Hell', after which Benjamin adds: 'For the flaneur [Baudelaire], there is a veil over this picture. The veil is formed by the masses.'[15] In contrast, Shelley's poem fixes its gaze on the masses, and in this gesture lifts the veil on 'the horrible social reality' of the city he describes even as it simultaneously casts the veil of its own measured language over that same reality. Veiling and unveiling. Now you see it, now you don't.

Notes

1 I discuss this episode in 'Allegorical Realism: Bertolt Brecht and Walter Benjamin's Reading of Percy Bysshe Shelley's Political Verse', in *The Politics of Romanticism*, ed. by Pascal Fischer and Christoph Hauswitschka (Trier: Wissenschaftlicher Verlag, 2019), pp. 171–84. See also Robert Kaufman, 'Legislators of the Post-Everything World: Shelley's *Defence* of Adorno', *ELH*, 63.3 (1996), 707–33.
2 [J81,6], *AP*, p. 370; *GS5*, p. 468.
3 'Exposé of 1935', *AP*, p. 10; *GS5*, p. 55.
4 [J59a,4], *AP*, p. 336; *GS5*, p. 423.
5 [J59a,5], *AP*, p. 336; *GS5*, p. 423.
6 'On Life', *SPP*, p. 508; 'Exposé of 1939', *AP*, p. 26; *GS5*, p. 77.
7 [J59a,4], *AP*, p. 336; *GS5*, p. 423.
8 *Peter Bell the Third*, ll. 21–5.
9 *Peter Bell the Third*, l. 147; emphasis added.
10 *Peter Bell the Third*, l. 196, ll. 174–6.
11 *Peter Bell the Third*, ll. 187–90, ll. 212–21.
12 Eric Lindstrom, '"To Wordsworth" and the "White Obi": Slavery, Determination, and Contingency in Shelley's Peter Bell the Third"', *Studies in Romanticism*, 47.4 (2008), 549–80 (p. 559).
13 [J69,2], *AP*, p. 351; *GS5*, p. 443.
14 'The Paris of the Second Empire in Baudelaire', *SW4*, p. 34; *GS1*, p. 562.
15 'The Paris of the Second Empire in Baudelaire', *SW4*, p. 34; *GS1*, p. 562.

Bibliography

Abrams, M. H., 'The Correspondent Breeze: A Romantic Metaphor', in *English Romantic Poets: Modern Essays in Criticism*, 2nd edn (London: Oxford University Press, 1975), pp. 37–54
Agamben, Giorgio, *The Fire and the Tale*, trans. by Lorenzo Chiesa (Stanford, CA: Stanford University Press, 2014)
An, Young-Ok, 'Beatrice's Gaze Revisited: Anatomizing "The Cenci"', *Criticism*, 38 (1996), 27–68
Anon., *Homeric Hymns, Homeric Apocrypha, Lives of Homer*, ed. and trans. by Martin L. West (Cambridge, MA: Harvard University Press, 2003)
Arendt, Hannah, 'Introduction: Walter Benjamin: 1892–1940', in *Illuminations*, ed. by Hannah Arendt, trans. by Harry Zohn (London: Jonathan Cape, 1970 [1968]), pp. 1–51
Azoulay, Ariella Aïsha, *Potential History: Unlearning Imperialism* (London: Verso, 2019)
Balfour, Ian, 'Reversal, Quotation (Benjamin's History)', *MLN*, 106.3 (1991), 622–47
Bari, Shahidha K., *Keats and Philosophy: The Life of Sensations* (New York, NY: Routledge, 2012)
Beaumont, Matthew, 'Imagining the End Times: Ideology, the Contemporary Disaster Movie, Contagion', in *Žižek and Media Studies*, ed. by Matthew Flisfeder and Louis-Paul Willis (New York, NY: Palgrave Macmillan, 2014), pp. 79–89
Benjamin, Walter, *The Arcades Project*, ed. by Howard Eiland and Kevin McLaughlin (Cambridge, MA: Harvard University Press, 2002)
Benjamin, Walter, *Briefe*, ed. by Gershom Scholem and Theodor W. Adorno, 2 vols (Frankfurt am Main: Suhrkamp, 1966)
Benjamin, Walter, *The Correspondence of Walter Benjamin: 1910–1940*, ed. by Gershom Scholem and Theodor W. Adorno, trans. by Manfred R. Jacobson and Evelyn M. Jacobson (Chicago, IL: University of Chicago Press, 1994)
Benjamin, Walter, *Early Writings: 1910–1917*, trans. by Howard Eiland and others (Cambridge, MA: Harvard University Press, 2011)
Benjamin, Walter, *Gesammelte Schriften*, ed. by Rolf Tiedemann and Hermann Schweppenhäuser, 7 vols (Frankfurt am Main: Suhrkamp, 1972–1999)
Benjamin, Walter, *The Origin of German Tragic Drama*, trans. by John Osborne (London: Verso, 2009)
Benjamin, Walter, *Selected Writings*, ed. by Marcus Bullock and Michael W. Jennings, 4 vols (Cambridge, MA: Harvard University Press, 1996–2003)
Brigham, Linda C., 'Count Cenci's Abysmal Credit', *Texas Studies in Literature and Language*, 38 (1996), 340–58
Bullock, Marcus, *Romanticism and Marxism: The Philosophical Development of Literary Theory and Literary History in Walter Benjamin and Friedrich Schlegel* (New York, NY: Peter Lang, 1987)
Butter, Peter, *Shelley's Idols of the Cave* (Edinburgh: Edinburgh University Press, 1954)
Cadava, Eduardo, *Words of Light: Theses on the Photography of History* (Princeton, NJ: Princeton University Press, 1997)

Carson, Anne, *Economy of the Unlost: Reading Simonides of Keos with Paul Celan* (Princeton, NJ: Princeton University Press, 1999)

Chandler, James, *England in 1819: The Politics of Literary Culture and the Case of Romantic Historicism* (Chicago, IL: University of Chicago Press, 1998)

Curran, Stuart, *Shelley's Cenci: Scorpions Ringed with Fire* (Princeton, NJ: Princeton University Press, 1970)

de Man, Paul, '"Conclusions" on Walter Benjamin's "The Task of the Translator": Messenger Lecture, Cornell University, March 4, 1983', *Yale French Studies*, 97 (2000), 10–35

de Man, Paul, 'Shelley Disfigured', in *The Rhetoric of Romanticism* (New York, NY: Columbia University Press, 1984), pp. 93–123

de Man, Paul, 'Shelleys Entstellung', in *Die Ideologie des Ästhetischen*, ed. by Christoph Menke, trans. by Jürgen Blasius (Frankfurt am Main: Suhrkamp, 1993), pp. 147–82

Derrida, Jacques, 'Des Tours de Babel', in *Difference in Translation*, ed. and trans. by Joseph F. Graham (Ithaca, NY: Cornell University Press, 1985), pp. 165–207

Derrida, Jacques, 'Force of Law', in *Acts of Religion*, ed. by Gil Anidjar, trans. by Mary Quaintance (London: Routledge, 2002), pp. 230–98

Derrida, Jacques, 'Living On: Border Lines', in *Deconstruction and Criticism*, ed. by Harold Bloom and others, trans. by James Hulbert (London: Routledge & Kegan Paul, 1979), pp. 75–176

Derrida, Jacques, '"Le Parjure," Perhaps: Storytelling and Lying ("abrupt breaches of syntax")', *Acts of Narrative*, ed. by Carol Jacobs and Henry Sussman (Stanford, CA: Stanford University Press, 2003), pp. 195–234

Donahue, Luke, 'Romantic Survival and Shelley's "Ode to the West Wind"', *European Romantic Review*, 25.2 (2014), 219–42

Farnell, Gary, 'Rereading Shelley', *ELH*, 60 (1993), 625–50

Fenves, Peter, *'Chatter': Language and History in Kierkegaard* (Stanford, CA: Stanford University Press, 1993)

Fraser, Jennifer, 'Intertextual Turnarounds: Joyce's Use of the Homeric "Hymn to Hermes"', *James Joyce Quarterly*, 36 (1999), 541–57

Freer, Alexander, 'Unbinding Forgiveness: *Prometheus Unbound*', *European Romantic Review*, 33.5 (2022), 697–711

Getsy, David J., *Body Doubles: Sculpture in Britain, 1877–1905* (New Haven, CT: Yale University Press, 2004)

Gines, Kathryn T., *Hannah Arendt and the Negro Question* (Bloomington, IN: Indiana University Press, 2014)

Grabo, Carl, *A Newton Among Poets: Shelley's Use of Science in* Prometheus Unbound (Chapel Hill, NC: University of North Carolina Press, 1930)

Hamacher, Werner, '"Lectio": de Man's Imperative', in *Premises: Essays on Philosophy and Literature from Kant to Celan*, trans. by Peter Fenves (Cambridge, MA: Harvard University Press, 1996), pp. 181–221

Hamacher, Werner, 'The Word *Wolke* – If It Is One', in *Benjamin's Ground: New Readings of Walter Benjamin*, ed. by Rainer Nägele, trans. by Peter Fenves (Detroit, MI: Wayne State University Press, 1986), pp. 147–75

Hamilton, Paul, 'Poetics', in *The Oxford Handbook of Percy Bysshe Shelley*, ed. by Michael O'Neill and Anthony Howe (Oxford: Oxford University Press, 2012), pp. 177–92

Hartman, Geoffrey, *Saving the Text: Literature/Derrida/Philosophy* (Baltimore, MD: Johns Hopkins University Press, 1981)

Hartman, Saidiya V., *Lose Your Mother: A Journey Along the Atlantic Slave Route* (New York, NY: Farrar, Straus and Giroux, 2007)

Hill, Geoffrey, 'Poetry as "Menace" and "Atonement"', in *Poetry in Theory: An Anthology 1900–2000*, ed. by Jon Cook (Malden, MA: Blackwell Publishing, 2004), pp. 464–73

hooks, bell, 'Choosing the Margin as a Space of Radical Openness', *Framework: The Journal of Cinema and Media*, 36 (1989), 15–23

Hörisch, Jochen, *Kopf oder Zahl: Die Poesie des Geldes* (Frankfurt am Main: Suhrkamp, 1996)

Hörisch, Jochen, 'Der Satanische Engel und das Glück – Die Namen Walter Benjamins', *Spuren – Zeitschrift für Kunst und Gesellschaft* (1986), 38–42

Howard, Luke, *On the Modifications of Clouds* (London: J. Taylor, 1803 [repr. 1969])

Hunt, Leigh, *The Autobiography of Leigh Hunt*, ed. by J. E. Morpurgo (London: Cresset Press, 1949)

Jacobs, Carol, 'The Monstrosity of Translation', *MLN*, 90 (1975), 755–66

Jacobs, Carol, *Uncontainable Romanticism: Shelley, Brontë, Kleist* (Baltimore, MD: Johns Hopkins University Press, 1989)
Jacobus, Mary, *Romantic Things: A Tree, A Rock, A Cloud* (Chicago, IL: University of Chicago Press, 2012)
Kabitoglou, E. Douka, *Plato and the English Romantics* (London: Routledge, 1990)
Kahan, Claudine T., 'Shelley's "Hymn to Mercury": Poetic Praxis and the Creation of Value', *Studies in Romanticism*, 31 (1992), 147–69
Keats, John, *John Keats: The Complete Poems*, ed. by John Barnard, 2nd edn (Harmondsworth, Middlesex: Penguin Books, 1976)
Knight, G. Wilson, *The Starlit Dome: Studies in the Poetry of Vision* (London: Methuen and Co. 1968)
Kohler, Michael, 'Shelley in Chancery: The Reimagination of the Paternalist State in "The Cenci"', *Studies in Romanticism*, 37.4 (1998), 545–89
Kraus, Karl, 'Es war die Nachtigall und nicht die Lerche', in *Die Fackel*, 2 August 1916 (Vol. 18, No. 431-436), 24
Lindstrom, Eric, '"To Wordsworth" and the "White Obi": Slavery, Determination, and Contingency in Shelley's "Peter Bell the Third"', *Studies in Romanticism*, 47.4 (2008), 549–80
Lorde, Audre, *Your Silence Will Not Protect You* (London: Silver Press, 2017)
Mallarmé, Stéphane, 'Crisis of Verse', in *Divagations*, trans. by Barbara Johnson (Cambridge, MA: Harvard University Press, 2007), pp. 201–11
Malt, Johanna, 'The Space-Time of the Surrealist Object', in *Thinking Through Relation: Encounters in Creative Critical Writing*, ed. by Florian Mussgnug, Mathelinda Nabugodi and Thea Petrou (Oxford: Peter Lang, 2021), pp. 85–96
Marx, Karl, *Selected Writings*, ed. by David McLellan, 2nd edn (Oxford: Oxford University Press, 2000)
Mbembe, Achille, *Necropolitics*, trans. by Steven Corcoran (Durham, NC: Duke University Press, 2019)
McFarland, James, 'Sailing by the Stars: Constellations in the Space of Thought', *MLN*, 126 (2011), 471–85
McNulty, Tracy, 'The Commandment against the Law: Writing and Divine Justice in Walter Benjamin's "Critique of Violence"', *Diacritics*, 37 (2007), 34–60
Menninghaus, Winifred, 'Walter Benjamin's Exposition of the Romantic Theory of Reflection', in *Walter Benjamin and Romanticism*, ed. by Andrew Benjamin and Beatrice Hanssen (London: Continuum, 2002), pp. 19–50
Miller, J. Hillis, 'The Critic as Host', in *Deconstruction and Criticism*, ed. by Harold Bloom and others (London: Routledge & Kegan Paul, 1979), pp. 217–53
Mitchell, Robert, *Sympathy and the State in the Romantic Era: Systems, State Finance, and the Shadows of Futurity* (New York, NY: Routledge, 2007)
Morgan, Jennifer L., *Reckoning with Slavery: Gender, Kinship, and Capitalism in the Early Black Atlantic* (Durham, NC: Duke University Press, 2021)
Nabugodi, Mathelinda, 'Allegorical Realism: Bertolt Brecht and Walter Benjamin's Reading of Percy Bysshe Shelley's Political Verse', in *The Politics of Romanticism*, ed. by Pascal Fischer and Christoph Hauswitschka (Trier: Wissenschaftlicher Verlag, 2019), pp. 171–84
Nägele, Rainer, 'Echolalie', in *Übersetzen: Walter Benjamin*, ed. by Christiaan L. Hart Nibbrig (Frankfurt am Main: Suhrkamp, 2001), pp. 17–37
Neely McLane, Lucy, 'Sound Values in "The Cloud"', *The English Journal*, 22 (1933), 412–14
Newsome, David, *Two Classes of Men: Platonism and English Romantic Thought* (London: John Murray, 1974)
O'Neill, Michael, 'Emulating Plato: Shelley as Translator and Prose Poet', in *Shelleyan Reimaginings and Influence: New Relations* (Oxford: Oxford University Press, 2019), pp. 28–44
Phelan, Anthony, '*Fortgang* und *Zusammenhang*: Walter Benjamin and the Romantic Novel', in *Walter Benjamin and Romanticism*, ed. by Andrew Benjamin and Beatrice Hanssen (London: Continuum, 2002), pp. 69–82
Philip, M. NourbeSe, *Zong! As told to the author by Satey Adamu Boateng* (Middletown, CT: Wesleyan University Press, 2008)
Phillips, Tom, 'Unapprehended Relations', *Classical Receptions Journal*, 12.1 (2020), 109–27
Plato, *Plato in Twelve Volumes*, trans. by Harold N. Fowler, 12 vols (Cambridge, MA: Harvard University Press, 1921). Accessed via http://www.perseus.tufts.edu/ [accessed 1 June 2022]

Pulos, C. E., *The Deep Truth: A Study of Shelley's Scepticism* (Lincoln, NE: University of Nebraska Press, 1962)
Quillin, Jessica K., *Shelley and the Musico-Poetics of Romanticism* (Farnham, Surrey: Ashgate Publishing, 2012)
Reiman, Donald H., *Percy Bysshe Shelley: Updated Edition* (Boston, MA: Twayne Publishers, 1990)
Rieger, James, *The Mutiny Within: The Heresies of Percy Bysshe Shelley* (New York, NY: George Braziller, 1967)
Roberts, Hugh, *Shelley and the Chaos of History: A New Politics of Poetry* (University Park, PA: Pennsylvania State University Press, 1997)
Ryder, Robert G., 'Walter Benjamin's Shell-Shock', *New Review of Film and Television Studies*, 5 (2007), 135–55
Schestag, Thomas, 'Lampen', in *Übersetzen: Walter Benjamin*, ed. by Christiaan L. Hart Nibbrig (Frankfurt am Main: Suhrkamp, 2001), pp. 38–79
Schiller, Friedrich, *On the Aesthetic Education of Man in a Series of Letters*, ed. and trans. by Elizabeth M. Wilkinson and L. A. Willoughby (Oxford: Clarendon Press, 1967)
Scholem, Gershom, *Tagebücher nebst Aufsätzen und Entwürfen bis 1923*, ed. by Karlfried Gründer, Herbert Kopp-Oberstebrink and Friedrich Niewöhner, 2 vols (Frankfurt am Main: Jüdischer Verlag, 2000)
Scrivener, Michael, *Radical Shelley: The Philosophical Anarchism and Utopian Thought of Percy Bysshe Shelley* (Princeton, NJ: Princeton University Press, 1982)
Sharpe, Christina, *In the Wake: On Blackness and Being* (Durham, NC: Duke University Press, 2016)
Sheffield, Frisbee C. C., *Plato's Symposium: The Ethics of Desire* (Oxford: Oxford University Press, 2009)
Shelley, Lady Jane (ed.), *Shelley Memorials: From Authentic Sources* (Boston, MA: Ticknor and Fields, 1859)
Shelley, Percy Bysshe, *Essays, Letters from Abroad, Translations and Fragments by Percy Bysshe Shelley*, ed. by Mary Shelley, 2 vols (London: Moxon, 1840)
Shelley, Percy Bysshe, *The Letters of Percy Bysshe Shelley*, ed. by Frederick L. Jones, 2 vols (Oxford: Clarendon Press, 1964)
Shelley, Percy Bysshe, *The Poems of Shelley*, ed. by Jack Donovan, Cian Duffy, Kelvin Everest, Geoffrey Matthews and Michael Rossington, 4 vols to date (Abingdon: Routledge, 1989–)
Shelley, Percy Bysshe, *The Posthumous Poems of Percy Bysshe Shelley*, ed. by Mary Shelley (London: John Hunt, 1824)
Shelley, Percy Bysshe, *Shelley on Love*, ed. by Richard Holmes (London: Anvil Press Poetry, 1980)
Shelley, Percy Bysshe, *Shelley's Poetry and Prose*, ed. by Neil Fraistat and Donald H. Reiman, 2nd edn (New York, NY: W. W. Norton and Co., 2002)
Shelley, Percy Bysshe, *Shelley's Prose; or The Trumpet of a Prophecy*, ed. by David Lee Clark (New York, NY: New Amsterdam, 1988)
Singleton, Theresa Ann, 'Archaeology of Marronage in the Caribbean Antilles', *Revista do Museu de Arqueologia e Etnologia*, 35 (2020), 1–13
Sperry, Stuart, 'The Ethical Politics of Shelley's "The Cenci"', *Studies in Romanticism*, 25 (1986), 411–27
Steiner, Uwe, 'Exemplarische Kritik: Anmerkungen zu Benjamins Kritik der *Wahlverwandtschaften*', in *Benjamins Wahlverwandschaften: zur Kritik einer Programmatischen Interpretation*, ed. by Helmut Hühn, Jan Urblich and Uwe Steiner (Berlin: Suhrkamp, 2015), pp. 37–67
Stoll, Timothy, 'Nietzsche and Schiller on Aesthetic Semblance', *The Monist*, 102 (2019), 331–8
Taylor, Michael, *The Interest: How the British Establishment Resisted the Abolition of Slavery* (London: Vintage, 2021)
Wallace, Jennifer, 'Shelley, Plato and the Political Imagination', in *Plato and the English Imagination*, ed. by Sarah Hutton and Anna Baldwin (Cambridge: Cambridge University Press, 1994), pp. 229–41
Ware, Tracy, 'Shelley's Platonism in A Defence of Poetry', *SEL*, 23.4 (1983), 549–66
Wasserman, Earl J., *Shelley: A Critical Reading* (Baltimore, MD: Johns Hopkins University Press, 1971)
Webb, Timothy, *The Violet in the Crucible: Shelley and Translation* (Oxford: Clarendon Press, 1976)
Weber, Samuel, *Benjamin's -abilities* (Cambridge, MA: Harvard University Press, 2010)
Wilson, Ross, *Shelley and the Apprehension of Life* (Cambridge: Cambridge University Press, 2013)

Wilson, Ross, 'Shelley's Plato', in *The Routledge Handbook of Translation and Philosophy*, ed. by J. Piers Rawling and Philip Wilson (London: Routledge, 2018), pp. 345–57

Winnubst, Shannon, 'The Many Lives of Fungibility: Anti-Blackness in Neoliberal Times', *Journal of Gender Studies*, 29.1 (2020), 101–12

Wohlfarth, Irving, 'Das Medium der Übersetzung', in *Übersetzen: Walter Benjamin,* ed. by Christiaan L. Hart Nibbrig (Frankfurt am Main: Suhrkamp, 2001), pp. 80–130

Woodman, Ross, 'Figuring Disfiguration: Reading Shelley after de Man', *Studies in Romanticism*, 40 (2001), 253–88

Index

Abrams, M. H., 29
Adorno, Theodor, 98
Aeschylus, 84, 135
Afterlife, *see* Death
Agamben, Giorgio, xvi, 4, 8
Aphrodite, 15, 38
Archive, 102, 129, 135
Arendt, Hannah, 2-3, 98
Ariosto, 68
Aristotle, xvi
Atonement, xviii, 107, 116, 118, 124-5
At-one-ment, 117, 121, 136
    See also One
Autoimmunity, 121
Azoulay, Ariella Aïsha, 102
Babel, 33, 107
Barbarism,
    A costume, 92-3
    And civilization, xix
    And criticism, 133-4
    In the figure of Socrates, 82-3
    Of two genders, 88
    Philosophical, 61
    Sound of foreign languages, 55
    Where we came from, 130
Bari, Shahidha, 41
Baudelaire, Charles, 140-4
Belmore, Herbert, 88
Benjamin, Walter,
    'Agesilaus Santander', 14-15
    Berlin Childhood around 1900, 22-23, 34-5, 43-4
    Charles Baudelaire: A Lyric Poet in the Era of High Capitalism, 140
    'Conversation on Love', 82-3
    'Critique of Violence', 16, 104, 111, 128
    'Epistemo-Critical Prologue', *The Origin of German Tragic Drama*, xii, xiv, 28, 54-5, 67-8, 71-2, 74-6
    'Fate and Character', 98-9, 104, 110, 116
    'Goethe's *Elective Affinities*', xii, 15-16, 38, 59-64, 92-3, 99
    'Karl Kraus', 129-30, 136-8
    'Monument to a Warrior', 130

    'On Language as Such and on the Language of Man', 27-30
    On the Concept of History, 97
    'Socrates', 82, 89-90, 97
    'Teaching and Valuation', 83-4
    The Arcades Project, xiii, 134, 140-2, 144
    The Concept of Criticism in Early German Romanticism, 5-6
    'The Meaning of Time in the Moral Universe', 108, 110
    'The Metaphysics of Youth', 88-9
    The Origin of German Tragic Drama, xi, 66, 142
    'The Paris of the Second Empire in Baudelaire', 144
    'The Storyteller', 2, 5
    'The Task of the Translator', 8, 26-7, 30-4, 67, 73
Blasius, Jürgen, 43
Brecht, Bertolt, 140
Brigham, Linda, 105, 112
Bullock, Marcus, 6
Butter, Peter, 14
Byron, George Gordon, Lord, 1, 7
Carson, Anne, xv
Chandler, James, 124
Chatterton, Thomas, 7
Choreography, 79, 103, 117, 121
Cloud,
    As undistinguishable mist, 116-17, 121
    Its likeness to words, 44, 47-9
    Of guilt in tragedy, 98, 116-7
Constellation, xiii-xv, xviii, 32, 72, 134-5
Corngold, Stanley, 63
Curran, Stuart, 120
Dancing,
    Feet of the shape all light, 41
    In the youth of the world, 73
    Karl Kraus before the burial vault of the German language, 130
    Of represented ideas, 75-6
    Of truth in language, 57
    See also Choreography
Dante, 70

De Man, Paul, 3, 26-7, 39-45
De Saussure, Ferdinand, 27
Death,
    And afterlife, 7-8, 90-1, 122, 125
    Beatrice Cenci's sentence, 98, 101-2, 107-8, 112-13
    Benjamin's, 2-3
    Shelley's, 1-4
    Thought trampled into the dust of, 41, 49
Derrida, Jacques, 7-8, 16, 113 n.9
Donahue, Luke, 8
Duchamp, Marcel, 58-9, 137
Dürer, Albrecht, 142
Evelyn-White, H. G., 19
Fall of Language, 30-2, 35, 54, 82, 129
Farnell, Gary, 13
Fenves, Peter, 23
Flow,
    Beautiful (Schönflies), 15, 38
    Etymological root of *eros*, 59
    Of broken language (un-telling), 132
    Of Platonic prose, 75-6
    Of Sapphic speech, 88
Flower,
    Absent from every bouquet, 35
    In a crucible, 26
    Its colour as it fades and changes, 69
Flowery,
    Herbage, 18
    Language, 130
Ford, Edward Onslow, 2
Fournier, Louis Édouard, 2
Fraser, Jennifer, 17
Freer, Alexander, 133-4
Gisborne, John and Maria, 79
Goethe, Johann Wolfgang von, xii
Grabo, Carl, 69
Grünewald, 89
Güntert, Hermann, 55
Hamacher, Werner, 23, 34-5, 44-6
Hamilton, Paul, 3
Hartman, Geoffrey, 13-14, 16, 123
Hartman, Saidiya, 123
Harmony,
    Of a literary work, 117-18
    Of a lyre and a bow, 72-3
    See also Musica universalis
Heinemann, Moritz, 2
Hill, Geoffrey, 117-18
Hölderlin, Friedrich, 34, 73-4, 99, 136
Homeric *Hymn to Hermes*, 13
Shelley's translation of ('Hymn to Mercury'), 17-22, 43
hooks, bell, xvi
Hörisch, Jochen, 15
Howard, Luke, 44, 48
Hunt, Leigh, 23 n.3
Imperative,
    Of literary criticism, 46
    To love, 86
Interruption,
    By what cannot-be-said, 99
    In the composition of 'The Triumph of Life', 4
    In the rhythm of contemplation, 74
Jacobs, Carol, 31, 131
Jacobus, Mary, 47
Kafka, Franz, 97

Kahan, Claudine, 19
Keats, John, xii, 6, 41
Kraus, Karl, 129-31, 136-8, 141
Lacan, Jacques, 13-14
Lewis, Matthew 'Monk', 133
Lindstrom, Eric, 143
Lorde, Audre, 87
Lucan, 7
Mallarmé, Stéphane, 32-35, 43, 68, 74, 135, 138
Margin,
    As a site of resistance, xvi
    At the bottom of the page, 3, 132
Marx, Karl, 106-7, 130
Mbembe, Achille, 118
Measure,
    Deliberate, 18-19
    Contra semantic failure, 32-3, 42-3
    Of eternal music, *see Musica universalis*
    Of knowledge, 28-29
    Of money (fungibility), 105-7
    Of thought, 67
    Prosodic, 71
    Syllabic, 34, 73
McFarland, James, xv
McLane, Lucy Neely, 48
McNulty, Tracy, 110
Menninghaus, Winifred, 9 n.21,
Miller, J. Hillis, 49
Milton, John, *Paradise Lost*, 68, 127-8
Mitchell, Robert, 110
Moore, Thomas, 7
Morgan, Jennifer, 108-9
Mosaic, 117
    Of citations, xii, 66-7
    Of linguistic shrapnel, 31
    Of social relations, 116
    Sonic, 72-3
Musica universalis,
    Language spheres, 32, 136
    Platonic Ideas, 76, 92
Nägele, Rainer, 32
Nakedness,
    Of truth, 47, 56, 92
    Of the biblical Noah, 100
Newsome, David, 53-4
Novalis, 5-6
One,
    'a setting at one', at-one-ment, 117-8
    Choice that is not one, 104
    Cloud that is not one, 48
    Word that is not one, 44-5
One word,
    As threat, or nothing at all, 119
    For a diversity of things, 82
    Meaning several things, 32
    Really a cloud, 43
O'Neill, Michael, 79
Osborne, John, 28, 75
Petrarch, 69
Phelan, Anthony, 110
Philip, M. NourbeSe, xviii, 132
Phillips, Tom, 21, 135
Plato,
    And the gods of myth, 97
    Cratylus, 59
    Republic, 58

Symposium, xiii, xvii, 53-5, 59-60, 70-3, 79-84, 90-1, 122, 124-5
Poetics,
    And politics, 4, 70, 73, 76, 136
    Of criticism, xii, 74
    Of measure, xiv, 19, 33, 42-3
    Of translation, 21-2, 26-7, 33, 67
    Romantic, 29
Point of indifference, xvii
    Between critic and text, 8
    Between genders, 89
Proper name,
Its 'romance', 13-14, 16, 123
Mathelinda, 15, 19, 30
    Shelley, and shells, 13-14, 16
    Spectral, 132
    Suffering (*Lida*), 34-5
    The Cenci name, 122-4
    The Hartman name, 123
    The Schönflies name, 15-16, 24 n.13, 30
    Walter, and Julius Walter, 15-16
    Walter, and *Gewalt*, 16, 74
Pulos, C. E., 70
Purple,
    See St Lydia of Thyatira
    See Violet (colour)
Quillin, Jessica, 19-20
Rang, Florens Christian, 55
Roberts, Hugh, 3
Ryder, Robert, 23
Yeats, W. B., 117
Schiller, Friedrich, 58-9
Schlegel, Friedrich, 5-6
Schlegel, August Wilhelm, 9 n.25
Scholem, Gerschom, 66-7, 139 n. 14
Scrivener, Michael, 102, 106
Seed,
    Of divine name, 28, 67
    Of knowledge, 5
    Of poetry, 5, 33
    Rhymed with 'deed', 42
Shakespeare, William, 137
Sharpe, Christina, xvi
Sheffield, Frisbee, 59-60
Shell,
    Benjamin's self-portrait with a, 23
    Fotuto, 138
    Homeric shell-lyre, 13, 18-22
    Shelley's signature, 14
    Translated into German as *Grenate* (artillery shell), 137-8
    Translated into German as *Hülle* (shell, husk, casing, veil), 62, 143
Shelley, Jane, Lady, 1
Shelley, Mary, 79
As editor, 3
Shelley, Percy Bysshe,
    'A Defence of Poetry', xii, 4-5, 21, 26, 33, 68-70, 75-6, 92, 103
    'A Discourse on the Manners of the Ancient Greeks Relative to the Subject of Love', 84-8
    'A Philosophical View of Reform', 109
    Adonais, 6-7
    'Essay on the Devil and Devils', 128, 131
    'Hymn to Mercury', 13, 17-22, 38, 43, 48
    'Julian and Maddalo', 1
    'Ode to Liberty', 47, 49

'On Life', 56-7, 141
Peter Bell the Third, 140, 142-4
Prometheus Unbound, 14, 127, 131-6
'Sonnet: "Lift not the painted veil"', 53, 62-3
The Cenci, 97-108, 111-13, 116-25, 127-8, 131-2, 135
'The Cloud', 48-9
The Mask of Anarchy, 140
The Necessity of Atheism, xi
'The Triumph of Life', 3-4, 7-8, 38-41, 45-8,
'The Witch of Atlas', 49
Translation of Plato's *Symposium*, 75-6, 79, 83-4; *see also* Plato, *Symposium*
Sidney, Sir Philip, 7
Slight adjustments,
    In citation, 137
    In translation, 18
Sobriety, 74
Sophocles, Hölderlin's translations of, 34, 73
Sperry, Stuart, 111
Split between,
    Art and the real, 58-9
    Beautiful bodies and Beauty itself, 60
    Poetry and philosophy, xii
Splitting,
    Criticism as the art of, xi, xvi, 91
St Lydia of Thyatira, 26, 30, 35
Standstill,
    History at a, 110
    In the blanks, 34, 68, 74
    Sapphic conversation, 89
    See Mallarmé
    See Hölderlin
Steffin, Margarethe, 140
Steiner, Uwe, 7
Steps,
    Mercury's incomprehensible, 20
    Of meaning (*Sinnstufen*), 67-8, 70
    Of measured feet, 18-21, 38, 40-2, 47-9, 54, 131
    On the Platonic ladder, xvii, 60, 69-70, 80, 86
    Tottering, 119-20
Unpremeditated,
    Composition, 68
    Song, 18
Vico, Giambattista, 32
Violence,
    Semantic, 41
    Sovereign, 16
Violet (colour), 26, 35
Violet (flower), 26, 33, 35
Violins, 35
Wallace, Jennifer, 57
Walter, Julius, 15
Wasserman, Earl, 14
Webb, Timothy, 26
Weekes, Henry, 2
Wilson, Ross, 3, 76
Wilson Knight, G., 14
Winnubst, Shannon, 105
Wohlfarth, Irving, 28, 32
Wollstonecraft, Mary, 85
Woodman, Ross, 42
Wordsworth, William, 13, 142

Lightning Source UK Ltd.
Milton Keynes UK
UKHW021257140223
416998UK00032B/594